ROOM *for* IMPROVEMENT

ROOM *for* IMPROVEMENT

Jan Orchard

B. Mitchell

Editor: *Donna Wood*
Art Editor: *Glynis Edwards*
Production: *Richard Churchill*

This edition published for W. H. Smith,
Toronto.
Exclusive to W. H. Smith/Classics in Canada.

Published by Marshall Cavendish Books Limited
58 Old Compton Street, London W1V 5PA

© Marshall Cavendish Limited 1987

ISBN 0-99994-332-4

Typeset in 10/11pt Cheltenham Book by
ABM Typographics

Printed and bound in Italy by L.E.G.O.
S.p.a. Vicenza.

CONTENTS

Taking Stock, page 12

PART TWO: ROOM-BY-ROOM IMPROVEMENTS 70

One Room Living, page 175

INTRODUCTION

"A house is a living machine" said French architect Le Corbusier. Our aim in *Room for Improvement* is to make the machine function in the most space-efficient, comfortable and economical way possible and to add those essential touches of style which mark the difference between a house and a home.

I've never been able to resist improving, simply because the end results are so satisfying. Even something as simple as moving a piece of furniture, or adding a plant or a new lamp can transform a room and, as we show in this book, lack of space need never be an insurmountable problem.

Clever use of color, pattern and mirrors can make a small room seem much bigger. Well-organized storage will remove clutter and create space – and it's surprising where extra storage room can be found if you look carefully. Bigger projects, such as removing a wall or adding an extension, can completely change the way the whole house is used.

I hope that this book will encourage you to think about your home in a constructive way. Make the building work for you. List the features you dislike and those which don't work within your lifestyle and you have the basis for successful change. Remember, moving is the last resort. After all, why uproot your family and disrupt your way of life when a few well-planned changes can make the home you already own a more comfortable, spacious place in which to live?

Today, there's a greater awareness of good design than ever before. Equipment, colors and techniques once only available to interior designers can be found in almost any shopping center. Modern, easy-care fabrics and wallcoverings come in hundreds of colors and patterns. Well-designed furniture is available at budget prices, thanks mainly to improvements in the structure and appearance of chipboard and veneers. New non-drip paints and prepasted wallcoverings make doing it yourself a possibility for even the most inexperienced.

Room for Improvement is divided into two sections. The first deals with using space, adding on, dividing and opening out; the second is packed with inspiring ideas for every room.

At the back of the book, you will find a list of names and addresses of manufacturers.
Happy improving.

Jane Orchard.

Far left: *Thinking of building on? This light, airy dining room is part of an imaginative extension that begins to erase the dividing line between house and garden.*

Top: *Hallways need not be drafty, characterless places.*

Above: *A gleaming, high-tech kitchen to propel your home into the 21st century.*

PART ONE

ASSESSING
WHAT YOU HAVE

Use Every Inch, page 39

Paint Effects, page 58

TAKING STOCK

Left: *Clever use of color, paint techniques and imaginative accessories have transformed what used to be a large, drafty hallway with little character into an extremely pleasant area with useful overhead storage capacity.*

The old adage that you never know anyone until you've lived with them can be applied to homes as well as people. Drawbacks not apparent on casual acquaintance with a house or apartment can become major irritations once you have moved in. Lack of space, rooms that are dark, awkwardly shaped, cramped or simply in the wrong place are major causes of discontent. Moving may seem the best solution to the problem, but the search for another property, upheaval and the costs of buying, selling and moving drive many homeowners to stay put and suffer. The other option is to change what you have. The level of change can range from simple redecoration and new furniture to major structural alteration.

IDENTIFY YOUR NEEDS

Change of any kind needs careful consideration. Even something as simple as redecoration can be a failure unless color and pattern are decided on before work starts. Bigger structural changes are often irrevocable; once the extension is built or the new staircase installed, there's no going back.

Before you decide on a home improvement plan, assess your home in relation to your needs, the features you hate (and those you like) and what you can afford.

Begin by listing your needs. You may, for instance, want an extra bedroom or bathroom because another baby is expected, existing children are too old to share or because the pressure on the family bathroom is too much. Or perhaps the need is for a quiet spot to do homework, or somewhere to keep an expanding collection of records or books. Don't confuse needs with wants. You may want a giant-size whirlpool bath, but do you need it?

The next step is to make a room by room plan of action. It could look something like the table above right.

Once the problems have been identified, you can think about the possible solutions. There are several things to consider.

Budget: How much can you afford to spend? Do you need a loan? If so, how much can you realistically repay every month? Where will you raise the money?

Investment value: Will you get the money back if you sell the house? A large project may seem attractive but it may be impossible to recoup the cost as even the best-equipped

ROOM	PROBLEMS
▶ Kitchen	Too small. Not enough storage space. Not enough work surface. Nowhere to eat. Appliances take up too much of the existing space.
▶ Living room	Too dark. Not enough power sockets. Storage needed for TV and video.
▶ Dining room	Not used often. Inconvenient in relation to the kitchen.
▶ Bathroom	Lighting inadequate. No storage space. Fixtures stained. Morning bottleneck.
▶ Master bedroom	More clothes storage needed. Dark and tends to be untidy. No full-length mirror.
▶ Children's bedroom	Needs more space to store toys. Constantly untidy. Children tend to squabble. Nowhere for older child to do homework.
▶ Entry hall	Tends to be dumping place for bikes, coats, etc. Dark.

house will only attract the ceiling price for the area. A real estate agent will advise you on the best possible price.

Disruption: Will the work be worth the upheaval? Expanding a kitchen may seem an attractive prospect but, on average, work takes around 13 weeks. If you have small children, life without proper cooking or laundry facilities can be hell. It's better to improve the kitchen as much as possible

Above: *Sometimes extra light is all that is needed to change the feel of a room. This small kitchen was transformed by replacing the old back door with glazed French doors.*

Left: *A simple square opening can act as a picture frame for a cleverly arranged room beyond. Strong colors make this a particularly successful scheme.*

Left: *An extended kitchen, made by removing a wall between the original kitchen and dining room. The conservatory beyond adds light and extra space.*

using nonstructural means, leaving major work until the children are older.

The future: Major structural work is the sort of thing most people only want to experience once. Think about the future. Might you need more than one extra bedroom within the next five to ten years? Try to get everything done at the same time.

When you have the answer to these questions, solving problems will be easier because you'll have a framework. If adding on is out of the question because of the cost, you'll be able to spend time considering other possibilities. Or, if you can afford to add on, you'll be able to start thinking about the type and size of home addition needed.

Consider how the house is used by you and your family. You will probably find that some rooms are used more than others. Children, for instance, may ignore their bedroom during the day, preferring to play downstairs in an already overcrowded living room. Perhaps the bedroom is cold, or uncomfortable, or badly equipped for play. Ensuring that heating is efficient, installing smooth cushioned vinyl flooring (a good surface for toy cars, model railways and games) and adding a work surface, portable TV and some storage space could put a swift end to the discomfort of trying to relax against a background of Space Invaders and squabbles. Another solution could be to convert the attic into a playroom.

Location of rooms is important too. A corridor between a dining room and kitchen can make serving meals difficult. A child's bedroom sited at the front of the house, where there is noise from the street and from the living room immediately below can cause sleeping problems.

Look at the size and shape of the rooms and list the features you like or dislike about each one. Think about light. Would a bigger window, a change of color scheme or a mullioned door help?

Does the decoration suit the purpose of the room? Children's rooms should have either washable (vinyl) paper or latex paint on the walls. Wallpaper tends to peel in a steamy bathroom.

Perhaps the problem is simply one of style. Rooms with no identify, packed with a jumble of furniture and with no decorative theme make a home that looks and feels disorganized. An eclectic mixture of objects can work, provided the objects are attractive in themselves. Style is a matter of personal

Left: *A folding table provides dining space in this small kitchen. The side leaves are let down and the table is put aside when not in use.*

Left: *A glass-topped table occupies less visual space than one with a solid top and makes a bridge between kitchen and dining areas.*

preference. Think about the things you like. It's likely they'll be similar in design. Once you've established this and eliminated the things you hate, you are well on the way to establishing a home that works as a whole. When you've assessed what is wrong and how much you can afford to put right, go back to your problems chart and add the solutions that you have decided upon.

CHANGING SPACES

LIFE ON THE LEVELS

The conventional arrangement of upstairs and downstairs isn't the only way to divide rooms. This modern house was built into a cliffside, and designed to work on several interconnecting levels. The house has no ordinary interior doors; instead all the rooms have sliding doors, framed in pine. The whole interior is an exercise in intelligent use of space, and is packed with ideas to inspire.

Right: *Sliding pine frame doors are used all over the house, either to link areas or to close them off whenever necessary.*

Below: *This staircase leads from the lower level to the loft living room.*

Left: *There's no space wasted in this kitchen. Light comes through the roof, and from narrow strips of glass set between wall and base cabinets.*

Left: *Windows at ceiling level flood the living room with light. A minimum of furniture makes the most of the long, narrow space.*

Far left: *The study leads off the living room and is an oasis of calm.*

Left: *The central hall with its high, tilted ceiling. Glazed walls mean that anyone sitting in the hall can see all over the rest of the house.*

Left: *Rooms are clutter-free to make the most of light. Color comes from vibrant soft furnishings, like this Marimekko bedcover.*

A HOUSE WITH A HEART

Clever organization of space is the secret of this stunning modern house. A central living area with a ceiling higher than the rest of the roofline creates a focal point, rather like the great hall in medieval manor houses and castles. The central room is 15 feet high with a tilted ceiling. Partly glazed walls mean the hall is connected visually to the rest of the house, so the rooms work as one space, rather than as a collection of boxes.

This central room idea is easy enough to copy. Visualize a typical hallway and living room, then think of the space with the hall wall and most of the ceiling removed, with a stairway running to a gallery at the second-floor level. It may even be possible to remove the ceiling as far as the attic and install skylights or windows in the gable end.

The house shown in our picture is square. Existing corridors between rooms were removed, so there is no wasted space. Light floods in, encouraged by large expanses of double glazing. The doors around the high central hall are corner mounted, allowing for a wall of glass through to the living room.

Above: *The house from the outside. Double glazing and an efficient central heating system keep every room comfortably warm, despite the large amount of glass.*

Left: *Windows and doors were made to the same width so that the owners could have some corners with doors and some without. Open rounded shelves mean that the ends of a row of cabinets can be used without any risk of impeding the doorway.*

The Grand Plan

Above: *This house was planned so that all rooms would radiate off from the central area, the "heart" of the house. This arrangement ensures that all of the rooms work together as one large space rather than a collection of separate boxes.*

MAKING IT WORK

A custom-built home is a dream few of us ever achieve. In reality, most houses are less than ideal. Older buildings were designed for a different lifestyle, when domestic staff were cheap and readily available to deal with the dusting of high ceilings and the inconveniences of a large house. Modern "production line" homes are built to a price, often with little regard for the way the space will be used by future occupants.

Change in family circumstances also affects the way a house works for those who live there. Two children may share a room in perfect peace until one reaches the age of seven or so, and begins to resent the younger child's toys in his/her space, or small hands interfering with a pet project. Likewise what seemed a perfectly reasonable living room for Mom, Dad and a couple of youngsters will become uncomfortably cramped when toddlers turn into teenagers.

Moving isn't the only solution to the problems of a space that doesn't suit your needs. Walls can be moved, new levels established and rooms changed around, often at little cost and certainly with less upheaval than would be entailed in moving.

SIMPLE ALTERATIONS

The easiest alterations are those which don't involve structural work. If one room is bigger than you really need and another smaller, consider changing them around. A big kitchen is usually more useful than a spacious dining room, for instance. If you have a large living room and would like to make the area more intimate, screening sections off with bookcases or room dividers can work wonders.

If a room is underused, think about using it for more than one purpose to ease the strain where there's a shortage of space. Add a comfortable sofa to a big kitchen and it becomes an extra living space. Dining rooms can double as a place for hobbies or homework. Either organize the work so it can be cleared away without fuss, or screen off a corner.

STRUCTURAL WORK

Removing internal partition walls is the time-honored way to change the way a house is arranged. Living and dining rooms are the favorites for this treatment, or you can be more adventurous and knock living room, dining room and kitchen into one. Consider combining a small split bathroom (found in older homes) into one bigger, easier-to-plan space. The project doesn't have to be enormous to be effective. Removing a chimney breast, provided it can be done safely, can add 3 to 4 feet to a living room; moving the position of a doorway can make a room very much easier to plan.

Walls can't be removed at will. There are often structural and legal constraints which affect what can be moved and where.

There are two types of walls used in house construction. Load-bearing walls carry the weight of the wall or floors above. If this wall is removed, a support girder must be installed in its place. Non-load-bearing walls can be removed without adding extra support. However, you will need to reroute service pipes and electrical wiring and make good the floors and ceilings.

Working out which walls are load-bearing and which are not can be difficult. The best clue is given by the floorboards on the second floor. If these run at right angles to the wall, the wall is probably not load-bearing, since the joists it would be supporting are parallel to it, though it may be supporting a wall above. If the floorboards are parallel, the wall is likely to be load-bearing. It is essential to seek professional advice before removing walls that may be load-bearing – and you will need to comply with all your local building regulations.

Cutting into or removing floors is a more spectacular way to change space. Removing a whole floor gives a spacious double height room. Where there are doors on the second floor, a section can be cut away, leaving a loft or gallery. This sort of work involves cutting through the floor joists and providing alternative support. Again, this is work for an expert, as extremely complex calculations are involved.

There are legal restrictions which affect alterations to internal layout. Any alteration to the way a building is supported needs expert advice. In general, habitable rooms must have a ceiling height of at least 8 feet over a percentage of the total area of the room. A habitable room must also have a window or windows that provide an opening at least tenth the size of the floor area.

ORGANIZING THE SPACE

Knocking down walls can create problems unless the new space is well planned. Many "through rooms" where a living room and dining room have been made into one are wasted space because the family still congregates at one end. Making one room from two smaller ones presents a number of alternatives to complete removal of the center wall. If the wall to be removed is load-bearing, you'll have to install a beam, which will be visible at the top of the new opening, plus ribs of the old wall at each end. Why not open up with an archway instead? Or, if the partition wall houses a fireplace, consider leaving the chimney breast intact to make an attractive central feature.

Whichever option you choose, unify the two spaces by using the same floorcovering and decoration throughout. Remember to replace the cornice and baseboard too, as a break is visually disturbing.

Knocking a living room, dining room and kitchen into one makes a big, airy space out of three little boxes. Cooking, however, is a messy business and there are times when the kitchen would be better if screened off from the living area. The way around this is to run open shelves halfway across the division between the dining room and kitchen. Leafy plants will let the light through and hide the clutter. Make sure that the kitchen area is well ventilated with an appropriate hood or other ventilation system; otherwise cooking smells will filter into living areas and take a long time to disperse.

In a small, typical brownstone or row house, where the staircase runs up between the living room and kitchen, knocking the dividing wall down and replacing the closed stairway with an open plan or spiral design will add both space and light. Not all such changes are as satisfactory. Think carefully before you knock down a chimney breast or remove a fireplace; the room may look featureless without this focal point.

Dividing can be just as effective as combining. The space in a big bedroom can be more effective if divided into a bathroom and bedroom suite, bedroom and study or two small bedrooms (a good solution to the problem of children no longer willing to share). Erecting partition walls willy nilly will not work as there are practical considerations. Light is the most important. If the room has only one window, how will the second room be lit? Avoid running a partition up the middle of a window as the effect is ugly. Think about

Left: *A large kitchen like this one is a real bonus. It becomes so much more than a place to prepare food; the insertion of a fine, solid wood dining table means it can be used not just for eating but for hobbies and homework too, and a small sofa extends its use even further as a place for reading and relaxing. Modern, functional-looking cabinets would be out of place here.*

Above: *Knocking the living room, dining room and kitchen into one is a courageous step toward big, open spaces. Sensitive lighting is important in a room of this size, and ventilation must be good to prevent cooking smells from filtering into the living room area. Here, a feeling of warmth and comfort has been created by the use of glowing wood tones.*

Above and right: *Adding a room divider or partition wall is an easy way to break up or make space within a house. The least expensive way to install one is with a prefabricated kit, as no special skills are necessary.*

access. Unless the new room is a study or bathroom suite, it will be inconvenient to use if the only access is through the adjoining bedroom. The partition wall itself is easy to build. All that is needed is a wooden stud frame, braced with horizontal pieces and covered with plasterboard and a skimming of plaster. An alternative is to use folding or sliding doors which can be pushed out of the way when not in use. Reckless removal or addition of walls can spoil both the proportions and the character of your home. Turning a cozy country cottage into a big, open space, or dividing an elegant Georgian room are two extreme examples of the sort of thing to avoid.

TWO-LEVEL LIVING

In a room with a high ceiling, more than half the space is useless. Adding a loft or mezzanine is an effective way to use generous headroom and can add an interesting and useful feature to your home. Changing levels is popular in Germany and Scandinavia, less so in the UK and here in the US. Adding or removing floors and ceilings seems a radical move but can reap enormous benefits in terms of space and light. Removing a ceiling gives a dramatic, airy feel. Adding a loft creates an area that is cozy and intimate, yet still very much in touch with the mainstream of family life.

Cutting away: Here a section of floor is removed, leaving a gallery at the second floor. This treatment can work well in a building where the ground floor ceilings are very low. The ground floor room then becomes a modern version of the medieval great hall, a heart for the restructured house.

To make the most of the new light well, try to add skylights, a gable window or extra windows at ground and second-floor level. Cutting away requires the skills of an architect and a qualified builder, however.

Adding a loft: A loft is a floor between first- and second-storey levels. If floor space is limited and the ceiling is high enough, adding a loft will prove valuable. In a living room, the loft can be used to take TV, stereo or reading away from the main area. In a bedroom, the platform can be used as a bed with storage space beneath. Don't do this if you have small children who may fall from the ladder. Don't ignore corridors, halls and the stairwell. If there is enough ceiling height, adding a wooden loft will provide a spare bed or some storage, study or work space.

Anyone reasonably good at woodwork can make a wooden loft. The platform is made from high-density chipboard and the supports from wooden joists that must span two load-bearing walls if the loft is a proper floor. Access can be by ladder or by a proper stairway if there is room. The bottom of the platform should line up with the top of interior doors.

Position the loft away from the windows or it will obstruct natural light. If the platform is to be used for sleeping, there should be at least enough headroom for an adult to sit up in bed. Platforms for reading or watching TV need enough space for a tall adult to be able to stand upright.

Above: *Adding a wooden loft is a bold way of making use of the empty space above head level. It can only work in a house with very high ceilings, however. Apart from the extra space such a structure provides, it can make a room very much cozier. High ceilings create a lovely, airy feeling in the warmer months but can be rather bleak when colder weather sets in.*

MAKING A PLAN

Making a floor plan of each room in your home will help you to understand proportions and how the space can be used to best advantage.

Equip yourself with some graph paper, a ruler, pencil, eraser and a tape measure. A metal tape is the most accurate or, for easy measuring, look for a mobile tape with a handle which measures as you push it around the room.

Carry a notepad with you as you measure. Mark down the length and height of each wall and the position and size of doors and windows. If the room has alcoves, measure them carefully. Mark the position of plumbing fixtures, power outlets and light switches.

Once you have all the details, draw up the shape of the room on graph paper. A ratio of ten squares to a foot is easiest to work with. Mark the position of doors, windows and alcoves or other features in red. Also mark

Left and above left: *Lack of wall space made my own living room, pictured here, particularly difficult to plan. The room measures 21 × 12 feet but has very little free wall space. One end is completely occupied by windows while the two long walls house heaters.*

Originally, we had two long sofas in the room, placed at right angles to each other. The wall behind the sofas was covered with floor-to-ceiling bookshelves, giving a boxed-in effect which made even this generous space seem cluttered.

We decided to break up the floor area by replacing the two sofas with a three-seater sofa and two comfortable chairs. The sheer bulk of the sofa meant it had to back onto one of the long walls. Turning it at a slight angle toward the two chairs (divided by a low coffee table), makes a comfortable, welcoming setting.

The old floor-to-ceiling bookshelves were replaced with half-height models to that lamps could be positioned around the room to add soft, indirect lighting.

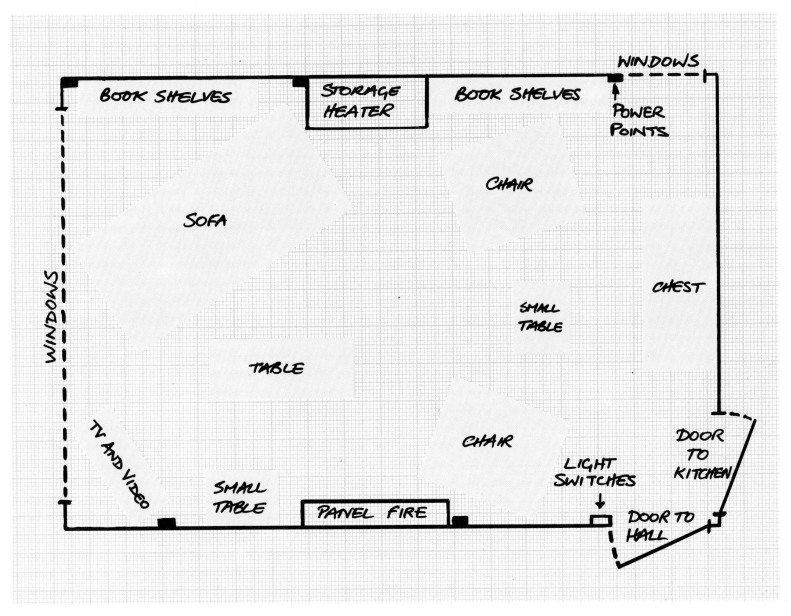

BOOK SHELVES

STORAGE HEATER

BOOK SHELVES

WINDOWS

POWER POINTS

CHAIR

SOFA

CHEST

WINDOWS

SMALL TABLE

TABLE

TV AND VIDEO

CHAIR

DOOR TO KITCHEN

LIGHT SWITCHES

SMALL TABLE

PANEL FIRE

DOOR TO HALL

the position of plumbing, power outlets and light switches. When you have rearranged your room, you may decide you need more.

POSITIONING FURNITURE

Making cut-out scale plans of furniture to move around your floor plan is much easier than heaving the real thing from place to place in search of a successful arrangement.

To make furniture templates to scale, measure the length and width of each piece of furniture and note the measurements. Using graph paper and the same scale as the floor plan, draw up the furniture shapes. Label each piece, then color it in so that the furniture stands out when laid on the basic floor plan.

Where furniture has opening doors or drawers, measure how far they project into the room when open. With outward-opening side-hinged doors, measure how much space is needed for the door to open fully.

To work out the position of furniture, place the larger pieces on the room plan first. Remember that some pieces will need to be near power outlets and light switches. Think too about the traffic flow. It will help to mark the main pathways through the room. This will show how much space is needed between the pieces of furniture.

Try out the furniture in different arrangements until you find one you really like.

Above: *This simple plan allowed us to move furniture around on paper until we found the best arrangement for the room shown on the left.*

EXPANDING YOUR HOME

Left: *A pleasant combination of old and new, this modern addition with glazed sliding doors provides a light and airy living room for a country cottage.*

When space simply won't stretch any further and tempers become strained as a result, moving is usually the first idea that springs to mind. But moving can prove more expensive than expanding your existing home. Before you visit the real estate agent, consider the following:

A bigger house in the same area will cost more, so mortgage payments will rise.
Legal fees and taxes involved in the move.
The cost of moving.
Time spent looking for a suitable property.
Cost of new carpets, curtains and extra furniture for the bigger house.
Change of schools and general upheaval to family life.

These "hidden extras" can add up to several thousand dollars, possibly more than enough to pay for the cost of adding a good-quality addition onto your present home.

An addition can be added to the back or side of the house and used for a bigger kitchen, a dining room, extra bedroom, bathroom or playroom. More ambitious plans to consider are a two-story addition (in effect, a new wing to the house), building over an attached garage to add another bedroom or bathroom, or conversion of the attic.

WHAT SORT OF ADDITION?

Think carefully before plans are drawn. It's wise to add as much space as possible. Remember that this is your chance to decide exactly what you want, so take advantage of the opportunity. There are several options, depending on the sort of house you live in.

SINGLE-STORY ADDITIONS

As long as it conforms to the building code, a single-story addition can be built onto almost any part of the house. The space can be used as a kitchen, a bathroom, an extra bedroom, a study or a living area. Additions can range from simple aluminium or wooden conservatories, to a specially designed extra room or wing. If the existing kitchen and dining room are at the back, consider knocking the two rooms into one and joining it onto the addition to make a really spectacular space. Other possibilities include siting the addition at a lower level than the room it backs on to, and raising the ceiling to the level of the windows on the second floor. Add a loft and an internal spiral staircase and you've created an inspired addition rather than just an extra room. If you want this sort of effect, tell your

architect, who will advise you on what is possible and show you different drawings of how the building might work.

If the addition has a flat roof and it is possible to create access from the second floor, you'll be able to replace lost garden space with a raised deck.

TWO-STORY ADDITIONS

If space is needed at both ground and second-floor levels, a two- or three-story addition will provide two, three or more extra rooms. At the simplest level, this sort of extension simply matches the rest of the house. More interesting examples can have large sections of glass, with a sloping roofed conservatory at ground-floor level jutting out into the garden and two narrower glazed or part-glazed rooms above. An extra staircase gives access to the new upstairs rooms. Another possibility with this sort of addition is to make one of the upper floors a loft, creating a stunning high-ceilinged interior.

If the house has an adjoining garage, it may be possible to build another story above it. The garage can be left as a garage, or can be turned into a room with a staircase to the floor above. You could follow Victorian and

Edwardian style and add a glazed garden room at this level. Whether this is possible depends on the structure of the garage: some were built with the possibility of future expansion in mind.

GETTING THE WORK DONE

Once the decision to add on has been made, the next step is to get work under way. There are several options.

DOING IT YOURSELF

To an enthusiastic do-it-yourselfer, building an addition may seem a straightforward job. The building work itself may well be, but drawing proper plans and considering the legalities can be a minefield for the amateur; you can't simply buy the materials and start building. To get building permission if you need it, proper plans must be submitted to the relevant local authority. A rough drawing won't do. This can mean supplying up to two different sets, depending on the work and on local regulations. Add to this months of back-breaking labor, renting special tools and the possibility of meeting a problem beyond your skills, and going it alone becomes a daunting prospect.

Building an addition yourself isn't impossible; it is simply the most time-consuming, disruptive and difficult way to do the job. An attic conversion will often inmvolve major structural alterations, including repositioning headers and strengthening the floor. This part of the work is something best left to a professional, though you could do much of the finishing and decorating work yourself, provided that you have the necessary time and a few basic tools.

DOING IT YOURSELF WITH HELP

The most difficult part of building an addition from the do-it-yourself point of view can often be dealing with building and zoning regulations. If you are determined to do some or all of the building work yourself, employ a contractor or architect to do the planning and estimating. Many contractors can draw plans, submit them to the local building office and obtain building permission and advise on the amount and type of materials needed. For a more complex addition, consult an architect who will be able to deal with planning permission and help with estimates and materials. For the construction work, you

may want to employ tradesmen for the parts of the work you can't or won't want to do – such as bricklaying, plastering, wiring or plumbing. Most are self-employed and can be hired on a daily basis. Always agree terms in advance.

USING A KIT

Many companies offer "build it yourself" kits for single-story additions. They supply the addition in kit form and you assemble it. The company may deal with planning regulations. The drawback is that designs are limited and usually only for a simple one-or-two room building with window and door. Using an architect to design an addition with your needs in mind gives better results.

Companies offering kits usually also offer a service where they supply and build the addition. Again, design is limited. Many companies contract the work out and therefore have little control over the builders.

ARCHITECT AND BUILDER

This is the best, although the most expensive, choice. The architect will design a building tailored to your individual needs. He will deal with legal aspects, oversee the building work and the materials. Some builders will design an addition for you, but their work is unlikely to be as interesting as that of an architect.

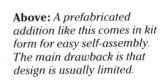

Above: *A prefabricated addition like this comes in kit form for easy self-assembly. The main drawback is that design is usually limited.*

CHECKPOINTS

Ask yourself these questions before deciding how to proceed.

DOING IT YOURSELF

▶ Can you cope with the plans?

▶ Do you have time and the necessary skill to deal with any legal or zoning problems?

▶ How long will it take to do the building work?

▶ What will the work cost in terms of missed holidays and loss of time spent with the family?

▶ Will you have to rent or buy special tools?

DOING IT YOURSELF WITH HELP

▶ How much time would using an architect or surveyor to deal with the plans and legal aspects save?

▶ How much time will the building work take?

KIT OR ALL-IN-ONE SERVICE

▶ Does the company offer designs you like and that will suit the house?

▶ Are you capable of putting the kit together?

▶ Will you need to rent or buy special tools?

▶ Would it be cheaper to build using your own materials?

▶ How much control does the company have over the builders who erect the addition?

▶ Is there a guarantee covering the addition?

▶ Is it reasonably burglar-proof, or can it be made so?

Right: *This smart, compact kitchen addition revolutionized a small row house.*

FINDING AN EXPERT

If you decide to use an architect or builder, the next step is to find someone properly qualified to do the work.

ARCHITECTS

A good architect will discuss your ideas, point out any pitfalls, then transform them into a design that suits both your style and your pocket. The best way to find an architect is by word of mouth. Barring that, contact the nearest office of the American Institute of Architects for referrals to qualified architects in your area. Be prepared to explain your needs so that the AIA can match you up with an architect who is qualified to do the kind of work you have in mind. Another approach is to find an addition you like and ask the homeowner who the architect was who designed it. As you search for an architect, beware of unqualified architects, who may describe themselves as "architectural designers" or "design consultants." An unqualified architect can cause disaster, so be careful and make your choice through official sources.

Once you have a list of names, contact the architects and explain the sort of building you have in mind. Ask what kind of work they have done and whether it is possible to see a local example. Ask about fees too. Most architects charge by the hour for the initial stages (although some will offer this advice free of charge in the hoipe that you will like the design and offer the firm the job). If you decide to see the architect to design, plan and oversee the work, the fee is usually a percentage of the total building cost. The fee includes design, drawing and presentation of plans, and may include finding a builder and supervising the construction. Don't choose the first architect you see. It's better to visit a few and find one whose ideas you like.

BUILDERS

Everyone knows a builder horror story. Tales of builders who disappear for weeks on end, leaving the job half done, shoddy workmanship and overcharing are common. Firms like this are the exception rather than the rule, and a few elementary precautions at the early stages will protect you.

Personal recommendation is the best way to find a good builder. If you are using an architect, or or she may be able to recommend a firm whose work he or she knows. Neighbors and friends are another good source of information.

There are various professional organizations of building contractors, and these can be a good source of referrals if your architect or friends have no suggestions. Among these are the Associated General Contractors of America, the Master Builders Association and the American Building Contractors Association. Contact your local library for the national headquarters or for local branches. You might also phone your local office of the Better Business Bureau to see if their membership includes any contractors.

In searching for a reputable contractor, make sure the candidates you are considering are licensed and qualified to do the proposed work. Ask for references and don't be shy about following them up.

Make a shortlist of three or four builders and send them all a set of plans and a written specification (your architect will supply these) and ask for a written estimate and a schedule of when the work would begin and how it would progress. Allow three or four weeks for the estimates to come in.

Once the estimates have been received, you can choose the builder offering the best service and value for money. Take warranties into account when assessing the estimates. It is better to use the builder with the warranty, even if his estimate is a little more expensive than the others. Also ask to see the builder's insurance certificate to make sure that he has liability coverage. If he doesn't and a brick falls through your neighbor's greenhouse (or worse still, on his head), a nasty legal wrangle could ensue.

When the choice has been made and plans approved by the local building office, you must draw up a contract between you and your builder. This is essential and is your protection should something go wrong at a later stage. Word of mouth, or a confirming letter is not good enough.

The contract should specify every aspect of the work, from starting date to the materials to be used. A penalty clause may sound severe but the builder is more likely to finish on time if he will lose money by going beyond the agreed date. Your architect or lawyer will help with the contract.

Organize how interim payments will be made before the work starts – and don't part with any cash in advance. Equally, don't make the final payment until you are happy with the work. Above all, be firm. You are paying. The builder is not doing you a favor by turning up or by doing the work as specified in the estimate.

SUPERVISING THE WORK

It will probably take between four to six weeks to reach a starting date, so there's plenty of time to clear the rooms affected by building work. Dust spreads everywhere, so remove carpets from the rooms around the new addition. Remember that the workmen will need somewhere to store tools, lunch facilities and a toilet.

If you are employing an architect, he will probably supervise the work. If you are supervising the work, make sure the builder knows where to contact you at all times.

CHECKPOINTS

A home addition is a big project, so bear the following in mind.

▶ If you are using an architect and don't like the first design submitted, say so. You have to live with the new building, use it and pay for it.

▶ Make sure the new building suits the style of your house. An addition that is an eyesore, or just plain unattractive, will make the house hard to sell.

▶ If you are adding a kitchen or bathroom, choose the fixtures before the addition is planned. It is easier to plan a new space to suit the cabinets or fixtures you really want than it is to make the fixtures work in a building of the wrong size or shape. And make due allowance for manufacturers' delivery dates, bearing in mind that it is possible that these will not necessarily be met.

▶ Go for the biggest space you can afford. Eventually you are sure to want more cabinets or equipment, and if you think big now, you will have the space when you need it.

▶ Make sure the new space does not reduce light to the rest of the house or make access inconvenient.

CONVERSIONS

ROOM ON TOP?

Most homeowners would deny wasting any usable space, and would be astonished to be told that there's a whole room standing empty above their heads, or at least the scope for creating such a room. When there isn't room to add on at street level, or when the need is for a quiet spot, away from the rest of the house, the roof space can offer a wealth of interesting possibilities. Conversion can be as simple as the addition of skylights (windows set into the roof), a floor, ceiling and access, or more complex with dormer windows to extend the usable floor area inside the attic. If the house is of suitable construction, it may even be possible to add an extra story, though you will need planning permission for such a venture and it is a very expensive one.

An attic room can be used as a bedroom, a second bathroom, a bedroom with a bathroom or shower room suite if there is enough space, a playroom, hobbies area or even a small apartment. Because the attic is quiet and well away from the main part of the house, conversion is the ideal way to make a retreat where parents can create an area of their own, children can play without causing chaos in the living room and teenagers can entertain friends, play music and watch TV without the inevitable disputes with the rest of the family. If one of the family has the kind of hobby that occupies a lot of space, the attic can become a tailor-made home for the model railroad, amateur radio rig, sewing, painting or pottery project.

An attic room is not, however, usually suitable for a grandparent's apartment. Elderly people may find the stairs difficult or could be worried about being cut off from the family when living at the top of the house. If a grandparent's room is needed, convert ground- or second-floor rooms and use the attic for younger, fitter members of the family.

Even the simplest attic conversion affects the structure of the roof, so design must be carried out by an architect or structural engineer, and the work done by a builder experienced in attic conversion.

Not all buildings can be extended at roof level. Obviously, a flat-roofed building has no attic space to convert, but it may be possible to add an extra story. Many modern houses where the roof is of trussed rafter construction (*see diagram*) cannot be extended. To extend an attic where the roof is built like this means removing the roof itself and doing a great deal of expensive support work. The

older style roof (*see diagram*) is ideal for attic conversion. If the house is of historic interest, or in a conservation area, planning permission for adding simple skylights, converting the attic with dormers or adding an extra floor may be refused. Check before contacting an architect or engineer.

Left: *Here, roofspace has been converted into a spacious second bathroom. Water-resistant wall-coverings have been used; textured tiles, vinyl wallpaper and tongue-and-groove cladding on the sloping ceiling. Twin rooflights let in the sun.*

Right: *A self-contained apartment with trap-door access, this pine-clad loft conversion makes maximum use of every inch – notice the cupboards in the eaves.*

Below left: *This is an older-style roof construction, suitable for loft conversion.*

Below right: *A roof with trussed rafters is not suitable for conversion. This style is common to modern houses.*

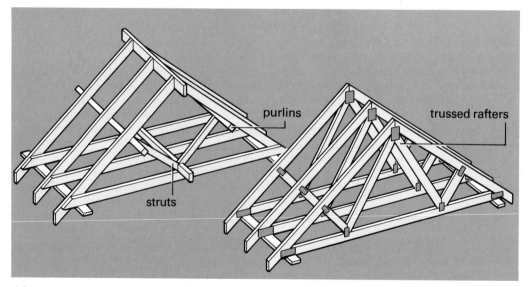

purlins

trussed rafters

struts

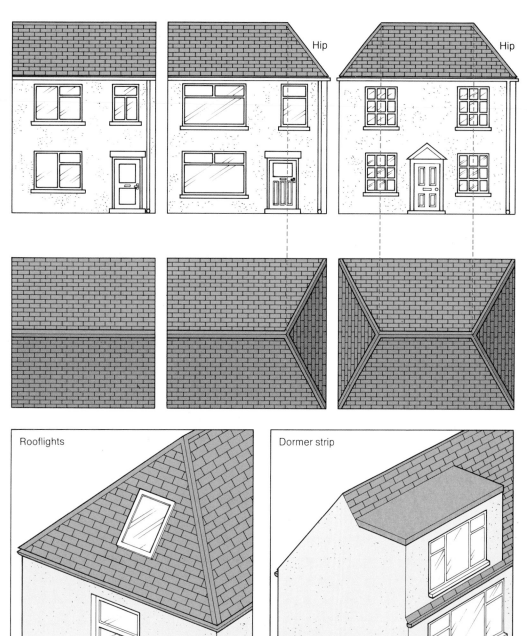

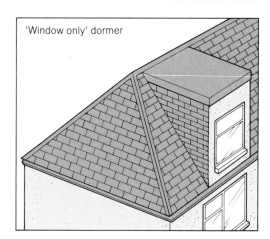

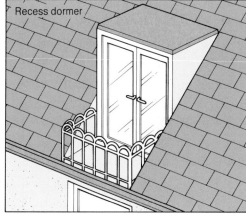

HOW MUCH SPACE WILL I GAIN?

The amount of usable space gained by attic conversion depends on the design of the house. A row house (*see diagram*) has no hips (sloping sides) on the roof so the whole roofspace is available. A semi-detached house has only one hip, so more than half of the roof can be used. A detached house has hips at both ends, so only the center portion can become a full-height room. The lower areas in the roof of a house with hips need not be wasted. Custom-built shelving or storage can be installed, or the sloping section can be partitioned off as a storage area or for a water heater. The architect or builder will advise you.

Space gained also depends on the way that the attic is converted. There are three options. Which you choose depends on the amount you have to spend and on the space that is actually needed.

ADDING SKYLIGHTS

If there is headroom of $7\frac{1}{2}$ feet inside most of the roofspace, and all you need is a playroom or a room for teenagers where restricted space around the edges won't matter too much, conversion can be as simple as adding skylights, a suitable floor and ceiling and a safe form of access. A retractable attic ladder really will not suffice for a room that is to be used regularly.

Skylights are flush windows, supplied ready-made with weatherstripping. As installing them involves cutting into the roof, it is best to have the work done by an expert. Most skylights open on a pivot system, so it is easy to bring fresh air into the new room. Blinds will be needed in summer; otherwise the room will become very hot. Insulating blinds, with foil on the outside to reflect heat, are best. Greenhouse shading blinds are also suitable.

Top: *A house with no hips* **(left),** *a semi-detached house with only one hip (center) and a detached house with two hips.*
Above left: *A roof window has been fitted into the gable end.*
Above right: *A lowline dormer.*
Far left: *'Window only' dormer.*
Left: *A recess dormer leaves room for a balcony outside.*

ADDING DORMER WINDOWS

Adding dormer windows increases the usable floor area inside the attic. Dormers jut out of the roof and have their own ceiling. This extends the amount of full-height ceiling inside the room. Maximum space is gained by adding a dormer strip. Windows can be installed at intervals, or along the full length of the strip. Installing at intervals gives more wall area for furniture inside the attic. In an older house, where the roof is steeply pitched at the front and shallow at the back, it is possible to use dormers to add almost a complete extra floor at the rear without coming above the roofline at the front.

Adding "window only" dormers means that the room will have small "bays" where the windows are. This does not add a lot of extra space, but may be the only acceptable way to add dormers on some older buildings. At the least, you should have room for a small, built-in cupboard, the top of which can be fitted

with cushions and used as seating. Or you might be able to put shelving there.

Dormers should be in character with the rest of the house. Nothing looks worse than a modern framed window on the roof of a Victorian house. A good architect or builder will make sure that the windows are in style.

The other option is to recess dormers into the roof – a style sometimes seen on old country cottages. This has the effect of creating a balcony. Recessing a strip of dormers makes a terrace, an attractive way to add a garden to a house with no land available at ground level.

The drawbacks are cost – recessing is an expensive operation – loss of space inside the roof and the problems of weatherproofing the terrace floor as it is part of the ceiling of the room below. This sort of terrace can be glazed to create a conservatory in the clouds. The roof will need greenhouse shading during the summer. This sort of addition is not suitable for buildings exposed to high winds.

Above: *This is a window-only dormer. Installing this type of window creates a bay into the room. If you want to make extra floor and ceiling space, the best way to do it is by installing a row of dormers to give an extended bay.*

Dormer windows are more expensive to install than skylights but are well worth the cost if extra space is your real need.

ADDING AN EXTRA STORY

This is a big project and should be considered carefully. Get some cost estimates first and work out whether the expense is worth the space gained. The other point to consider is if the money would be recouped in the selling price of the house. Houses have a "ceiling price" for the area – ask a local real estate agent to assess the value of your home with and without the extra story. If the difference in price is more than the cost of the addition (and remember to add on "hidden" costs such as carpet cleaning, redecoration and other wear and tear caused by major building work), then it may be worthwhile.

Not all houses are suitable for this sort of extension.

A Victorian-style row house with cross walls that stand up from the roof may be suitable as the new floor won't be too obtrusive. If the house has a front parapet or a mansard roof, an extra story can be added without spoiling the look of the street. Adding an extra story to a semi-detached house is unlikely to be allowed because it would unbalance the look of the building. Even if the house is detached, problems can occur if it stands in a street of buildings of the same design. Again, because it would disrupt the line of rooftops, permission to add an extra story will probably be refused.

Planners are more likely to favor a detached house in a country setting or in its own grounds for this kind of alteration. Permission will probably be refused if the house is of historic interest or if it is located in a historic area. Adding an extra story needs the expert advice of an architect.

USING THE NEW SPACE

To gain real benefit from the space, an attic conversion should be used for more than occasional extra sleeping space or storage for toys and games. Access is important – if the attic is difficult to get to and from, it won't be used. The stairway should not be too steep and it should be possible to carry things up and down without difficulty. If the attic is to be a studio, or a bedroom and bathroom that will be used every day, install a proper internal staircase.

You will need to extend the household wiring and central heating up into the converted attic space – to provide heat, light and electrical power. If you have a bathroom in the converted attic (or even a bedroom basin), this will mean routing the plumbing to accommodate the converted room. Check with a plumber to make sure that water pressure in the new bathroom will be adequate to support a shower or any other fixture you're planning to include. Nothing is worse than a shower that turns out to be a trickle, especially after the expense of installation.

Well-planned furniture and fittings are another way to make sure that you gain maximum benefit from the new space. Sloping walls need not be a problem. Custom-built shelves and closets can be used to fill spaces where there is not enough room to stand upright. Shelves running across above head height are a good place to keep boxed games or books. Stacks of wire baskets on castors provide cheap, portable storage. Compact fixtures, such as a continental-style sit-up bath, or a shower cubicle with a bi-fold door will make it easier to add a bathroom.

Far left: *The roof space must be used effectively if it is to be worth the cost of conversion. Adding an extra bathroom is well worthwhile and ensures that the new room will be used to the fullest. This bathroom was built using a custom-made range of built-in fixtures, designed to make the most of the available space.*

Left: *White paint and skylights flood this attic with cool, clear light. A second level, tucked under the apex of the roof, makes a sleeping platform – an arrangement strictly for the young and agile.*

SUN ROOMS

Cool, green and faintly mysterious, or light, warm and sunny, a sun room or conservatory can be more than just a place for plants. In some areas conservatories can be added without going through the time-consuming business of planning permission, so this can be a quick way to expand. The conservatory can't be used as a bedroom, bathroom or kitchen, but can become a leafy dining room, a study, extra play space or a second sitting room providing that it is double-glazed and properly heated for all-the-year-round use. Styles can range from a simple lean-to at the side or back of the house to an architect-designed addition from roof to ground level.

The simplest and cheapest sun room is a front or rear semi-glazed porch. A porch may seem a small space but can be useful. At either front or back, a semi-glazed porch protects the house from the full force of the weather and is a barrier between dirty feet and the hall or kitchen flooring. If you choose a porch with a solid bottom half, cupboards can be installed to hold outdoor clothing, shoes and shopping bags.

You can ask a builder to design and build a porch for you; buy a porch kit and assemble it yourself or ask the builder to do it. Porch kits come supplied with front and two sides, door, roof and drainage equipment. The glazing is installed separately.

ADDING A CONSERVATORY

The biggest decision you'll have to make is between a ready-made conservatory and a custom-designed model. Ready-made conservatories are cheaper than custom-built designs, but are mainly modern in style and not always suitable for an older house.

Ready-made conservatories are usually of lean-to design and come in a variety of sizes, or as component parts which you can assemble to the size needed. Both aluminium and wooden frames are available. Aluminium frames will not warp or rust and are available with double glazing to reduce condensation and draughts. Many aluminium-framed conservatories have a rounded roof, space age design. Wooden-framed models are more traditional and usually have a corrugated plastic roof. Remember that the wood will need regular treatment with preservative. Some companies supply Victorian-style conservatories in ready-to-assemble form, either for you or a builder to erect. Most have the traditional Victorian rounded end, are spacious inside and make an attractive addition.

If you want an individually designed conservatory, contact one of the companies specializing in this field, or ask an architect. There is no need to limit ideas to ground floor. Stunning effects can be achieved with a conservatory that encloses more than one level. A top to bottom design, with access from each floor of the house, either from balconies or landings onto a spiral stairway is ambitious, expensive and absolutely stunning. On a more modest scale, a simple lean-to can rise as far as the second floor with a loft at the upper level. This has the effect of extending the bedroom above, and increasing the energy efficiency of a large area of the house.

If you decide to use a firm of conservatory specialists, don't give the job to the first company you see. Contact two or three, study their suggestions, then make a decision. Some conservatory companies charge for initial survey and drawings, so find out if this is the case before they make a site visit.

WHERE TO PUT IT

The most useful site for a conservatory is at the side or back of the house, where it will extend the space inside. It is an attractive idea to remove the dividing wall between the house and the conservatory so that the kitchen, dining or living room flows unobtrusively into your extended indoor garden. The sun should reach the site for a reasonable period every day, so a south-facing orientation is best. Check the position of other buildings and trees that may cast too much shade over the conservatory. This will be pleasant in summer but will make the building chilly during the winter. And it is a simple matter to install blinds for use in the summer so natural shade is not necessary.

Check also that no nearby tree drips a sticky sap (as for instance, sycamores do). This makes constant cleaning of the glass areas a great chore.

Ground level isn't the only option. The Vic-

Left: *Top-of-the-range conservatories look good when the furniture is in keeping with their elegant design. Willow, cane or rattan seating is ideal, as are painted iron tables with heavy marble or slate tops.*

Far left: *A simple brick built conservatory adds extra space for relaxing.
It can be used to house a washing machine, freeing space in the kitchen.*

Left: *This stunning glazed addition is built at second-floor level and has a staircase down to the garden below. It is possible to build an extension like this, glazed at both ground and second floor, with a spiral staircase linking the two.*

Right: *Shading is essential in the summer. You can use greenhouse shading, or something more unusual and attractive, such as the rattan blinds shown here. Without shading, the conservatory will become uncomfortably hot on a sunny day – to the detriment of both plants and people.*

Far right: *There's no need to stick to a conventional conservatory shape. This conservatory/dining room has interesting sloping walls which lead the room out into the garden beyond.*

torians and Edwardians liked to build their "winter gardens" at second-floor level, an idea worth copying if you have a flat-roofed section at the side or back of the house. Imagine the fun of a bedroom leading onto a plant-filled sitting room, the perfect place to sew, knit, paint or simply enjoy a few moments of quiet reflection.

OUTFITTING AND FURNISHING

Whatever type of conservatory you choose, it will need a vapor barrier and a sound base. This concrete floor will need a covering of something pleasing to the eye and comfortable to walk on. Ceramic tiles or paving slabs are the traditional choice, but both are cold and hard underfoot. To encourage full use of the conservatory, choose warmer, softer vinyl tiles. Good quality tiles come in herringbone brick, paving, ceramic tile, parquet, marble, granite and slate effects and are surprisingly convincing. Cushioned sheet vinyl is cheaper and is comfortable to walk on and easy to clean. Woodstrip flooring looks good, but you must be careful that water from plants doesn't drip onto it or the boards will swell and distort.

If the house is centrally heated, it should be easy enough to add another one or two vents or radiators in the conservatory. Heating the conservatory means that it can be used as an extra room all the year round and will greatly extend the range of plants you can grow there.

Glazed buildings become very hot during the summer months, so add roller blinds or greenhouse shading at roof level. Curtains or blinds can be hung at the side windows but this rather spoils the effect of bringing the garden indoors.

Keep the garden theme with cane, wrought iron or plain white furniture. Look for upholstery in shades of green, with leafy patterning. To make the most of the space, limit planting to the edges of the conservatory. A plant shelf set just below the angle of the side walls and the roof will show off small vines. Big specimens can hang from the ceiling. Choose a mixture of leafy green, permanent plants, then fill in the spaces with seasonal blooms. Ficus, yucca, grape ivy, monstera, bromeliads, dracaena, ferns, wandering Jew, parlor palm and trailing ivies are all good permanent choices. Fill in with daffodils, tulips, crocus, primulas and narcissi in pots during the spring; geraniums, fuchsias, petunias, pansies, hydrangeas and impatiens in summer, azaleas, African violets and pot

chrysanthemums in the autumn and seasonal favorites such as Christmas cactus, solanum, poinsettia, cyclamen and pot-grown hyacinths between early December and January. Plants in pots are more adaptable than plants in beds, as less-successful specimens can be moved from the display. It is worth investing in a few big, permanent plants to get the new room off to a good start. One or two beds around the perimeter can look effective, but don't position them against the walls of the main house or you may bridge the vapor barrier. A grape vine trailing across the roof of an Edwardian- or Victorian-style conservatory is a traditional and charming feature. The leaves provide shading in summer and a well-established vine will produce grapes suitable for home winemaking.

Delicate tropical plants will need the extra protection of 24-hour heating during the winter months. A separate thermostat in the conservatory will guard against the room becoming too cold.

To get full use from the conservatory, you'll need lighting. Avoid spoiling the line of the glazed roof by choosing plug-in floor and table lamps. Uplighters can be positioned at floor level, so that the light beams through a screen of leaves. Downlighters can be used to show off a prize specimen, or light a corner used for reading or study.

Spectacular two- or three-level conservatories need careful thought. Establish seating at each level and use big vines so that there is a sense of continuity from ceiling to floor. You will also need to light the levels, either with angled spotlights at roof level, or with individual lighting at each level. As this sort of conservatory is likely to be designed by an architect, he or she will include lighting in the initial drawing.

MAINTENANCE

To keep the conservatory looking good, check plants daily. Remove dead or withered leaves. If watering isn't your strong point, invest in some self-watering planters. These are pots with a reservoir in the base, available at good nurseries. Feed the plants once a week during the growing season and repot and prune once a year.

Greenhouse owners will know how quickly glazed roof panels can turn green unless treated with a fungicide. Nurseries sell various wash-down products for use on both conservatory and greenhouse glazing.

USE EVERY INCH

It is easy to see the space-making potential of big projects, such as installing a new staircase, removing a dividing wall or installing a loft in a high-ceilinged room. But every home has a number of neglected corners that can be converted to efficient, effective space with little effort and at reasonably low cost.

CHECKPOINTS

Assess the potential by going around the house with a notepad. Look at these areas:

▶ Under the stairs. If the area is paneled in, why not consider opening it up?

▶ How big is the landing? Is it used for anything?

▶ What about the entry hall? Is it wide enough to allow a run of floor-to-ceiling shelves along one side?

▶ If the house has bay windows, is the bay area used? Consider installing window seats with a lift-up lid.

▶ Look inside built-in hall closets. Is all the space being used? Could the closet become a downstairs cloakroom or a wine cellar?

▶ If the house has long, thin corridors, think about using the space between the top of the doors and the ceiling, and about making use of wall space. Don't neglect the space above head height.

▶ Would wire baskets attached to the back of kitchen cabinet doors and clip-on baskets in closets help with storage problems?

▶ What about the space under the washbasin and at the end of the bath? Both these areas could become quite large cupboards.

▶ If a bed is not outfitted with drawers, how about making some pull-out storage boxes to go underneath it?

UNDER THE STAIRS

Even though the area under most staircases is an odd shape, the space is usable and shouldn't be wasted as a family dumping ground for everything but the family skeleton. The way in which the space can be utilized very much depends on the pitch and length of the staircase.

If the staircase is long and steeply pitched, the space beneath could be high enough to stand up in at the outside edges. It is well worth opening the area up and using the space for the telephone, or for a small table with a lamp and display.

If the house is a row house and the wall between the hall and living room has been knocked down, the space could be used to make a private corner, away from the rest of the room. Install a small, comfortable sofa, *chaise-longue* or chair, install lighting above, and add a low table for the ideal retreat. For even more privacy, use a screen to section the space from the rest of the room. Alternatively, the space could become a miniature office and house a table or desk for homework, hobbies or for writing letters.

In large houses, the under-stairs space is sometimes roomy enough to house a shower, or a continental sit-up bath, provided water supply and drainage are close by. A mini utility room is another possibility, with a washing machine and tumble dryer either side-by-side or stacked. You may also have room for a hamper and small sink. Bi-fold doors can be used to close the area off from the hallway when not in use.

Narrower, smaller under-stairs spaces lend themselves to all sorts of interesting building ideas. The space can be filled with wine racks (many wine merchants will make them to your size and specifications). Wine purists will probably recoil at the thought of a wall-mounted light shining through the bottles, but the effect is pretty and won't spoil the kind of wine most of us buy for everyday drinking.

Glass shelves installed from side to side, lit from behind and filled with plants or a collection of colored glass make an effective display. On a more practical level, the space can be filled with storage shelves, either open or with bi-fold doors. Use the shelves for books, magazines, shoes, shopping bags and odds and ends. A hanging section for coats is a neater idea than a hall tree.

Properly planned and insulated (to reduce vibration), shelving could be used to house stereo and a record and tape collection.

Above left: *This flip-down table is designed for maximum seating in a small area. When it's not in use it simply folds out of the way.*

Left: *The ultimate space saver, this platform bed combines storage, sleeping and seating in a tiny area. Some people may find an unconventional sleeping*

arrangement like this unnerving.

Above: *The space under the stairs is often one of the most wasted areas inside a house. A little imagination can turn the slightly awkward space into a practical and good-looking work area – an "understair office."*

ON THE LANDING

Landings can vary from a tiny area to almost small room size. In most cases, the space is ignored, used, at most, for a small table or a plant stand. If book storage is your problem, think about installing floor-to-ceiling shelves around the landing walls. Don't ignore the area above the doors and windows. Shelving can carry on above to link up at the other side. Add a set of library steps and a chair if there is space, and you've added a reading room. The same idea can be used for a record or tape collection.

A big landing may have enough space for a built-in cabinet to provide extra wardrobe storage or for bedlinen. Cabinets are easy to build. All that is needed is wood for the framework and ready-made louver doors for the front. Bi-fold louvers are space saving and available from good home improvement stores. Use single louver panels if sides are needed. One of the best landing cabinets I've seen was built straight across the wall, and around a window, adding a recessed window seat as well as useful storage.

Because the landing is a quiet spot, it's the ideal place to create a corner for homework, hobbies or reading. All that's needed is a desk or table, a comfortable chair and perhaps a screen. If the lighting is not very good, include a reading lamp there, too.

Sleeping on the landing may seem an odd idea, but if space is no problem it can be a good spot for an emergency sofa bed so that there is always a stand-by should you have an unexpected extra guest. A screen can be used for privacy and remain folded away when the bed is not being used.

Right: *This long, narrow landing is just big enough to accommodate a seat and some pleasant accessories. The floor-to-ceiling run of cabinets on the far wall is ideal for concealing household cleaning equipment.*

WINDOW SEATS

There's something wonderfully comforting about a window seat filled with plump, colorful cushions.

Building a window seat is an easy way to add an attractive feature to a room with bay windows, and there's a bonus as the space beneath the seat can be used for storage, accessible either through a hinged top or from doors at the front.

Like most good ideas, window seats are simple to make and well within the scope of a do-it-yourselfer equipped with an electric drill and screwdriver. Build a frame from wood, then add ready-made panels to the front. Louver doors can be used, or replacement wooden kitchen doors (available from home improvement stores in cathedral arch and fielded panel styles). If the top is to be covered by a padded seat, make it from chipboard. If the top will be seen, use 1½- to 2-inch-thick wood. Use a router to make a rounded edge at the front, then stain both the seat and top to match the front. If you buy plain louvers or doors, they can be stained to almost any color or wood effect.

If a radiator has been installed under a window where you might want to build a window seat, double glazing the window will mean the radiator can be positioned elsewhere in the room.

A deep window recess or other alcove can be turned into a miniature spare bedroom. All you need to do is build a base wide enough to take a single size mattress and hang curtains so that they pull across the front of the space to give some privacy. The mattress can be concealed with a slipcover made from upholstery fabric (quilted fabric looks effective) and throw cushions for day-to-day use. If you are building a bed in an alcove, add some narrow shelves to act as a bedside table.

THE LINEN CLOSET

In many homes the linen closet already is a multi-purpose repository for towels, sheets, tablecloths and even sundries like toothpaste, shampoo, soap and toilet paper. But there may still be more effective ways to use the space. See if any of the add-on storage accessories can mobilize inaccessible corners. Clip-on wire baskets, for example, can double your storage by making full use of the space below shelves. These baskets are available at good department stores in various sizes. Slide two baskets underneath each shelf and use the space below to stack towels, etc. Small baskets attached to the inside of the door will make it a good storage spot for toiletries and cleaning materials.

The inside of the linen closet door can be a good place to store the ironing board and iron, or the vacuum cleaner. Storage racks for ironing boards and irons are available from good department stores. These days, a vacuum cleaner may even come supplied with a hanging kit.

Of course, a small, shallow linen closet built into a hall wall may simply be the best use of space – in which case, organization will be your best friend.

Left: *Window seats should be cozy corners where you can curl up with a good book, or sit gazing at the view outside. Painted in shades of sunshine yellow, this delightful niche has the added attraction of underseat storage.*

BE SPACE-EFFICIENT

There's no truer saying than the old maxim "a place for everything and everything in its place". Clutter will make a small home seem even smaller. Cleaning materials, makeup, shoes, magazines and toys are difficult to store when there's no obvious place to put them. The answer is to look for under-used areas. Hang storage baskets on the backs of doors. Inside closets, they can be used for shoes, for makeup in the bathroom and for small toys in children's rooms. Hanging tiers of wire baskets are equally useful for kitchen odds and ends, fruit and vegetables, toiletries and the bits of broken toys, car wheels and old crayons most children seem unable to live without. Consider adding floor-to-ceiling shelves in hallways if there is enough width. Don't ignore the space under the bed. Either buy a storage bed (*see bedrooms section*), or invest in some plastic boxes on castors so that sheets, pillowcases, toys or shoes can be easily within reach.

If it is an effort to put things away, people will tend to find excuses not to be tidy. The best place to store anything is close to the place where that object is most often used, in a space that is easy to get in and out of.

Finding the space for storage may not seem easy in a small house, so think about the less obvious areas. Tall, narrow cabinets set at either side of a door with a shelf or matching bridging cupboard running over the top are unobtrusive and will hold a surprisingly large amount. If space is really tight, replace conventional doors with pull-down blinds suspended from the ceiling.

In a small bathroom, it will probably be worth replacing the basin with one which can be built into a counter with a cabinet beneath. There isn't much space around most bathtubs, but take a look, especially at the end opposite the faucet. If there is a useful area, build a small cabinet to fit the space, and attach a hinged door to hide the contents. Use the cabinet for cleaning materials. It will also be worth adding shelves above the bath to use for toiletries and towels. Glass shelves look attractive and won't be too badly affected by steam. But take care not to put shelves where you might bang into them when getting into or out of the bath. Make sure that glass shelves (or indeed any shelves) are firmly attached to their supporting brackets or studs so they cannot be accidentally dislodged.

Above all, never say "there isn't room." There is . . . if you look for it.

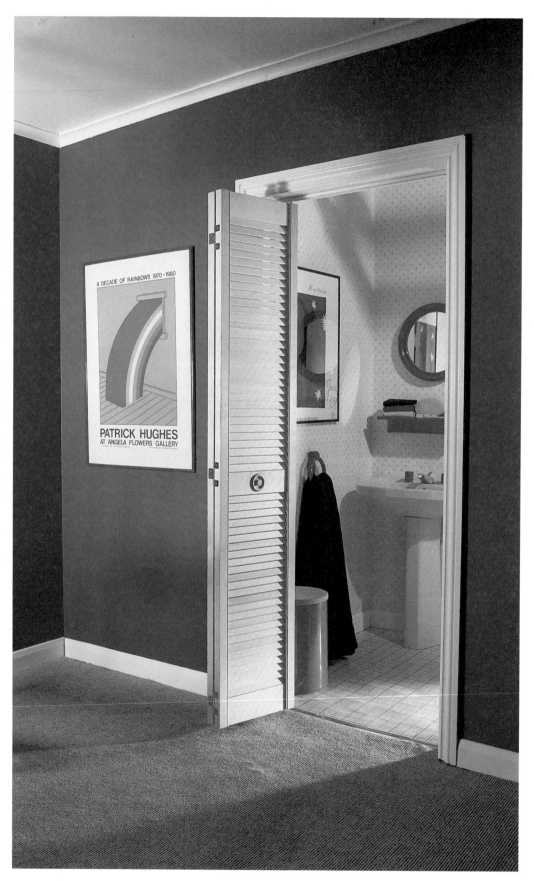

SPACE-SAVING DOORS

Doors which open into a room are restricting when space is limited. The area behind the hinged side of the door cannot be used and the floor area in front needs to be clear. There are various types of space-saving doors available.

Bi-folds: Bi-fold doors hinge at the center and fold one against the other. A typical bi-fold is about a third of the width of a conventional opening door. Their only disadvantage is that when open they project a small amount into the room. They still allow better access than hinged doors in crowded areas and take up less floor space.

Concertina doors: Concertina folding doors are pleated if made from fabric, or divided into narrow sections if made from a solid material. When the door is opened, the sections push together to lie flat against the door frame.

Sliding doors: A sliding door can be installed so that it slides along the wall adjacent to the doorway. This does mean that this section of wall cannot be used for anything else.

Shutters: Pull-down shutters are usually only seen in offices and industrial buildings but can look effective in the home. Wooden shutter doors have a warmer, friendlier feel than the metal type.

Curtaining: The cheapest solution is to remove the door and replace it with a curtain hung from a track fitted at the top of the door frame. The curtain fabric can be light in the summer and thick in winter.

Facing page: *Bi-fold doors consist of hinged panels which concertina as the door is opened. They do project a small amount into the room. The louvered type look good with this bathroom.*

Far left: *The bathroom with its original door. See how much floor space the door takes up with its opening arc.*

Left: *Concertina doors are the simplest of all to install, since they only have one top track. Unlike bi-folds, they don't project beyond the width of the frame or protrude into the room space.*

Below: *Rigid sliding doors are ideal provided there is enough room to one side of the opening for them to slide open. This tiny bathroom suddenly becomes much more accessible.*

A PLACE FOR EVERYTHING

A rigidly tidy home, with no clue to the likes and dislikes of its occupants, is a depressing and unpleasant place to be. Conversely, there's nothing quite so uncomfortable as a home which is chronically untidy. Attractive objects are worth displaying; old newspapers, discarded toys, shoes and the like are not. Consider too, the practical aspects of "a place for everything and everything in its place." A devil-may-care attitude to possessions usually means that keys, schoolbooks, passports and the like can never be found when they are wanted. On the other hand, a well-planned storage system means things can be found with a minimum of search and effort.

All families have an incredible amount of possessions, some used daily, others kept for sentimental reasons. For the home to work well and be comfortable, possessions need to be controlled so that things on display are visible only because you want them to be seen. If a frantic tidy up is a must before anyone comes to visit; if opening a cupboard is fraught with hazard as the contents are likely to descend and hit you on the head; if you have drawers jumbled full of pieces of string,

empty pens and broken cigarette lighters, installing storage to cope with it all can have the effect of a miraculous transformation.

Before you hang so much as a shelf, be ruthless with the clutter. Go through the house and throw away everything broken. Get rid of old newspapers and magazines. Sort through your mail. Put important letters to one side for filing and throw the rest out. Remember, if you don't use it, you don't need it, a policy which can apply to everything from furniture to clothes. Items in good condition can probably be sold or given to the Goodwill or Salvation Army.

Children are great hoarders but will usually respond to a plea for toys for a hospital or orphanage. Adopt the policy that if the offending object isn't put away after a couple of days, out it goes – very effective if your tidy-up campaign initially meets with loud cries of opposition.

Freed from the bonds of clutter, most rooms look larger, lighter and cleaner. There will be a reduction in wear, tear and breakages too. Most things last longer when removed from the risk of being trodden on, doused with coffee or chewed by the dog.

Top left: *The deep V of a pitched roof is a difficult space to use effectively. Here, narrow shelves make the most of every available inch.*

Above: *Ready-made modular storage can be combined in many different ways to suit your needs. Here, base cabinets, boxes and open shelves mix to make useful living room storage. When buying ready-made modular furniture, look for good, solid construction. A unit that is wobbly when empty will be even more insecure when loaded with books and other possessions.*

Above: *The stereo and television can be difficult to organize. Custom-built storage, with units specially designed to hold equipment is the answer. Usually, you can buy units individually and combine them as wished. A mixture of open and closed storage, as shown here, works well.*

Right: *Well-organized bedroom storage is a must for clothes and shoes. This row of cabinets offers full- and half-length units and a makeup mirror.*

IDENTIFY YOUR NEEDS

When the great sort-out is over and possessions have been pared down to the things the family wants to keep and enjoy using, you can decide on the type of storage needed. There are four basic choices.

WALL-MOUNTED SHELVES

Wall-mounted shelves are cheap to buy and easy to install. All that is needed is a power drill, some wall anchors, a spirit level and a screwdriver. Shelves look best in quantity, especially if they can be fitted into a recess and run from floor to ceiling. Try to avoid open-ended shelves, as it is difficult to prevent things from falling off. The strength of the shelves will only be as good as the installation fixing method used: thin chipboard shelves will need supporting at least every 16 inches; plywood or softwood every 27 to 30 inches. On solid walls, the brackets (or uprights for adjustable shelving) can be attached with screws into wall anchors; on hollow walls (plasterboard or lath-and-plaster), hollow-wall anchors will take only light loads – for heavier loads, screw directly into the vertical wooden studs or the cross members screwed across the studs.

FREESTANDING STORAGE

Freestanding means bookcases, cabinets, wardrobes and units not attached to the walls. As the furniture isn't custom-built for the room, space can be wasted. Well-made freestanding storage won't need the support of a wall to stand upright. Some self-assembly furniture tends to sway if unsupported; diagonal bracing will prevent this and avoid the possibility of it being accidentally toppled, with consequent breakages and/or injuries.

CUSTOM-BUILT UNITS

These are closets, bookcases, cabinets and shelving built to fit the room. Custom-built storage can be designed to fill oddly shaped or awkward areas which might otherwise be unused.

MODULAR STORAGE

Modular storage is a combination of shelf, drawer and cupboard units. Systems have a number of components which can be arranged to suit your needs. The advantage of most modular systems is that furniture can be added on as needed or when your budget permits further expenditure.

As well as the outside appearance of the storage system, consider what happens inside. If space is needed for a record collection, shelves must be wide enough from back to front to accommodate an album. The maximum practical length for bookshelves is around 30 inches. Longer shelves will bow in the middle because of the weight of a row of books. A front to back measurement of 9 inches is large enough for book storage. Deeper shelves have wasted space at the front. Don't buy storage furniture without thinking about what will be stored in it and whether or not it will be easy to put things in and take them out.

It will help to make a list, like the one shown on the right, of what you want to store, where you want to keep it and the space available before you go shopping for storage units.

Making this sort of list will help to identify where and what type of storage is needed. The answers are straightforward for our sample home. Adjustable shelving will cope with books in the kitchen, while a modular or custom-built system can house the TV, stereo, video, records, tapes and books needed in the living room. In the children's room, a combination of adjustable shelves and simple wire trays on castors tucked away under a worktop (to double as a desk) is a budget-conscious alternative to modular furniture.

Think too about how often things are used. Luggage, for instance, can be tucked away on the top shelf of a closet, as can Christmas decorations, buckets and shovels and other things used only once or twice a year. Remember to find a handy place for a hammer, screwdriver, fuses and washers, as these are needed more often than other tools.

FINDING THE SPACE

In a small home, finding a place for a storage system can be difficult. You'll see some good ideas throughout the pages of this book, but the most important thing is to make the most of the space available by adapting storage to suit your needs. If there isn't room for a conventional outward opening door, fit bi-fold doors or a roller or shutter blind instead. Narrow shelves can be used in confined spaces and are easier to manage than deep shelving. Remember not to block electrical fittings or ventilators.

STORAGE CHECKLIST

Items	Room
Records Stereo Tapes Video TV Books	Living room
Cookbooks	Kitchen
Sewing equipment	Spare room
Children's books Games Toys	Children's bedroom
Bicycle	Garage
Family documents	?

Below: *Don't forget the space beneath the stairs in your search for extra storage. This stylish Japanese-influenced staircase features open and closed storage boxes in the space beneath. Simple shelves or a cabinet can work just as well if your skills do not extend to something as ambitious as this.*

VISUAL IMPACT

Storage furniture is as important visually as upholstery, soft furnishings or any other component of your home. Storage units should be part of the look of the room. If, for instance, your living room is in traditional style, a modern stereo storage unit will be intrusive. Ready-made storage is available in many different finishes. Simple shelves now come in a selection of primary and pastel colors, with brackets to match. Plain white laminate-faced shelving goes with almost everything and is available in ready-cut lengths, or assembled into bookshelves and units of standard sizes.

As well as the obvious function, storage furniture can double as a room divider, be used to hide an unsightly wall or fill an awkward space. If you plan to use storage as a room divider, leave some shelving areas open to let light filter through to both parts of the room.

Remember small details, such as handles. These may seem unimportant in the store but could spoil the feel of the room. If the furniture is perfect for your purpose in every other way, see if the handles are easy to remove and replace with something more suitable.

One way to make a large row of shelves less obtrusive is to paint the woodwork to match the walls. You will have to use solid wood, as chipboard is usually laminate or wood veneer faced and can't be painted.

If you plan to use storage furniture for display, make sure that shelves are high enough from top to bottom to house your treasures. Choose a material which will enhance the objects on display and show them to best effect. Glass shelves or glass-fronted cabinets provide a good background for china, glass and sculpture. If you attach mirror panels to the wall between the shelves, you will not only enjoy the attractive reflections of your treasures, but make them seem more plentiful. Or you could use concealed lighting to highlight them.

If your budget won't stretch even as far as simple shelving, improvise. Wicker baskets, wire trays, plastic boxes on castors or simple shelves made from lengths of faced chipboard separated by bricks are all attractive storage solutions. Second-hand office equipment is often a good buy. Battered filing cabinets gain a new lease on life if resprayed in bright colors. Use two as a support for a length of wood or kitchen counter and you'll have a desk or dining table and handy storage combined.

Below: Simple industrial-style shelving and storage boxes can turn the garage into a useful warehouse for tools, paint, gardening and do-it-yourself equipment.

ADDING A STORAGE ROOM

A service porch, the garage, or any unused space with enough headroom to stand upright can become a walk-in storage room, the best possible solution for a big collection of books or records, toys, games or clothes. A storage room is a strictly functional space. It must be well-lit and ventilated, weatherproof and accessible – it defeats the object if the room is cold, damp, unlit and hard to get to, so don't use an unconverted attic or basement. A room too small to be habitable, or without a window is ideal.

Plan the room to suit the things to be stored there. For clothes, a tubular hanging rail on castors, wire racks for shoes and tiers of wheeled wire baskets for sweaters is all that is needed. If you want to use the area as a dressing room, add a mirror to one wall and surround it with light strips. A kitchen counter, hinged so that it will fold flat against the wall, makes a good makeup table. Above it attach a mirror surrounded by lights. Industrial metal shelving can be installed from floor to ceiling to store records, books and games. Add a ladder or a set of library steps for access to top shelves. Provided your storage room is reasonably cool, it can be used as a wine cellar, outfitted with either ready-made or custom-built wine racks. Avoid the temptation to treat the storage room as a dumping ground. It will quickly become cluttered and you'll be back to the "can't find a thing" situation.

One very simple way to gain extra space in a storage room is to change the door so that it opens outward, or replace it with bi-fold or sliding doors. This frees the section of wall running at right angles to the door for yet more shelves or perhaps a wall-mounted cabinet.

In the living room, or in a child's bedroom, a wall of storage will cope with books, games, toys, drinks and glasses. Include a pull-down flap to use as a bar or a desk and vary open shelves with glazed or solid-door cabinets and sets of drawers. There is a huge selection of custom-made modular furniture incorporating all of these features. Some have a special section for TV or stereo, with holes to take cords.

As a safety measure always make sure that open shelving in a young child's room is easily reached by the child. Otherwise, it is inevitable that he or she will attempt to climb up to retrieve a favorite toy or other desired object – and perhaps slip and fall.

Above: *A collection of family portraits stretching back through different generations looks attractive if displayed in a variety of interesting frames. As here, the grouping should be kept small and limited to one wall only to avoid dominating the room.*

COLLECTIONS

A collection on display adds a touch of warmth and personality and can add an important focal point to a featureless area such as a hall, landing or stairway.

Collectors collect because they like looking at their acquisitions – so always display your finds in a part of your home where they can be admired at any time of the day without having to get them out specially.

The word "collection" summons up visions of valuable antiques or priceless paintings, but often simple, inexpensive things make the best display. A group of flourishing green plants, arranged in a wicker basket or on a tray of colorful beach pebbles is as beautiful and interesting in its own right as precious pieces of china.

What you collect depends on your taste. Jugs, plates or cups and saucers are easy to find and look good if you choose the work of one particular potter, or decide to collect only blue or some other favorite color. Other inexpensive but effective collections include framed restaurant menus, straw hats, fans, matchbooks (cleverly displayed in a box frame), small wooden boxes, stone and wooden eggs, candlesticks and china. When the collection becomes too large for display, replace some of the less attractive objects with something prettier and more expensive.

The collection should never overpower the room in which it is displayed. One wall with a big grouping of pictures is pleasing; two or three walls treated in the same way will make the room feel crowded and have the effect of making it seem short of space. The collection should be small enough to stay in its allotted spot, and should not be allowed to spill over onto surfaces used by the family.

Display the collection where it can be seen and enjoyed. Pictures should be shown in good light (but not in direct sunlight as it will fade watercolors and prints). Arrange pictures for maximum impact. If you have a large, dramatic picture, or one you particularly like, hang it in the center of the group, or alone with strong lighting from a concealed source. Picture lights, or ceiling-mounted downlights will help to make art a focal point in the evening. Beam spotlights at a collection on shelves, or fit under-shelf lights. A light shining up through glass shelving will show amber, fine china or glassware to perfection.

A grouping of pictures will look more effective if the frames are interesting. Secondhand wooden and gilt frames can often be found in junk shops and will transform the most undistinguished print or simple collection of matchbook covers or labels.

Small objects, such as interesting pebbles, enameled pill or snuff boxes, tiny silver picture frames, lead soldiers and the like look good arranged together on a small table or chest beneath a wall or floor lamp for maximum impact.

Whatever your collection, remember that it is there because it is a part of your taste and a reflection of your interests. Clever, thoughtful display will allow others to share your pleasure and bring the warmth of your personality to the room in a way no contrived interior design can ever achieve.

Left: *An imaginative and dust-free way to display a collection is to incorporate it into a specially made glass-topped coffee table.*

Below: *Groupings of pictures look best if they follow a particular shape. If you want to make your ceiling look higher, a vertical arrangement will help. Equally, to lower a high ceiling try a horizontal grouping. To achieve the right balance when hanging pictures follow the guidelines given here.*

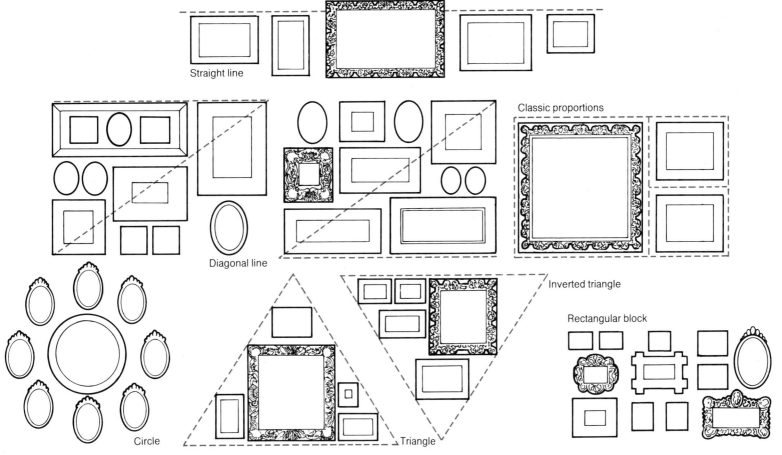

Straight line

Classic proportions

Diagonal line

Inverted triangle

Rectangular block

Circle

Triangle

COLOR AND PATTERN

Successful color scheming is a combination of personal preference and the character of the room where the colors will be used. Use of color is a subject that attracts more than its fair share of pretentious (and sometimes nonsensical) advice, ranging from the old saws on the folly of using blue and green together to the amateur psychiatrists who declare that blue is depressing, gray indicates a repressed personality and yellow is associated with mental illness.

Color and pattern are important features of any room. Both can affect the visual size of the room, and the amount of reflected light. The way in which we see color depends on the surface it is applied to and on the light source. Everyone has experienced the problems of buying carpet or fabric and finding the shade is quite different at home, in daylight, than it was in the store when displayed under harsh fluorescent lighting.

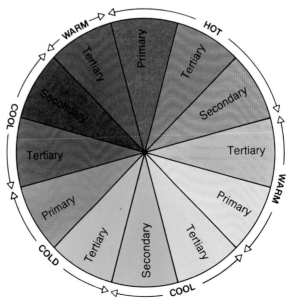

Above: *The bedroom should be a relaxing place, so look for a harmonious, gentle color scheme. This room was painted in a natural lavender-tinted white flat latex paint, with primrose-tinted natural white on the baseboard, door and window frames and headboard.*

Left: *A color wheel shows how colors graduate. A secondary color is produced by equally mixing the primaries on either side of it, a tertiary by equally mixing the neighboring primary and secondary colors. The wheel can be used to determine contrasting colors (opposites) and harmonizing colors (neighbors).*

If you cast your mind back to school art classes, you will remember the color spectrum. Red, blue and yellow are the primary colors, and orange, green and violet are the secondaries, each made by mixing two primaries in equal proportions. The spectrum falls into two groups, warm and cool. Warm colors include red, yellow, orange, tan, beige, cream and autumn shades. Used in a north-facing room, their effect is warming and comfortable. Cool colors suggest light, and space, the seascape shades. Blue, green, and monotones from palest gray to violet are all cool colors. A small, dark room painted in one of the cool shades will appear instantly larger.

Fashion affects the colors used by paint and wallcovering manufacturers. At the moment pastels and soft effects achieved by using paint techniques such as marbling, rag rolling and sponging are the kind of thing you will see on paint charts and in wallpaper sample books. Response to color is individual. Pink and peach may both be fashionable, but a room in either of these colors won't work unless you have a positive feeling about the color.

Present trends in color are almost all easy to live with. The advent of natural whites (white with a hint of rose, apricot, green, blue, lavender or beige) makes choosing a complementary scheme easy. Major paint manufacturers help too by grouping their shade cards in color sets.

CHOOSING A COLOR SCHEME

To work well, a color scheme must take into account every element in the room. Take a tip from interior designers and make a color board. Unless you are starting from scratch,

Above: *Now look at the same room and the same furniture with a different color scheme. The effect is just as relaxing, even though the colors are darker. The secret of success lies in choosing muted shades. The walls are painted in a dusky pink, with washed-out sea blue on the headboard, baseboard, door and window frames. Instead of white, which would have provided too much contrast in this scheme, the cornice is painted in a magnolia shade.*

Right: *Be brave with color and you'll achieve an effect that is both unusual and relaxing. Hot, bold shades of apricot and terracotta blend to give an exotic feel to this living room, in which patterns and textures are skillfully mixed.*

the scheme will probably have to work around an existing carpet or upholstery. Attach a small sample piece to your board, then experiment until you find the best possible combination for walls, floor, upholstery and soft furnishings. Remember accessories; the best-planned scheme can fail if lampshades, vases or bric-a-brac fight with the basics. A good way to choose accessories is to use them to pick up a predominant color in upholstery or wallcovering. If, for instance, upholstery and curtains have a blue background and pink, cream and beige pattern, adding pink lamps and shades, picture frames or vases will unify the scheme.

Many manufacturers now produce co-ordinated collections of tiles, wallcovering, upholstery and accessories to make mixing and matching simple. If you are unsure of your own skills, choosing from one of these collections guarantees that the scheme will succeed.

When planning a color scheme, you may find that your favourite color won't work if used on a whole wall. Think instead about introducing it in splashes, and using a more successful, complementary color on the walls. You may, for instance love turquoise, a color that is overpowering when used over a large area, but stunning if added to a white, pale green or pale gray room in the form of lamps or ornaments, cushions, upholstery or curtains.

White is a safe choice, but can be boring. Experiment instead with shades and textures. Walls painted in a natural white, combined with open-textured, off-white upholstery and crunchy pure white crochet cushions looks effective and inspired. White walls, combined with white net curtains and pale beige upholstery is simply dull.

The surface to which color is applied will affect the way it reacts to light. Flat paint absorbs light so that the color seems flat. Semi gloss and gloss reflect light and will bring life to a dark or cramped room.

Most people feel uncomfortable in rooms where one shade predominates. Beige, the "safe choice" is a case in point. Beige upholstery, beige carpet, magnolia walls and beige curtains are a combination guaranteed to depress. Visual relief, in the form of a more positive color, such as a dash of terracotta, some creamy, textured cushions, or an Indian dhurrie in burnt umber shades gives an instant lift. Adding contrast, even if it is only in the form of leafy green plants, will bring interest and vitality to a subdued background color scheme.

Pattern is important to the success of a color scheme, adding visual relief in the same way as splashes of color. If, for instance, you have decided to paint the walls pale pink, and have selected a gray carpet and upholstery, using plain pink or gray curtains would be a safe, but dull, choice. Look instead for a pattern. You might, in this instance, choose curtain and pillow fabric with a gray background, patterned in pink, blue, cream or gray shades. Add pink accessories, or break up the floor area with a plain or patterned rug and a static scheme has warmth and life. Repetition is an important part of any successful scheme. Picking up upholstery colors in piping, on cushions or curtain tie-backs may seem fussy, but it is this attention to detail that makes the difference between a pleasant room and one that attracts admiring comments.

Patterns can be used together, providing they are of the same basic design. You could, for instance, use a smaller version of the pattern on upholstery for curtains and lampshades. Avoid using patterns that "fight" with one another. Unless carefully chosen, a heavily patterned carpet, wallcovering and upholstery can be disastrous. Bold pattern can be used as a single focal point in an otherwise plain room. Remember that pattern does not necessarily mean fabric. Carved woodwork, textured blinds, loosely woven upholstery and architectural details all add pattern to a room. A simple way to accentuate the pattern of a cornice or molding is to paint it in a deeper or paler shade than the rest of the walls. Sometimes, pattern can be the starting point for a color scheme, when a particular wallpaper or fabric is the dominant element.

Light can add pattern too. Sunlight streaming through a venetian blind, or a table lamp shining through the leaves of a well-established plant can do as much to enliven a plain wall as a patterned wallcovering. A pleated lampshade will produce a different effect than a plain one in the same color.

Never rush headlong into a color scheme. You will have to live with the results for quite a long time, so tread carefully until you are sure that the combination of color and pattern is the right one. Making a color board will help. Some paint manufacturers sell small sample cans of paint, so you can try it out on a small area of wall (paint always looks different up than it does in the can or on the shade card). It is better to invest in one roll of wallpaper, stick a length up and decide you don't like it, than to discover you and the pattern can't live happily together once all the paper has been paid for. But ask the wallpaper salesperson to hold the requisite total number of rolls while you try the first one. Otherwise you could find the remainder comes from another dye batch and doesn't quite match up. Study room schemes in magazines and make a file of those you like. It is likely that they will all be of one type, a clue to the sort of schemes you will be comfortable with.

USING STRIPES

Wallcovering can have a dramatic visual effect on a room, particularly if the pattern runs in a distinctive direction.

Everyone knows that vertical stripes will make a room seem higher while horizontal lines will make the space seem lower and sometimes wider.

In practice, it isn't quite as simple as that. Thin stripes in a soft color on a white or neutral background have a better effect than wide, boldly colored stripes. Diagonal stripes, particularly if they are incorporated into a trellis pattern, widen space and are a good idea for the short walls in a narrow room.

The color you choose for paint and wallpaper can alter the apparent size of the room. The cool colors – blues, pale greens, lilacs and misty grays – recede, pushing back

the walls of a small room. This is why thin, soft gray stripes work better than the much more assertive bright red ones.

ON THE BORDER

Wallpaper borders provide tremendous scope for the creative decorator. They can be used to add interest to plain walls where a room is too small to stand strong pattern; add definition when used around the edge of a sloping ceiling or make tall, featureless walls seem lower and more interesting when added as a dado rail at waist height.

Borders can be run along the top of walls as a substitute for cornice. If the walls are very high, position the border at picture rail height (about 18 inches) below the level of the ceiling. This can also distract attention from an uneven ceiling line. Decorate the space above to match the ceiling. Many modern border designs have been made to look like stencils, a boon for those who aren't confident or artistic enough to attempt the real thing themselves.

Using a border is a good way to mark the dividing line between different patterns, or between paint and patterned wallcovering. Apply the border at waist height and run it up the sides and around the top of any doors or windows in the room. Use paint, either sponged or stippled on the lower half of the wall and a complementary patterned wallpaper above. The new coordinated collections of wallcoverings, borders and paint make this sort of mixing and matching well within the scope of the adventurous amateur home decorator.

Left: Bold striped wallpaper could be overpowering if used on every wall, but here it is seen to best effect, broken up by closets, reflected by a mirror and making the ceilings of this small room look much higher than they are. The crisp, cool atmosphere of the room has been achieved by the use of blue and white, both rather cold colors. Extra warmth comes from the glowing brass bed frame and the gold trim on the fittings.

THE ART OF ILLUSION

Don't be cast into despair if there's no structural rescue for a small, dark or awkwardly shaped room. Clever use of color, pattern, mirrors, light and texture can work wonders with the most unpromising location. Simplicity is the key. Remember, clutter crowds and dark colors have the effect of drawing walls inward. Pale colors, simple patterns and well-organized space have the opposite effect. Choose semigloss paint, as it has a slightly shiny surface that will reflect light and make the room seem bigger.

The quickest, easiest transformation for a small room is to paint the walls in a pale color and re-cover upholstery to match. Pale needn't mean white. Tinted white paints (whites with a hint of rose, yellow, blue or green) are all good. So are the very palest shades of yellow, blue, green and gray, the cool colors. Pale pinks, apricot, lavender and brown are warm colors and have the opposite effect. Use variations of the main shade for upholstery in self-patterned or textured fabric for a look that's cool and calm.

Pattern can create space, providing you choose the right type. Vertical stripes will make a low-ceilinged room seem higher. Diagonal lines have the effect of pushing walls outward and are particularly good used in carpeting. Pale trellis designs have a 3D effect. Most wallpaper manufacturers have a trellis in their line, or you can paint ordinary garden trellis white and attach it to an end wall in a rectangular room. Leaf green looks wonderful behind painted trellis.

As well as these simple tricks, there are more complex and effective ways to give the illusion of space.

Above: *Always position mirrors so that the reflection is interesting. This series of mirrored sliding-door closets reflects the room facing. Placing mirror at right angles to a window, as here, has the effect of visually lengthening the room. Big green plants add a cool, spacious air.*

MIRROR MAGIC

When Alice stepped through the looking glass, she found another room. In real life, the room itself won't be beyond the mirror, but you can exploit the illusion to add both space and light.

A wall of mirrored glass, cleverly placed, can give the impression that the room is longer, wider or that there is another room beyond. Mirror attached at right angles or opposite a window increases light. Arched mirror panels placed along a wall at evenly spaced intervals will suggest that the room leads on to more space.

Large pieces of mirror glass were once only available to interior decorators and the trade. Happily, this has changed and most home improvement centers now stock tall mirror panels in various widths, mirror arches and mirror tiles. Various finishes are available, including plain silvered, smoked, bronze veined and even etched glass.

Mirror panels and tiles are easy to install. Some small mirrors have self-adhesive pads on the back; others are attached to the wall using mirror screws, clips, adhesive or wood. Packs bought at home improvement centers come with full instructions.

Wherever you put mirror panels, make sure that the reflection works well; otherwise the illusion will be destroyed. Avoid reflecting posters or books – writing will be back to front. Likewise, steer clear of seating areas as most people find it disturbing to be constantly aware of their mirror image. Plants or a small table displaying an interesting object are both good subjects for reflection.

Mirror tiles only work well if the backing wall is completely flat. A bumpy wall will make it impossible to align the tiles, giving crooked, visually disturbing lines. Mount mirror panels on wood strips instead.

Left: *You can make a short, narrow area such as a hallway seem twice as long by positioning a mirror at the end. Here mirror doors conceal a useful storage closet and visually lengthen the hall.*

MIRROR TRICKS

Mirrors can work miracles all around the house. Try these simple tricks.

▶ Add length to a hallway or corridor with a mirrored wall at the end. If there's a storage cupboard, replace wooden doors with mirrored closet doors.

▶ Widen a narrow hallway or corridor by putting baseboard-to-ceiling mirrors along the entire length of one wall.

▶ Add height and light to a low room by completely covering the ceiling with adhesive mirror tiles.

▶ Make a garden niche by surrounding a piece of arched mirror glass with trellis. Trail ivy around the trellis and position a big plant against the facing wall to give the illusion of a beautiful, unreachable garden which exists beyond the archway.

▶ Fit mirror panels into alcoves on either side of the fireplace.

▶ Make a worktop, desk or sideboard top seem wider by covering the wall behind it with a row of mirror panels or tiles.

▶ Ordinary mirror glass will steam up in a bathroom, so a wall of mirror tiles can be a waste of time. Ask for plastic or acrylic steamproof tiles.

▶ Make a mirrored corner by attaching two half arches or rectangles of mirrored glass at right angles to each other.

▶ Make a fake cornice by attaching mirror strips at angles between the ceiling and walls.

▶ Cover the back and sides of a niche or alcove with mirror glass. Attach glass shelves and use the niche to display a collection. Installing recessed ceiling lights or spotlights at the top will reflect light.

Bottom left: *A soft, swirling paint technique, like the effect shown here, will help to make walls recede. Sunny colors make this north-facing room seem bright and warm. The paint technique is achieved by swirling paint over a base coat, using the back of an old plastic hair brush. Experiment with paint until you find an effect you really like.*

Bottom right: *Several shades and textures of white used together make this small space seem uncluttered – despite the big pieces of furniture and elaborate curtains. Color comes from the fabric used on the sofa, and picked up by stencils around the walls.*

PAINT EFFECTS

Paint can be as clever as mirrors in deceiving the eye, especially if the effect is expertly applied. Simple sponging with two or three colors from the same group will add depth to an alcove and interest to a plain wall. You'll find details on how to sponge paint on *pages 60-61*. When sponging, put the pale base coat on first, then the darker of the sponging colors with the palest on top. The effect is cloudy and insubstantial, a pleasant way to blur confining boxy spaces.

Dragging is an effect with finely graduated lines, ideal in pale shades for making a small room larger. Choose color combinations such as very pale blue over natural white with a hint of blue, or two very pale greens or yellows. Details on how to drag paint appear on *page 64*. Like sponging, dragging softens lines, making shapes seem insubstantial and creating an airy look.

Ragging on and rag rolling both give walls the texture of crushed velvet. This can be claustrophobic in dark shades, but works well in pales, especially if the scheme carries through with soft furnishings in one of the ragged colors. Ragging is a way of introducing pattern without reducing space. Again, choose pale shades of green, blue, yellow and gray when the intention is to make the room seem bigger.

Trompe l'oeil is the most complicated of all paint effects and is a technique for professionals. *Trompe l'oeil* is the art of deceit, a clever visual trick, which can be used to create anything from a row of marble pillars to a window scene with a garden beyond. The secret lies in creating perspective so that the painting has depth with the result that a row of fake bookcases looks like the real thing, doorways, stairs, windows and scenes can appear in otherwise impossible spots, a niche can sport a permanently fresh vase of flowers – the possibilities are endless provided that the work is done by a skilled *trompe l'oeil* artist.

Stenciling is simple enough for even the most unartistic. A stenciled border of leaves around a doorway, or a bouquet of flowers on an otherwise featureless wall adds interest to a small room. Cut your own stencils from oiled stencil board or acetate sheeting (both available at art and craft shops), or buy them ready cut from a decorating store. Work in one color at a time and allow each section to dry before you move on to the next. Vertical stenciling will have the effect of making a low ceiling seem higher.

If you have visited Italy, Greece or any other Mediterranean countries, you will know that interiors always seem cool and spacious, even though the room itself is small. Color washing is the secret of this subtle, luminous look. Color wash is made from thinned-down water-based paint and is applied with a big brush over an existing base coat. Use sweeping strokes to give the right effect. Color wash works well when applied in pale greens, yellows, pinks and blues but not in gray, where the effect generally tends to be muddy rather than attractive.

Below: *Dragging, where paint is applied on top of a base coat, then "dragged" by moving a brush over the surface, looks attractive on both furniture and walls. This solid wood kitchen was dragged in soft pink over an off-white base.*

DECORATING TECHNIQUES

SPECIAL FINISHES

Learning how to apply special paint finishes, such as sponging, rag rolling, stippling and stenciling, opens up a bright new world of color and effect. You can give walls a misty finish, add depth without pattern, disguise junk furniture, or add character to a plain room with simple stenciling.

SPONGING

Sponging is the easiest paint technique to master. It gives a soft, dappled effect, ideal in a room too small to support pattern. You can sponge light colors over a darker base, or dark over light; choose close harmonies or dramatic contrast.

Any good-quality latex paint is suitable for sponging. The only equipment needed is a paint tray and a natural sea sponge. Look for a medium-sized sponge with plenty of well-spaced holes. Synthetic sponge is not suitable as the surface is too even.

HOW TO SPONGE

Before you start, apply the base coat to the walls. The best effect is achieved by sponging in three colors, with either the palest or the darkest as the base, depending on the effect you want to achieve.

When the base coat is dry, soak the sponge in water and wring it out thoroughly. This is important. If the sponge is too wet, it will thin the paint and cause runs.

The paint is sponged onto the wall one color at a time. Try the colors on a piece of paper or cardboard first to see if you like them.

To sponge the walls, pour a little paint into a tray, dip the sponge in and scrape off the excess on the sloping part of the tray. Starting at the top of the wall, dab quickly and lightly in a

Above: *Sponging achieves quick overall impact. Color is sponged on with a rapid dabbing motion to create this pretty effect.*

Left: *In this room the three different techniques of sponging (upper walls), bag-graining (lower walls), and dragging (baseboard and table) are successfully combined.*

60

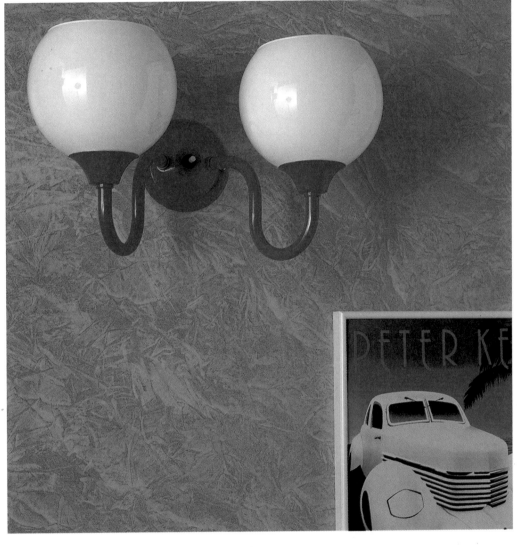

Left: *The ragging, or rag-rolling, effect is suitable for large areas.*

Below: *The effect is achieved by covering the wall with glaze in vertical stripes, then quickly rolling clean rags over the wet glazed surface.*

random direction, reloading the sponge with paint as necessary. Allow this first coat to dry, then repeat with the second color.

A coat of clear polyurethane varnish will protect sponging from the effects of steam in a kitchen or bathroom.

RAGGING

Ragging is a professional paint technique, giving effects ranging from softly blurred to crisply distinct. It can be used on walls or furniture and is a useful way to blend a bulky radiator into the room scheme.

There are two kinds of ragging; ragging on and ragging off. For both types, you must use a solvent-based paint (such as alkyd semi-gloss) for the base and a top coat made from a mixture of 70 percent scumble glaze (available through specialty paint shops and some-

times called transparent oil glaze), 20 percent alkyd semigloss paint in the color of your choice and 10 percent paint thinner. This mixture stays wet long enough for you to achieve the ragged effect.

Ragging really needs two people, one to apply the glaze and the other to rag while the glaze is still wet.

Start by applying the base coat of alkyd semigloss paint. This can be paler or darker than the color you want to rag. Allow the base coat to dry, then apply the first strip of glaze from floor to ceiling over an area about 18 inches wide.

Roll a bunch of clean chamois leather, mutton cloth or lint-free cotton rags into a sausage shape. Starting at the top, dab or roll the rags over the wet glazed surface. You can vary the pattern by changing the angle of your hand. When you reach the bottom, start again at the top of the next strip, overlapping

slightly with the first one as you progress.

When the room is complete, start again, using a glaze in a paler shade than the first coat and repeat the process. This will have the effect of revealing part of the dark base and give a soft, coordinating finish.

Rag rolling is a slightly different technique, giving an effect rather like moire or watered silk, perfect for a formal living room or pretty bedroom. It works best in soft pastels. Paint the wall in alkyd semigloss in a paler shade than the top coat. Mix up a glaze, as described for ragging. Ideally, the paint element of the glaze should be one or two shades deeper than the base.

Brush the glaze onto the walls, as described for ragging. Roll a bunch of lint-free rags into a tight sausage shape and roll it from top to bottom down the glaze. Overlap strips slightly and use an artists' brush to feather the paint at floor level.

STENCILING

Stenciling is a lovely way to add a touch of originality to any room. Designs can run around a door or window, liven up a dull piece of furniture or be used as a border. One of the best effects I have seen was a display of pictures "hung" from stenciled bows.

Stencils range from simple one-color designs, such as a row of ducks or toy soldiers for a child's room to complex swags of grapes, ribbons and flowers. Designs can be bought ready made, or you can cut your own.

To make a stencil, trace the design of your choice. If it is small, have it enlarged on a photocopier. To transfer the design to stencil board (available from most art shops), slip a piece of carbon paper between the board and the photocopy and trace the design.

Cut around the outline using a sharp craft knife. Have a thick piece of cardboard beneath the design. For a stencil to look effective, the spaces in the design must be distinct; otherwise you will have blobs rather than crisp paintwork.

When the stencil is complete, attach it to the required surface with double-sided tape. Alkyd, latex and acrylic paints are all suitable for stenciling. Apply the color with a stubby stencil brush, using just a minimum of color. If you overload the brush, the paint may run down behind the stencil causing smudges. Allow one color to dry thoroughly before you start to apply the next.

Stencil designs can be found to go with any style of decor, from an elegant dining room **(below)** *to a more whimsical child's bedroom* **(right)**.

Far right: *A pallette knife is used to hold the stencil firm while painting the pattern.*

If you are making a stenciled frieze, mark the position carefully before you start; otherwise the line will be wobbly.

When you have finished painting and the last color is dry, lift the stencil away from the wall and clean it with paint thinner, then store it away for future use.

COLOR WASHING

Color washing gives a soft, faded look, rather like well-worn cotton. It is a mellow effect, lovely in a country-style room. It is a rustic look, perfect with old pine furniture and cottage prints.

The time-honored way to color wash is with distemper but this can turn powdery. A better, more stable coating involves using a thin glaze over an alkyd semigloss base. Begin by applying a coat of white alkyd semigloss to the walls. Make up a mixture of 30 percent scumble, 20 percent paint thinner glaze (both available from specialty paint shops) and 50 percent alkyd semigloss paint in the color of your choice. Pale, soft shades work best when you are color washing.

Apply the top glaze with a wide brush, moving it in several different directions to prevent the glaze from running down the wall. Brush out obvious edges but leave some of the base uncovered. Allow this first coat to dry, then apply another coat, this time covering the visible white areas. This gives a varied effect. Wait until this second coat is thoroughly dry, then protect the color with a coat of clear polyurethane varnish.

Above: *Dragging creates strong vertical emphasis and consequently will make ceilings appear higher.*

Right: *When dragging a wall, one person should paint on the glaze while the other drags a brush down over it with a single stroke.*

DRAGGING

Dragging produces a faintly striped effect, achieved by applying a colored glaze over a pale base coat, then dragging a brush through the wet paint. It is an effect at its best in formal rooms, with rich, dark furniture. It also provides a good background for stenciled designs.

Dragging is a technique for the experienced. It can be difficult to keep the stripes straight, hard to do on a long wall. It can also be tricky moving from one stripe to the next.

To drag walls, first apply a pale base coat of alkyd or latex semigloss and leave it to dry. Make up a glaze using 70 percent scumble glaze (available from specialty paint shops), 20 percent alkyd semigloss paint in a darker color than the base coat and 10 percent paint thinner. Apply the glaze with a wide brush (a paper-hanging brush is best) with stiff bristles. Apply the glaze, working down the wall in bands about three times the width of the dragging brush. Starting at the top, pull the dragging brush in a light, steady movement through the glaze. Feather away any buildup of glaze at the base. Repeat on the next strip. You will need to clean the brush at intervals to keep the drag marks well defined but never stop to do this when you are halfway through a strip.

MARBLING

Marbling is the most complicated paint technique to master, but the most effective once you learn to do it well. You will need about a month of practice before you try marbling walls or furniture, during which time you should use a sheet of hardboard as your practice surface.

White marble is the easiest to imitate and it helps if you can find a small piece to keep by you as a guide to how the veins run through the stone.

THE PAINT

Marbling is applied using a base coat of off-white alkyd semigloss paint. Make sure that the surface is flat, dust-free and smooth before you apply the base, as every imperfection will show through and spoil the smooth, marbled effect.

Apply one or two coats of semigloss paint to give a smooth, slightly opaque finish. Apply a glaze made from 30 percent scumble (available at good paint shops), 50 percent bone-colored alkyd semigloss paint and 20 percent paint thinner glaze. Brush this over the painted surface, then fold a lint-free cloth into a neat pad and dab it over to give a soft, mottled background.

The next stage is to mix the paint for the veining. For this you will need black artist's oil, which is available from art supply shops, and some raw sienna oil paint. Mix a little of each together to make a dark gray paint. Using a pointed brush (also available from art shops) or a large feather, draw veins diagonally across the painted surface. Study your piece of real marble as you paint to see how the veins should run. You can then add a few darker veins in raw sienna, but be careful not to overdo this effect.

When you have painted about six veins, smudge them with a broad, soft brush. When the marbling is dry, you can protect it with a coating of clear polyurethane varnish.

Once you have mastered the marbling technique, you can work in other, more flamboyant colors.

MALACHITE

Malachite is an exciting finish, reflecting the texture of the natural stone. It is an easier technique to master than its appearance suggests and looks especially effective when used over a small area such as a shelf, a picture frame, trinket box or small piece of furniture.

Malachite works best on a smooth, pale surface. Lamanite-coated chipboard is ideal but it must be rubbed down with fine sandpaper first.

Start by applying a coat of alkyd semigloss paint. Pale pastel shades work best. Smooth the paint over the surface using a rag. Now take a piece of thin cardboard and drag it through the paint, wiggling it from side to side to make the contour lines so characteristic of malachite. There will be small gaps between the bands of pattern you have created. Take a small stubby brush and twist it in a circular motion in the gaps.

Allow the paint to dry, then cover it with one or two protective layers of polyurethane varnish.

OTHER TECHNIQUES

There are many other paint techniques, some too difficult for even a skilled amateur painter to attempt. Spattering, the art of flicking color over a painted wall is easy but messy and children love to help. Simply load your brush with slightly thinned latex paint and flick it at the surface you want to paint. Vinegar graining is the art of rolling putty or modeling clay over a glaze made from powder color and vinegar to produce a shiny veneer effect on furniture. Stippling, the art of producing a mottled effect, can be done with a special stippling brush or a dusting brush. Use a quick, dabbing motion.

Above: *Marbling imitates the colors and veining of real marble. It is one of the most difficult techniques to master.*

LIGHTING

Often the last item to be considered when decorating a room is the lighting. This can be a big mistake as lighting plays a very important role in the way a room looks.

Typically, the living room is a multi-functional space, so before attempting to light it, try to decide how you wish to make use of the light in order to divide off certain areas; illuminate particular features; "decorate" and even change the apparent shape of the room.

Lighting can be used to emphasize and enhance a feature – even to distort it – or you can use it to dramatize or minimize the decorations, as you can with color and pattern. Think of lighting as an interior design tool and you can use it to create atmosphere and style and to enhance certain attractive features or the whole look of the room.

There are three different types of lighting that can be used: background lighting; direct lighting and accent lighting.

Background lighting: This provides a soft level of light throughout the area, particularly important in the living room where it can add extra dimensions. The level can be further controlled by the use of dimmer switches or by using concealed lighting, for example, from behind valances or display shelving. Dimmable central pendants, recessed spotlights or even illuminated panels can all be employed.

Direct lighting: This is very useful for working under or by and is essential for reading, writing, sewing or working at a desk.

Accent lighting: This is used to shape a room and draw attention to particular details; for example, objects such as paintings or sculpture, even plants, can be made the focal point with the right use of this lighting.

All three types of lighting should be as flexible as possible so that you can make subtle alterations at the turn of a switch.

ILLUMINATING COLLECTIONS

Many living rooms contain works of art and with the help of creative lighting these can be made the focal point of the room. For example, a collection of pictures or drawings on a large wall are best served by the technique of "wall washing," which will evenly illuminate all the works of art displayed. All reputable manufacturers publish recommended spacing dimensions for their wall washers, so measure carefully; if you place them closer together than this you will not achieve an

Left: *A dramatic mixture of uplighters and downlighters creates interesting effects in this sitting room. The uplighter bounces light off the ceiling to the small corner table below. Painting the ceiling in a glossy finish increases the reflective effect. Background lighting can be added by concealing lights behind furniture.*

even effect, but a scalloped one. Remember, also, that it is not a good idea to try to "wash" a gloss or semigloss wall surface, as this will cause glaring. It will also reveal every imperfection in the wall's surface.

The neatest and most elegant way to wash a wall with light is by using downlighters recessed into the ceiling, or you could use a rather more convenient row of small portable uplighters.

Spotlights are probably the most obvious way of picking out a particularly interesting single object or small collection of objects. They may be designed to hold an ordinary bulb; a special spot bulb with an internal silvered reflector for intensity, or the spot itself may house a low voltage transformer which will cast a narrow beam of light on to a specific item. Tracks offer a flexible approach to lighting, as they can be attached across the ceiling or down the wall. Light beams can then be crossed at steep angles so that people in the room do not look directly into the beam of light.

High voltage accent lights are perfect for subtly highlighting various objects on display. For example, if you wish to "spotlight" pictures or collections of paintings on walls, then semi-recessed fixtures using lamps with parabolic reflectors can be adjusted to avoid glare and provide discrete accent lighting wherever you want.

Alternatively, theatrical spotlights, which are portable, are wonderful for being moved around to provide flexible lighting. Shutters on this type of light can be used to shape the beam while the lens train can be used to change the focus from sharp to soft. If your collection is gathered on a single table you could illuminate it directly with the bright source of downlighters, placing them above and around the area for best effect. Even industrial lighting is worth considering, with its curved and shaped tubes which can be used to cleverly outline a piece of modernist sculpture or painting. If you are really daring you could incorporate a colored neon tube into your plan, which can create marvelous effects in the right setting.

Many objects exhibited in the home are placed on some kind of shelf or protected within a cabinet. When illuminating shelving try using miniature strip lighting, either tungsten or fluorescent, or, provided the shelves are sufficiently wide apart, you can conceal the tube behind a slat attached to the leading edge of the shelf above the objects. Tungsten lighting is better for the living area, as it gives a warmer glowing light than

fluorescent bulbs, which are often too harsh.

The circle of light beneath a large, single table lamp is a favorite, traditional way of displaying small objects, whereas matching table lamps placed on either side of a larger collection can serve to concentrate the attention toward the pieces. Remember that the conical shades are a good idea as they cut down the amount of upward light, too much of which spoils the effect. With this type of arrangement the bulbs should not exceed 60W for the best effect.

Never use a bulb of a higher wattage than that recommended by the manufacturer anyway. With some shades, over-heating could have disastrous results. Those wattage limitations are decided by experts with safety very much in mind, and not applied just to frustrate your needs.

If the collection is arranged on a glass table, illuminating it from below with diffused uplighters can create dramatic highlights. The shadowing effect in itself is often very interesting, but beware of making people stare straight into the source of the light, as this can ruin the effect.

RESHAPING A ROOM WITH LIGHT

It is by manipulating the general illumination of the room that you will best be able to correct any faults, such as too-low ceilings, uninteresting shape layout, etc.

Ideally the general lighting should reflect all the different functions occurring in the various parts of the room; using dimmer switches is a very useful and versatile way of controlling the intensity of light in different areas.

Remember that pendants serve to emphasize the loftiness of tall rooms and spaces, while downlighters have the effect of making colors seem more brilliant and moldings more apparent. If you wish to use light to heighten your ceilings you could also use halogen uplighters which can be very intense as a light source, and will bounce all or most of the light off the ceiling, drawing attention to lofty proportions and giving an added sense of height and space. Use them sparingly in the living room where table lamps may be more appropriate, producing a

cozier atmosphere in which to relax.

A pendant or hanging light with interestingly colored or cut-out shade can have strange and attractive effects on the light thrown down. Remember that this form of lighting tends to flatten shadows but can cleverly divide the room, if you wish to exploit this feature. Groups of pendants are particularly useful for demarcation purposes and the lower the position of the shade, the more definitely the space is separated off. Even quite small light fixtures can be used to define spaces when deployed in pairs or groups. You can also use pendants to highlight seating areas, but avoid placing them directly over sofas or armchairs as they can produce unpleasant shadows and at the same time cause a glare where you least want it when reading or sewing.

Light acting upon a pale-colored surface will produce background light that can alter the apparent size of the room. To make a room appear more spacious use light paint for the walls and a white flat finish for the ceiling and cornice together with well-placed high-intensity light sources.

CORNER LIGHTING

A traditional-style table lamp placed in the corner of a room gives off a soft, mellow light particularly if the shade is a soft neutral or warm pastel shade and will draw attention in a very welcoming way. But there are many, less conventional ways to highlight a corner.

For instance, an attractive corner can be made by incorporating the fireplace, illuminating it with recessed lights or uplighters around the mantlepiece and inside the hearth – you could even use colored bulbs to mimick the warm color of flames.

Corners can also be lit with fluorescent or incandescent tubes, or try bulbs positioned around a large mirror, for reflected illumination. For a more unusual, high-tech look you could use an aluminium mesh shaded rise-and-fall pendant lamp placed over a corner table. Concealing a tungsten bulb with the upturned metal bowl reflects light into the shade. The mesh will allow some of the light to percolate through, while the rest is bounced downward onto the table with subtle effects. If you have an old faded parasol or

an oriental umbrella made from paper and bamboo you could invert these to make ingenious pendants for a romantic corner, with wicker chairs and lots of plants.

If you want to use your corner to work in then a task light is the best option. These are often complicated pieces of engineering, contrived to give maximum adjustability with fingertip control. Together these characteristics allow you to make small alterations to the lighting direction as you work, without interrupting your concentration. The original Anglepoise light designed in 1933 by George Carwardine, was the first design to achieve this degree of flexibility with great elegance. Modern types are increasingly using tungsten-halogen light sources often fitted with an integral dimmer. Clamp-on task lights are useful for saving valuable desk space.

The standard lamp has been the traditional mainstay of the corner setting – but this is increasingly giving way to the halogen uplighter which reflects all or most of its light output off the ceiling – the whole room can now be lit by a single fixture.

PART TWO

ROOM-BY-ROOM IMPROVEMENTS

Small Wonders, page 86

Bedroom Basics, page 146

THE CONTEMPORARY KITCHEN

Less than 80 years ago many women only set foot in their own kitchen in order to tell someone else what to do. Men, on the whole, remained in total ignorance of the goings on there.

In stark contrast to this was the life of many thousands of poor families, for whom the kitchen was also the living room and sometimes a bedroom too. The only facilities in the average working class kitchen were a cold water tap and a coal-fired range.

Today, the kitchen is a family room, used by everyone from toddlers upward. The head cook and maid of the early 1900s have been replaced by a battery of high tech, super-efficient appliances designed to make cooking and cleaning up afterwards easy, and only the rich have the luxury of a cook.

Kitchens have more than kept up with the fast pace of change over the past 80 years. Most homes have a modern range, a refrigerator and freezer and an automatic washing machine and dryer, with microwaves and dishwashers gaining in popularity. Some even include built-in toasters, coffee makers and food processors.

Skilled European designers lead the field in innovative kitchen design. As well as being smart on the outside, today's cabinets are packed with clever storage gadgetry on the inside. For those working to a very tight budget, but with some experience of assembling unit furniture, there are good self-assembly kits available. Mass production has brought ceramic tiling, once very expensive, within reach and there are paints, fabrics and floorings to match or complement every style of kitchen cabinet.

With so much to choose from, remodeling a kitchen can be difficult. It pays to shop around. Collect together as many manufacturer's brochures as you can. Study the way the rooms shown are designed, as well as the style of the cabinets. Most have good ideas that you could adapt to improve the kitchen you already have if you are not keen to spend the amount of money an all-new kitchen requires.

Installing a new kitchen is an expensive business, so don't rush in and live to regret your haste later. Making a list, like the one shown below, may seem a tedious business, but if you calculate your needs with as much accuracy as possible at this stage it can save you time and expense in the long run.

In this section, you will find ideas on improving what you have.

Above and right: *Both views of this kitchen show how much pass-through room has been allowed due to clever planning. Set-back wall cabinets allow improved headroom.*

ASSESS YOUR KITCHEN NEEDS

Your lifestyle
► What do you dislike about your present kitchen?

► Which features would you keep?

► If you could have your ideal kitchen, what would it look like?

► How many people use the kitchen at one time?

► Do pets use the kitchen?

Eating
► Do you want to eat in the kitchen?

► If so, which meals and for how many?

► What sort of table would you like (breakfast bar, pull out, or permanent table).

Activities
► What is the kitchen used for?

► Which activities cause you the biggest problem? If the answer is laundry, for instance, think about building a laundry room elsewhere.

Budget
► How much can you afford to spend?

► How will you raise the money (bank, savings and loan, etc).

► Are you thinking of moving within the next few years? If you are, spending a lot on a kitchen will be a waste.
Redecorate and install good-quality budget-priced cabinets instead.

Appliances
► Do you entertain a lot? This will affect the size and type of appliances you buy.

Space
► Is there enough space to make the improvement you want? If not, think about employing an architect or builder, either to find extra space within the existing structure, or to plan an extension.

► Do you need a dishwasher, a microwave, a deep fat fryer or food processor? They all take up space.

A NEW BEGINNING

Installing a completely new kitchen is a mammoth task, involving choosing cabinets, counters, appliances, tiles, flooring, lighting and ventilation, then fitting it all into the space available. It's a unique opportunity to make this important room an efficient, practical, pleasant place to be with the help of the huge range of kitchen fittings now available. Because there's so much choice, begin the thought process a couple of months before you hope to start work. Collect as many brochures and magazines as you can and make a file of kitchens you like as a starting point for the many decisions which you will shortly have to make.

BUYING NEW CABINETS

Just as computer experts have a jargon outsiders find hard to understand, kitchen cabinet manufacturers often speak in terms that baffle a newcomer. Before you go to buy new cabinets, it's worth learning a little "kitchenspeak" so you can hold your own.

Body: The back, sides and shelves of the individual cabinet.

Fronts: The doors and drawer fronts.

Lights: Glazed doors or windows.

Particleboard, high-density chipboard: Both terms for fiber or chipboard. In all but the most expensive kitchen cabinets, the

Right: *A new kitchen need not be expensive to look good. Just a few cabinets, carefully arranged, work as well as a complicated custom-built design. These budget-priced cabinets were given a touch of individuality by painting the toekick in soft blue to match the tiles and paintwork in the room. Blue accessories and a pretty floral tablecloth pick up the color.*

Far right: *Wood trim on laminate is a popular look that will never go out of fashion. It is a style which suits both old and new buildings.*

body is made from this material. It is actually more suited to use in a kitchen than wood because it doesn't move or warp unless water is allowed to soak into the material.

Wood fronts: Be careful. In many cases, all this means is that the frame of the doors or drawers is made from wood while the center is chipboard. On well-made lines, it is difficult to spot the difference between veneered chipboard and real wood.

Toekick: The area between the bottom of the cabinets and the floor (also called the "kickspace").

Cornice: Trim at top or bottom of wall cabinets. A light cornice has concealed lighting behind it.

Trim kits: Panels that can be fitted to suitable appliances so that they will match cabinet fronts. The appliance must be ordered with a decor frame. This is a door surround that unscrews so that the panel can be fitted over the existing front. Trim kits are available for refrigerators, freezers, trash compactors, some laundry equipment and dishwashers but not for stoves.

Refacing: Replacing existing cabinet doors and drawer fronts with different-style doors and drawers. There are a number of companies that specialize in refacing, which is a relatively inexpensive alternative to new

cabinets. For a nominal expenditure you can have a new-looking kitchen. The catch is that the quality can be cheap and you're stuck with your old cabinet layout.

Midways: Small units designed to go between wall and base cabinets.

Postformed edges: Worktops with rounded front edges.

Self-rimming sink: Sink that sits on top of the base cabinet.

Inset sink: Sink which fits flush with the surrounding worksurface. An inset sink costs more because the worksurface must be cut to accommodate it.

Balustrading: Decorative trim on the edge of open shelves. Usually seen in the more traditional designs.

Knockdown: Self-assembly kitchen cabinets that come in boxes.

Cabinets sized to match appliances, and designed for easy cleaning and maximum storage capacity are the backbone of a streamlined modern kitchen. The choice is enormous, ranging from budget-priced knockdowns for home assembly to expensive, made-to-measure custom designs. What you buy depends on what you can afford, your needs, your personal taste and the style and size of your house.

KNOCKDOWNS

Knockdown kitchen cabinets are designed for do-it-yourself construction so cost less than many ready-assembled lines. Cabinets are offered in standard sizes and in a number of finishes. At the lower end of the price scale, you will find white, teak effect and colored laminates. At the upper end, cabinets have either solid wood or wood-framed doors and traditional cathedral carving or fielded panels. Oven and sink housings are available. Trim kits, rounded, open-end storage and midway units are more unusual. All but budget-priced lines offer a selection of interior cabinet fittings, such as corner carousels, saucepan drawers and pull-out pantries – all of which help you to make use of the full depth of cabinets without the annoyance of trying to find items that have been pushed right to the back.

The advantages of buying knockdowns are price and convenience (you can take the kitchen home with you instead of waiting up to eight weeks for delivery). The drawbacks are the limited cabinet sizes available and the time it takes to assemble the kitchen at home. Sometimes, the instructions for assembly are so concise that they can be quite difficult for a layman to follow. And you need quite a lot of floor space in which to work. Even armed with a powered screwdriver, you'll be lucky to assemble and position more than two or three cabinets in a day.

You will also probably find that in an older home, where walls and floors are out of true, it may be very difficult to make the cabinets line up at the front and across the top of the counters. There is the problem of storage too – cabinets come in very large boxes and need to be kept under cover. You will have to plan the kitchen yourself, a time-consuming job which must be done before buying the cabinets.

If the room is an awkward shape, it may be difficult to work with the restricted number of sizes offered in most knockdown lines. Remember too, the plumbing and electrical work involved in a new kitchen, as this may affect the way the cabinets are positioned. Bearing all these possible snags in mind, before buying knockdowns, ask how they are assembled and if any special tools are needed. If possible, look at a copy of the assembly instructions and you'll avoid the frustration of getting the cabinets home and being unable to put them together for lack of the right tool, or because the work is beyond your skills.

Left: *This kitchen was custom built and hand-painted to suit the customer. If you decide that you can afford a custom-built kitchen, there are many advantages. Most builders will paint the kitchen any color and are willing to incorporate special features, like the slatted trellis-style wine rack shown under the island here, and the lacy carvings around the cornice and above the cooktop.*

Above: *Custom-built kitchens can be made in old, seasoned wood. Often, the wood comes from old churches, barns and other buildings. The advantage of using old wood is the rich patina which can only come with age. This kitchen was made of oak and includes many individual features, such as the shelf and hanging rail for utensils.*

MODULAR CABINETS

Modular cabinets are sold ready assembled for home or professional installation. Depending on where you buy them, the store may offer a planning and installation service. Low-priced modular cabinets are sold to take away in much the same way as knockdowns. All that you need to do is position them, attach them to the walls and add the counter, toekick, sink, taps, waste pipes and appliances. Low-priced models come in a variety of styles, from simple laminate to country look. There's a bigger choice of sizes and interiors than in most knockdown lines, but it can still be difficult to plan an awk-wardly shaped room.

If the room is a difficult shape or size, it will be worth seeing a kitchen planner. Kitchen planners are the selling arm of major kitchen cabinet companies. They operate from the kitchen studios to be found in almost every community. The planner will visit your home, measure the kitchen and plan the room to suit the cabinets you have selected from his or her store. The plan and order then go to the manufacturer, who makes up a package of cabinets of exactly the right size. Once the cabinets have been de-livered, the planner deals with installation, electrical and plumbing work and tiling. This is an expensive way to remodel a kitchen, but worthwhile if you want to make maximum use of the space. There are also many qual-ified independent kitchen planners and de-signers who offer similar services without re-stricting you to a single line. Problems well beyond your scope can be solved by profes-sional planning and made-to-measure build-ing.

CUSTOM-BUILT KITCHENS

If you want a kitchen hand-painted in raspberry pink, stenciled to match the pat-tern on a prized set of saucepans, built in antique wood, or in solid wood from toekick to counter, a custom builder can help. Cus-tom builders are skilled craftsmen, working mainly in wood, so the price is generally high. Most have no standard line but will design to suit your particular needs or whims.

Some will build a kitchen using antique fur-niture to give a "no cabinets" look. Planning, installation, plumbing and electrical work and tiling are all dealt with by the supplier. The cost of a custom-built kitchen will be ap-proximately the same as for a top-of-the-line modular kitchen.

THE PRACTICAL DETAILS

Once you have decided on the type of cabinets you will buy and the style, consider the practical details and list those you want to include before visiting a supplier.

Cabinets are now available in a number of different finishes.

Laminate: Used on cabinets across a wide price range. Hundreds of different colors are available, including wood effects. Laminate is easy-to-clean and hard wearing but can scratch and stain.

Textured laminate: Effects such as burlap or basketweave, usually in shades of cream or beige, often in combination with wooden handles and trims.

Polyester and lacquer: A high-shine finish used on more expensive made-to-measure modular kitchens. Polyester and lacquer look attractive but are not practical if there are small children in the house, as the material smears and fingermarks easily.

Wood and laminate: A combination used in many contemporary and traditional-style kitchens. The door frames are solid wood while the center panel is chipboard covered with veneer. The body is laminate-faced chipboard. A well-made wood and laminate kitchen looks almost as good as a solid wood one.

Wood fronts: Doors are all wood but the body is of laminate-faced chipboard. There is no great advantage in paying the extra to have an all-wood door unless quality is important to you.

All-wood: Offered by custom cabinetmakers and better modular cabinet lines. Everything is made from solid wood. An all-wood kitchen is expensive but will last for many years to come.

Hard-wearing, easy-to-clean worktops are a must as this is the surface which bears the brunt of hard wear. There are several materials to consider.

Laminate: Economical, hard wearing, easy-to-clean and available in hundreds of colors and effects. The laminate is bonded to chipboard. Most modern laminate worktops are postformed or have a wooden edging. Laminates are heat-resistant but will mark if used for chopping vegetables. Think about an inset chopping board positioned close to the range or sink.

Ceramic tiles: Provided that tiles are of the right grade for counter use, they make a hard-wearing surface. Most tiles will stand the heat from a pan of hot water, but not the thermal shock from a pan of hot fat. The top must be well grouted and sealed as spilled water will make the tiles lift. The tiles will break or crack should you drop onto them anything heavy. If you use the surface to knead pastry or make dough, the grout lines will quickly become messy and unhygienic. Consider having a generously-sized piece of marble or slate inset in the main preparation area if tiles are your choice.

Corian: DuPont Corian is a material which looks and feels like marble but is resistant to water and lighter in weight. Corian can be used for long lengths of worktop and does not stain or mark easily. It is however, a very expensive material.

Stone: Polished gray or pink granite are both fashionable but very expensive worktop materials. Granite is not porous and does not stain or mark. It looks effective, but base cabinets may have to be strengthened to take the weight. Marble is porous and stains too easily to make it a sensible choice for counter use. A marble pastry slab, set into a laminate, tile or wooden worktop is useful.

Wood: Only hardwoods are suitable for use as counters. Maple, cherry, beech and teak are best but expensive. Wooden worktops mark and dent easily, but the damage is easy to remove. All that is needed is a rub over with sandpaper for scratches and a damp cloth and warm iron for dents. The wood will need frequent treatment with cooking oil to remain in good condition. A wooden chopping board or butcher's block set into a laminate or tile worktop is a more economical and satisfactory alternative.

Stainless steel: An industrial material, now being offered by some manufacturers. It looks stunning when new, but if you have a stainless steel sink, you will know how difficult it is to keep the surface shiny and unmarked. Steel certainly looks stylish, especially if used in a long run with a self-rimming sink and matching cook top.

STORAGE

The other point to consider before buying a kitchen is the amount you need to store. Modern cabinets have an impressive line of storage solutions. If there is space, a giant double-door pantry, complete with cooled area, will cope with storage of nonperishable foods and vegetables. If space is tight, a tall, double-sided pull-out fitted into a narrow cabinet will hold cans, boxes and cartons of food. L-shaped corner cupboards should be equipped with a carousel, so that all the space can be used. The carousel will take either food or cookware. Modern kitchens have hundreds of storage options (see *page 79* for just a few), from small midway shelves for spice jars and herbs to a complete preparation area with chopping board, knife block and a hinged section for the food processor. Visit a kitchen showroom or one of the larger stores that provides a wide range of kitchen cabinets and see what is available before you make your choice.

Today's modern kitchens come equipped with a stunning array of special storage and well-thought-out details.

Above left: *Tall pull-out pantry with wire baskets for storage of cans and boxes.*

Left: *A corner carousel to make access easy. Most of these fittings are extra and are charged separately from the price of the main cabinet. The kitchen designer will advise on which interior fittings are suitable when you buy the kitchen.*

Above: *Special cabinet designed for a food processor.*

PLANNED TO PLEASE

Initially, the shape and size of the room will dictate how your kitchen is planned and whether it can include as many cabinets and appliances as you would like. Do-it-yourself kitchen planning is not easy but settling down with graph paper and pencil is a must if you are installing the kitchen yourself and it is worth drawing up a rough plan as a starting point before visiting a kitchen planner. If you are installing knockdown units, get a list of cabinet sizes before you start the plan, plus the measurements of the stove, cooktop, laundry equipment, refrigerator, freezer, hood and dishwasher. If the plan is being made by a professional, all that is needed is a rough sketch of the existing layout and a list of the features you would like.

Start your plan by measuring the room. Draw the shape up on graph paper; ½ inch to one foot is a good scale to use. Use the same scale to draw up cabinet and appliance shapes, using the measurements on your master list. You might make up templates for these so you can move them around on your plan. The way a kitchen is planned is personal and most home owners have their own ideas and priorities, but all of the points listed here are worth bearing in mind.

The work triangle: A planning rule discovered by researchers at Cornell University who sensibly concluded that the sink, stove and refrigerator should be close together for the room to work efficiently. If you imagine a triangle drawn on the kitchen floor, two elements (ideally the range and sink) should be on the base line with the other at the apex. The diagrams below show how the work triangle theory looks in practice.

Floorspace: You will need a clear area of at least 4 feet between facing banks of cabinets to allow ease of movement.

Practical considerations: Plumbing can be difficult to move (especially drainage) so it will be easier to leave the sink where it is in the new plan. If the kitchen includes laundry equipment and a dishwasher, both appliances should be sited near the sink.

Think about the cook: The main purpose of the kitchen is to cook family meals. Try to allow an area of countertop on each side of the range to provide a resting place for hot dishes. Incorporate as much work surface as possible in the rest of the kitchen. Try to plan centers for mixing, baking and clean up.

KITCHEN SAFETY

The kitchen is potentially the most dangerous place in the home. Heat, electricity, gas and water can all cause accidents.

▶ Fire is always a danger in the kitchen. Have a small extinguisher and a fire blanket close to the range. Fat fires are the most common cause of disaster. If a pan of fat catches fire, throw a fire blanket or dish towel over it. DO NOT ATTEMPT TO MOVE THE PAN AND DO NOT POUR WATER ON IT. Switch the heat off and close windows and doors. It is safe to remove the pan when the flames have died down. Remember that the pan will be very hot so use a damp cloth around the handle.

▶ If you smell gas, extinguish all naked flames immediately. Open the windows. Don't switch lights on – an electrical spark can ignite gas. Call the gas company immediately. Take children and animals out of the house.

▶ Faulty appliances or bad wiring can cause electric shock. A person receiving a severe shock may be throwh across the room, or may not be able to let go of the source of the shock. Turn electricity off at the main box. IF THE VICTIM IS STILL IN CONTACT WITH THE OBJECT GIVING THE SHOCK, DON'T TOUCH HIM/HER UNTIL THE POWER HAS BEEN TURNED OFF.
Phone 911 or your local emergency number immediately.

▶ Never touch plugs or electrical appliances with wet hands. Always make sure electrical appliances are properly wired.

▶ Water can make tiled or vinyl floors very slippery so always mop up spills immediately when they occur.

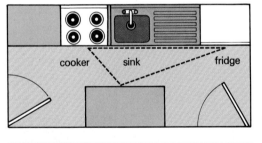

cooker   sink   fridge

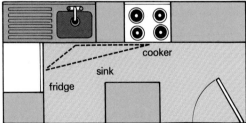

cooker
sink
fridge

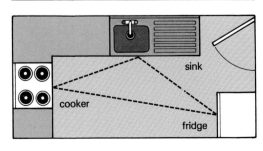

sink
cooker
fridge

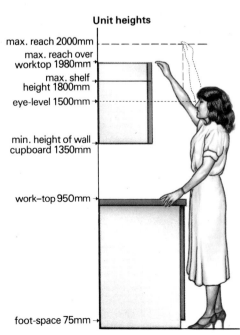

Unit heights

max. reach 2000mm
max. reach over worktop 1980mm
max. shelf height 1800mm
eye-level 1500mm
min. height of wall cupboard 1350mm
work–top 950mm
foot-space 75mm

Power plus: Don't be stingy with electrical outlets. Sockets for appliances built under a worksurface can be concealed. Plug molding is an effective way to power small appliances such as the toaster, food processor, kettle, coffee maker, etc.

Safety: Don't position the stove near a doorway, or plan the kitchen so that there is a doorway between the stove and the sink. It is dangerous if a main traffic area crosses the point where hot pans are likely to be *en route* to the sink. Don't put a wall cabinet above a low table or someone may receive a nasty blow on the head. Other things to avoid are sharp, jutting corners near a doorway, or at toddler head height, curtains close to the cooktop or any shelving that involves you leaning across the cooktop to reach it.

THE FINISHING TOUCHES

Heating, lighting and flooring are the three final decisions to make before work starts on your new kitchen.

Heating: Most people decide that extra heating won't be needed in a small to average kitchen as warmth from the stove and other appliances will keep the room at a comfort-able temperature. In a larger kitchen/diner, locate a radiator in the dining end. A portable fan heater is useful when a burst of warm air is needed to boost the temperature early in the morning or late at night.

Lighting: The time-honored overhead fluorescent tube is the worst possible way to light a kitchen because the light comes from behind the person working at the stove or preparation area. To avoid working in your shadow, position downlighters over the front of the counter or sink and concealed strip-lights beneath wall cabinets. Spotlights mounted on a track are usually the only extra light needed in a small to average-sized kitchen which is used only for cooking. If the kitchen is also used for dining, use a variety of lights to create different atmospheres in the kitchen and dining areas. Ceiling dimmers mean the cooking area can be in semi-darkness while the eating area is illuminated, or vice versa. A rise and fall pendant light above the dining table adds an intimate atmosphere.

If the kitchen is a small, dark room, make the most of light by installing pale-colored cabinets with a glossy surface.

Ventilation: Good ventilation is a must in all modern kitchens, not only to remove cooking smells, but to prevent condensation, which can quickly damage decor and furnishings.

A ventilation system above the stove will cope with steam and cooking smells. There are two different types of ventilation systems: updraft and down-draft.

An updraft system draws cooking fumes up through an exhaust fan and vents them outside, whereas a down-draft system works by sucking them down through the appliance cabinet and exhausting them outside through a vent.

Perhaps the most important difference between the two systems is that a down-draft system doesn't need an overhead hood. This means that you can place your range or cooktop in an island or peninsula without the visual obstruction of a hood. Remember, though, that a hood can hide downlighting for the cooktop.

Where you locate your cooktop or range dictates how strong a ventilation system you will need. All systems are rated according to the cubic feet per minute (CFM) that they exhaust.

A hood mounted on a wall has the back-splash to help channel the fumes into it and usually has a CFM rating of 450 or 650. A system for a peninsula requires 650 to 900 CFM. An island will need 900 to 1,000 CFM.

Far left: *The illustrations show alternative ways of planning your work triangle, and optimum heights for kitchen cabinets.*

Left: *Built-in lamps are a useful feature of this white/gray laminate and light oak kitchen.*

Left: *Skilled design means that a lot of kitchen can fit into a small space. Here the designer has made the most of the area by installing cabinets across corners. This type of cabinet is available through suppliers of modular cabinets. Other clever touches, such as setting the cooktop at exactly the right height for the person who will use it, make modular an option worth considering if you want to fit a kitchen into a difficult space. All the appliances in this kitchen (with the exception of the range) are hidden by trim kits.*

Far right: *Practical flooring is a must for the kitchen. Vinyl tiles are easy to install, non-slip when wet and can be cleaned by mopping. Good-quality tiles can effectively imitate ceramics and terracotta, without the disadvantage of being cold, hard and slippery.*

Flooring: Kitchen flooring comes in for a lot of punishment so must be hardwearing, water-resistant, comfortable underfoot and easy to clean.

Vinyl tiles: Available in hundreds of different designs and colors and at prices from cheap to very expensive. Tiles are easy to install if the floor is level, dry and sound. They are easy to clean but polish will eventually build up, so no-wax tiles are strongly recommended. Vinyl tiles can be slippery when wet and will begin to lift if laid in an area where water is often spilled.

Sheet vinyl: Available in thick cushioned and thin harder-wearing varieties and in hundreds of different colors and designs. Sheet vinyl can be laid on any sound, dry floor and is easy to install if there is enough space to unroll the flooring. Most vinyls are easy to clean but all can be slippery when wet. No-wax vinyl is especially easy to maintain.

Studded rubber: An industrial flooring, now available in primary and pastel colors for domestic use. Studded rubber is sold as large tiles or in a sheet and can be installed on any sound, dry floor. The textured surface means that spills can be difficult to wipe up, and the rubber is prone to scratches and wear.

Ceramic and terracotta tiles: Both of these look attractive but have many drawbacks. Tiles are cold, hard and uncomfortable underfoot and very slippery when wet unless you buy a textured type. If anything is dropped on the floor, both the object and possibly a tile or two will break. Both types of tile need professional installation. Broken tiles are difficult and expensive to replace. If you decide to have a tiled floor, it is definitely a good idea to have a few extras set aside for any such replacement. As with so many other commodities, styles, shapes and colors change, and even the most "basic" terracotta tiles may be difficult to match if you should need to replace some of them exactly in a few years' time.

Cork tiles: Warm, comfortable, easy to install and with sound-insulation properties, cork tiles are a good kitchen choice. The tiles must be ready sealed or spills will simply soak in and distort the material. Beware also, of using strong cleaners on such surfaces; the seal can be weakened by harsh liquids or powders. Fortunately, sealed cork usually responds well to a quick wipe-over with a damp cloth or floor mop.

A ROOM FOR THE FAMILY

It is a well-worn cliché that the kitchen is the heart of the home, a concept associated with comforting visions of a large but cozy room, complete with shelves of glowing preserves, snoozing cats, the mouthwatering smell of home-baking and a Mom, ever ready to dispense an endless supply of wholesome goodies. Like many old-fashioned ideas, the family kitchen still has something to offer even in a 21st-century style home. For a person with small children, a big kitchen can be a godsend as it allows them to play without getting under anyone's feet. There's also the bonus that a big, comfortable kitchen acts as a magnet for everyone in the house, guaranteeing company and a chat for the cook.

If you have a large kitchen, or a combined kitchen and dining room, turning it into a family center is an appealing way to deal with the space. A small kitchen won't be a success as there must be enough space to have clearly defined areas for cooking, eating and relaxing. A big table, comfortable dining chairs and a sofa or armchair are the perfect combination. A TV and a wall-mounted telephone will help to make the room the hub of the household. If your kitchen isn't big enough, it may be possible to add extra space by adding on or by removing a dividing wall (see page 18).

A family kitchen must be hard-wearing and easy to clean. Country style is the traditional choice, but there's no reason why you shouldn't use streamlined modern cabinets. Safety is an important consideration if there are small children in the family. Avoid sharp corners at toddler head height and hard, slippery flooring. Sheet vinyl or vinyl tiles in the cooking area, and carpet or coir matting in the sitting and eating areas is a good combination. If you have small children, install a pan guard around the cook top. You should also have a fire extinguisher and first aid box (see also page 80 on general safety considerations when you are planning your kitchen).

Above: *A good-quality veneer can look just as good as solid wood. A mixture of open and closed storage gives the kitchen a country-style effect, even though the design of the cabinets is modern.*

Right: *Soft, pastel yellow makes this kitchen sunny to look at and relaxing to work in. The L-shaped design has both open and closed storage, essential to avoid a boxed-in look which can come from solid walls of cabinets. The dining area has been positioned where it will get the best of the light from the glazed door.*

FAMILY-SIZE APPLIANCES

Super-size appliances can help to make life easier for a family of four or more. A dishwasher which will take 12 international place settings is a must. Look for a big capacity refrigerator/freezer and double ovens so that family meals can be cooked in bulk and frozen for future use. A microwave is useful as children can reheat freezer food for themselves without the danger of fire. As every farmer's wife knows, a large range is worth its weight in gold, able to cope with everything from making eggs for breakfast to drying damp clothes and generating extra heat. Try to find space for a separate laundry room where the family can dump dirty linen and where there is enough space to iron and hang clothes.

CREATING A STYLE

For the room to work as a whole, kitchen fittings, dining and relaxing furniture should be in harmony. Country style, with pine cabinets, a big stripped table, wheelback chairs, a dresser and a settee or friendly chintz sofa strewn with colorful cushions or an afghan has a timeless appeal. Pine kitchen cabinets are easy to find, but look for wood in a mellow, aged shade. Counters should ideally be tiled or wooden, but these can be impractical materials in a family kitchen. Look for a laminate in a natural stone, tile or burlap effect and add wood molding. Choose wall tiles in warm, country colors in a slightly bumpy "hand-made" finish, or mix old-fashioned junk shop finds with plains. Forget about coordination. So long as you stick to natural effects, you'll achieve the eclectic "grew with time" look of a real farmhouse kitchen.

A big range will add a comforting country touch, but for layout convenience you may prefer a separate cooktop and ovens. Happily, you can still achieve a country style. Many appliances are available in brown, gold or cream, all better colors for the country look (and less likely to show sticky fingerprints) than conventional white.

A wall-hung collection of transfer-printed plates or prints, dried flowers or bunches of herbs suspended from the ceiling and a hutch to display a favorite collection of jugs or traditional china are basic elements in the country kitchen. Wicker baskets, either hanging from the ceiling or stacked in piles of different sizes against a wall will add to the rustic atmosphere. But take care that any items hung from the ceiling are above head-height, do not have sharp edges and are properly secured. Children will appreciate a painted chest or a pine coffer to keep favorite toys close at hand.

A nice way to add to the family atmosphere is to attach a cork bulletin board to the wall with a picture light or down beam spotlight above and fill it with favorite family snapshots, shopping lists and reminders.

It is more difficult to achieve a warm, friendly effect with modern kitchen furniture, but possible if you choose a line that includes matching or complementary dining furniture, storage and seating. The high tech look, with its bright, easy-to-clean surfaces copes well with family life. You'll need the same elements as described in the country kitchen: somewhere to eat, somewhere to relax, functional, practical appliances and storage.

Whatever your style, avoid creating a room which is difficult to clean. Rustic, bare bricks look wonderful with old pine furniture but quickly collect airborne grease. Pale upholstery will soon look the worse for wear where there are small children, as will a beautiful hand-painted traditional kitchen. Think of your family kitchen as a cross between workroom, playroom, living room and office and the activities it will be used for. The easiest way to plan is to make a list of all the things you hope to do in the kitchen, then match facilities to the action. If you haven't room for all of them, at least it will help you to decide what are the priorities and perhaps to plan some dual-purpose amenities that might otherwise be overlooked until it is too late. Do not stint yourself at this stage; remember, you may never again have the opportunity to plan your dream kitchen. Your list might look something like this:

Below: *Creating desk space in your kitchen need not be a major undertaking. All you need do is adapt this clever design with its flap-down desk-top.*

ACTIVITY	AMENITY
▶ Cooking family meals	Big, efficient range and freezer Microwave Dishwasher
▶ Playspace for toddlers	Soft, easy-to-clean floor Storage for favorite toys Space for playpen or highchair Table to use for drawing and games First aid kit Pan guard for cooktop Lock for freezer
▶ Entertaining friends	Comfortable seating Big table to seat six or more
▶ Home office	Desk space (an area of countertop with a filing cabinet on castors is ideal) Bulletin board Phone and message pad (should be within reach of the cooking area)
▶ Eating	Dining area and comfortable chairs
▶ Relaxing	TV and radio Comfortable seating Relaxing lighting. Use table lamps to create pools of light around the seating area.

SMALL WONDERS

Clever planning is a must for a small or awkwardly shaped kitchen where it is vital to make good use of every inch of space. Standard-sized cabinets and appliances may prove impossible to fit, so you will need to think of alternatives, or use a kitchen planner, depending on your budget.

Look carefully at the space before you start buying cabinets or appliances. Measure it and draw up a plan on graph paper. There may be obvious ways to gain extra space: by removing a chimney breast, or taking the doors off a built-in cupboard. Make a list of the appliances you want to include and the things you need to store.

SPACE-SAVING EQUIPMENT

Equipment is the "bones" of the kitchen and must come first in your calculations. Do you really need a full-size stove? A compact all-in one stove/microwave or stove/dishwasher will meet the needs of a single person or a couple. A cooktop with a hinge-down cover will give you extra worksurface. Many space-saving small appliances are now available in small, under-cabinet models. Others combine several functions into one, like a microwave/toaster-oven. A dishwasher is worth having if there is space because it cuts down on clutter and will help to keep work-

Above: *When space is difficult or very restricted, special-sized cabinets can usually provide the answer to the problem of designing a working kitchen. This kitchen has been planned around the sloping ceiling. Instead of being mounted above the counter, the wall cabinets sit on top of it and have a useful shelf running around the top. The European modular cabinets can be moved around as wished.*

surfaces free of dirty dishes when you are preparing food. A compact refrigerator/freezer takes up less space and may be adequate for your needs, especially if you don't store large quantities of perishable food. If laundry equipment must be in the kitchen, a stacking washer and dryer occupy less space than separate appliances.

CABINETS AND STORAGE

If the kitchen is narrow, standard size cabinets will probably eat up too much floor area. This won't be a difficulty if money is no object as you can call on the expertise of a kitchen planner or have a custom-built kitchen. Many major kitchen cabinet manufacturers produce narrower cabinets or 3D cabinets where the doors are angled back from full to just over half width, corner mounted cabinets and midway shelving. Combined with the skills of a kitchen planner, these special-sized units can turn the smallest, most awkward kitchen into a well-designed, functional room.

For those on a tight budget, planning a small kitchen needs ingenuity and an imaginative approach to space. If there is no room for conventional base cabinets, cut a worktop down and fit shelves with bi-fold or sliding doors beneath, and use tiers of wire baskets on castors for drawers. Install narrow shelves in place of wall cabinets and either leave them open, or cover with bi-fold doors or roller blinds. Under-shelf baskets will increase the storage capacity of your shelves, or screw in some simple hooks for jugs, cups, etc. Provided that they are very stable, free-standing shelves can be used if you don't own a power drill, an essential when installing fixed shelving. Where there is not enough depth for a worktop of any sort, make the most of wall space with floor to ceiling shelves, just wide enough to house pots and pans. You will gain valuable space by replacing a conventional door with a pocket door, or by removing the door completely. A hinge-down or pull-out counter will add an eating area to the kitchen, or extra preparation space when needed.

Neatness is essential in a small kitchen. A build-up of clutter where space is already strained will make the room totally unworkable, so make sure utensils are hung up on rails or tidied away when finished with. Explore the possibility of storing rarely used kitchen equipment on top of cabinets or in any awkward gaps that may exist.

DECORATION

The right decor will make your small kitchen seem bigger. Choose light, shiny surfaces and steer clear of fussy patterns. In a confined space it may be necessary to put the stove quite close to the window – in which case blinds will not only be safer, but they will also look neater than curtains, or you can screen the window with glass shelves and plants. White, combined with a primary or pastel trim, is a guaranteed space maker. Use white shelves and counters with a primary edging and add matching colored handles to the cupboards and drawers. Spotlights mounted on ceiling track will bounce light off shiny surfaces, making the room appear larger, and can be adjusted at will.

Below: *A long, narrow kitchen is easy to plan if there is room for cabinets along both sides, as shown here. The task becomes more difficult when there is not enough space for facing rows of cabinets. A solution is to fill one wall with narrow shelves.*

THE VISUAL KITCHEN

Add character to your kitchen by mixing visible and closed storage. The visual kitchen, conceived by ever-ingenious West German designers, has much to offer the improver on a budget as expensive cabinets can be mixed with cheaper open shelving. You could, for instance, buy three or four special cabinets, such as a built-in pantry or corner carousel, then add your homemade shelving and wire basket storage. Ready-cut shelves with a wood effect or colored lipping give a professional look.

This simple but striking kitchen measures just 8 × 12 feet, an area that would look unpleasantly boxy if filled with cupboards and drawers. The mixture of closed cupboards and open, wood-edged shelves of different sizes gives more storage space than conventional cabinets. The sky blue bridging panel adds a smart note to an essentially businesslike layout: a hanging rail for dish towels, a work space, easily accessible chopping board and utensils and ideally placed narrow shelves around the vent for spices, oils and other ingredients in everyday use.

A small refrigerator with a trim kit is cleverly hidden beside the sink. The other side of the sink is filled by more open storage with one section fitted with boxes for keeping fresh vegetables.

A small freezer lives inside the built-in pantry at the end of the sink wall. A small dining area makes this the perfect kitchen for its businesswoman owner.

Below: *Ash and white open shelving with gently rounded edges gives definition and individuality and makes the most of a small space. The tall open shelf unit is an effective way to divide kitchen and dining areas.*

Above: *This cleverly designed kitchen is a good cook's dream. Kitchen utensils in everyday use are always at hand and there is plenty of space for preparation on both worktops and the central table.*

The preparation area at the far side of the kitchen, beneath the extension window, has a solid beech top which serves as a cutting and chopping board and is equipped with a pull-out leaf, allowing

comfortable working when seated. The ceiling element above the central butcher's block provides space for hanging utensils and storing condiments and brings useful light to the work table.

MAKING THE BEST OF IT

A complete remodel is a tempting way to deal with a kitchen which is lacking in space, badly planned or downright ugly. Unfortunately, the high cost of a brand new layout, even using budget-priced cabinets, makes it a step to be considered only if finances are no problem, or if the kitchen is completely beyond hope.

Shortage of storage and working space, worn or unattractive cabinets and lack of ventilation are problems that can be solved without breaking the bank. Start by identifying what is wrong with the kitchen. Plumbing and gas pipes are difficult and expensive to change, so you will probably have to accept that the sink and any gas appliances cannot be moved. With this in mind, draw up a list of the things you hate about the room, or simply find a little inconvenient, and the improvements you would like to make.

CABINETS

Provided that the bodies (sides and back) of cabinets are in good condition, ugly or damaged doors won't be a problem. It is possible to completely change the appearance of the kitchen with replacement door and drawer fronts. New fronts come in all styles, from traditional cathedral carved to modern laminates. Wood or wood frame and veneer panel doors are available either stained and sealed or unfinished. The advantage of buying unfinished doors is that they can be painted or stenciled, then sealed with a coat of clear polyurethane. Replacement doors come in a range of standard sizes. Odd sizes can be made to order by a carpenter or specialty cabinet refacing firm.

If your budget is really tight, louver doors are inexpensive and can be stained and

Paint can give an old kitchen a new lease on life. Laminate doors must be sanded down before painting, or the paint won't cling to the shiny surface.

Above: *This simple wooden kitchen was given a designer touch by sponging the cabinets in a combination of beige and red gloss paint. Red gloss was used to pick out the framework of the kitchen.*

Right: *In this kitchen, worn base cabinet doors were replaced by wooden louvers painted in gray gloss paint. Soft lilac walls complete the gentle, harmonious scheme.*

painted. Alternatively, battered cabinet doors can be removed, leaving open shelving, which can be stained or painted to match or contrast with the rest of the kitchen. Cleaning materials or any other odds and ends you don't want on display, can be hidden by a roller blind or a curtain hung from a wire. Colored laminates can be changed with a coat of paint, so there is hope for old fashioned fake teak and '60s-style orange, bottle green and navy blue.

Before you paint the doors, rub them over with fine sandpaper. This provides a "key," so that the paint will cling to the surface. Follow with two coats of primer, then the top coat of your choice. Flat latex is best. Avoid gloss as the paint will chip in use. The top coat can be a single color, or you can experiment with sponging, dragging, marbling, stippling and stenciling. The refrigerator can be painted to match, if you wish.

Stoves, washing machines and dishwashers need special enameling as the heat from cooking and hot water will melt ordinary paint.

Details of special paint techniques appear on *pages 60-65*. Protect the finished paintwork with a coat of the clear polyurethane.

Once you have completed all the painting and it is thoroughly dry you could screw cup hooks to the front edge of open shelves and use them to hang mugs, cups or jugs.

New handles will add an individual touch to plain white laminate cabinets and are easy to install. D handles, grip bars (to replace metal grips fitted to the tops of doors) and knobs are available in pastel and primary colors and wood effects.

If you have a steady hand, and an artistic bent, flat white doors can be given a paneled look with car trim tape. Measure in about 2 inches from the edge of the doors, mark with a pencil, then stick four straight lines of tape to form a square panel. Cut the ends of each piece of tape on a slant, so that the corners are mitered.

You can experiment with tape on a piece of cardboard until you find an effect that suits the style you wish to create.

ELIMINATE CLUTTER

Clutter can make cooking even the simplest meal an irritating business. If space is short, start by eliminating extraneous pots, pans and utensils. Preserving pans, fish kettles and very large serving plates probably aren't used often, so tuck them away on a high shelf. Use the lower shelves for pots, pans and other equipment which is in daily use. Take a tip from professional chefs and opt for visible storage. Fit a magnetic rack for knives above the counter.

Make use of the area between base and wall cabinets by hanging small shelves or wire baskets to hold spices, wooden spoons, the can opener, vegetable peeler and other small, often used objects. Wire wall grids are immensely useful; most come with a range of baskets or shelves which can be attached, and with S-shaped hooks to hold sieves, kitchen scissors, large spoons, etc.

Many fashionable functional-look European kitchens feature chrome hanging rails between wall and base cabinets, an idea easy to copy using either a length of metal pipe or wooden doweling, painted to match your color scheme. Metal pipe can be chromed or color-sprayed using car touch-up paint. Use S-shaped butcher's hooks to hang utensils from the rail.

Plates occupy a lot of space if stacked inside a cupboard. A pile of plates can be difficult to reach, and liable to crash to the floor if there are several different sizes in the stack. An old-fashioned wooden plate rack mounted on the wall will safely hold from 10 to 20 plates of different sizes. But be sure to use wall anchors when attaching it to the wall – otherwise the weight of the plates will send it crashing to the floor. This could leave you

with badly damaged wallplaster as well as shattered plates and nerves! If the rack is mounted above the sink, it can double as a drainer.

Space inside doors and beneath shelves is often wasted. Narrow wire racks can be attached to the back of doors and used for jars of herbs, canned foods and small cartons. Slide-on under-shelf baskets will extend storage space inside the cupboard.

Pull-out wire baskets will help you to make more efficient use of cupboard space. There are several designs available, including a corner carousel for deep L-shaped cupboards. Visit a kitchen showroom and take a look inside cabinets to see how storage is organized to give you some ideas on how pull-out units can be used.

Don't forget the ceiling in your search for extra storage space. A hanging rack can be used for pans, cookware, bunches of dried herbs and bags of spices. Black wrought iron is the traditional choice and brings a charming French provincial air to a country style kitchen. Good kitchen shops sell either long or circular racks which are designed to be suspended from the ceiling on chains. These ready-made units are expensive so make your own version, using copper pipe sprayed black. Hang it from the ceiling using chains or the type of bracket used for hanging towel rails. A broom handle or length of thick doweling stained or painted to match the kitchen is even cheaper. For a high-tech kitchen, use a stainless steel rod, or spray copper pipe with chrome paint and hang either shiny metal or black cookware from the rail. Three tier hanging metal or wicker baskets are an attractive and practical way to store herbs, spices and cleaning materials. Hang a "cook's basket" near the stove or main worksurface.

Take a tip from German kitchen designers and run shelves from wall to wall 12 to 18 inches from the ceiling or across the top of a window. Use the shelves to store preserves, baskets and cookware only needed once or twice a year. Glass shelves across a window won't reduce the light too much if used for drinking glasses or to display plants.

COUNTERS AND PREPARATION AREAS

Damaged or unattractive counters are easy to replace. If the top has square edges, the old laminate can be removed and new stuck in its place. If the edges are round (known in the kitchen trade as postformed), the whole top

will have to be replaced. Laminate-covered worktops are inexpensive and come in hundreds of different designs, including marble, granite and slate effects. Replacing laminate with laminate isn't the only choice. Both square-edged and postformed worktops can be covered with tiles. The tiles must be of a grade suitable for countertop use. Most wall tiles won't stand the heat of a saucepan. If the counter has a rounded postformed edge, look for tiles with matching round edgings. Tiles can be cut to fit square-edged counters, or the edge can be covered with a length of flat doweling, stained or painted to complement the tiles.

Butcher block wooden worktops are fairly expensive but look good and provide a practical, hardwearing surface for food preparation. Consider replacing just a section of counter with either a butcher block or a piece of marble.

An old marble-topped wash-stand built into a row of cabinets can be turned into a baking area with flour, dried fruit and baking trays and tins stored underneath. Suppliers

Above: *Take a tip from the French and hang pots, pans, utensils and dried herbs from a ceiling rack. A varnished broom handle, suspended from the ceiling by chains, works just as well as an expensive custom-made design. Add to the country feel by hanging an assortment of baskets, pictures, racks and bric-a-brac on the walls.*

Right: *This home-made kitchen with a designer touch was built using inexpensive louver doors stained blue. Simple stenciling above the tiles picks out the blues.*

of marble and granite sometimes have marble scraps that they will be happy to sell you at a fraction of the cost of a custom-made marble counter.

Lack of preparation and dumping space is frustrating. There is nothing worse than trying to prepare food in the midst of a muddle of pots, pans, and used utensils. Finding extra worktop space can be difficult in a small kitchen. A folding table is one option, or you can hinge a worktop and support against a wall. Some major appliances can offer a makeshift worksurface. Take advantage of this by butting appliances together to give a good run of work area. Bridging space between appliances with a worktop makes a combination of preparation area and breakfast bar.

A butcher block cart on castors means that the work surface can be moved as and when needed. Ready-made carts come in various sizes. Some are fitted with storage baskets beneath, a knife rack and space for a food processor and blades.

DECORATION

Wallcovering and paintwork are easy and inexpensive to change. Tiles are more difficult. Removing damaged or unattractive tiles from the wall may be impossible if the tiling runs behind cabinets. To give a completely new look you can either affix new tiles on top, or paint the old tiles.

To paint tiles, rub with fine sandpaper first so that the paint will cling. Follow with two coats of primer, then top with gloss paint. Plain colored tiles can be given a new look by changing the grouting. A combination of white tiles and primary colored grout is particularly effective. If you plan to install new tiles yourself, choose tiles that are self-spacing. This eliminates the need for spacers between each tile and gives good, even results.

Sheet vinyl is the cheapest and most practical way to cover the floor. Easy to lay, hard-wearing and wipe clean, vinyls come in a wide range of designs, including ceramic tile effects. They can be laid on top of tiles, floorboards or concrete. Most kitchen vinyls have an extra wear layer to cope with heavy use, spills and pressure from appliances. Cork tiles are inexpensive, easy to clean and warm underfoot. They can only be installed over a sound floor. Buy the ready-sealed type for kitchen use. Unsealed tiles are not suitable, as they absorb spilled liquids.

A PLACE TO EAT

Defining the space between cooking and eating areas is essential if you want more than a simple table for light snacks. The shape of the room may suggest a natural dividing line. If you are lucky enough to have an L-shaped room, the dining section can be tucked away in the short arm of the L.

Kitchen cabinets can be planned to act as a partition between cooking and eating areas. The cupboards will be twice as useful if they are accessible from both sides, or if the dining side has enough room to tuck stools beneath, thus providing you with a handy breakfast bar. The top half can be screened using open shelving, blinds, pierced wood paneling or hanging plants.

Light is a great mood maker and a simple way to define cooking and eating areas. Choose bright, functional lighting for the work center and softer, more intimate light for dining. A rise and fall pendant light above the table, combined with recessed ceiling dimmers works well. Install separate light controls so that the kitchen area can be left in darkness while the dining section is lit and vice versa.

Decoration can act as a dividing line too. Use tiles in the kitchen and a complementary wallcovering or paint in the dining area. Some kitchen cabinet manufacturers produce wall panels and dining furniture to match cabinet fronts, an expensive but effective idea. If you are buying a table and chairs separately, look for a design and finish to either match or complement kitchen cabinets. It can be difficult to match shades of new pine, so try to buy everything from the same line. Shade variations in old, mellowed pine blend together well. When the dining area is restricted, a glass-top table is visually less bulky than a table with a solid top, although some people find it disconcerting to look down at their own and chair legs through the glass. You could resolve this problem by covering the table with a cloth at mealtimes and whipping it off again afterward. Folding chairs, or a banquette built against a wall with seating beneath make spacewise seating.

Efficient ventilation is a must to keep the dining area free of lingering cooking smells. A ducted hood above the cooktop or an efficient down-draft ventilation system, plus a good through flow of fresh air from a window will clear strong smells before they begin to lurk. If the dining section has a window, you could think about setting a fan or ventilation duct in the room to whisk away irritating cigarette smoke and food smells.

Left: *It is wise to make some sort of division between the working part of the kitchen and the dining area. This unusual slatted metal screen is, in fact, a radiator, as is the multi-colored sculptural panel on the wall. A slatted or latticed screen helps to hide the kitchen clutter from the dining area without isolating the cook from family or guests . . .*

Above: *When all that is needed is a place for a daytime snack or a light meal for one or two, a pull-out unit like this one is a space-saving choice.*

A kitchen eating area can be anything from a simple pull-out or fold-down table for one-person snacks to an arrangement suitable for formal dining. Although it seems a sensible idea to eat food in the room where it is prepared, the conventional open plan kitchen/dining room arrangement has its drawbacks, mainly for the cook. Pots, pans and mess tend to pile up, and there's no hiding the odd mistake if guests or family are watching. It can be difficult to create a relaxing, dinner party "mood" in the place where the meal has been prepared and traces of this still exist. On the plus side, a kitchen/diner is a great space saver. You can add an extension to the kitchen and free the original dining room for another use, or combine a small kitchen and an adjoining dining room to make a spacious and more efficient layout.

DINING IN STYLE

A room set aside solely for dining is a space-gobbling luxury most families can't afford. These days, the dining room may be part of the kitchen, a section at the end of the living room, or if it is a separate room, will double for hobbies, homework and family pursuits. Whichever arrangement you choose, it makes practical sense to have the dining area close to the kitchen to save carrying hot food any distance. And do invest in a cart that is capable of carrying everything in one trip. It can be used for so many other carrying tasks too, that it merits whatever precious space it takes up.

THE SEPARATE DINING ROOM

A separate dining room needs little more than a good sized table (preferably extending) chairs and a hutch or sideboard. Having a separate room will be useful if you entertain friends and business associates regularly. A family dining room, used for hobbies and homework as well as eating, needs different treatment.

Eating should be relaxing and enjoyable, whether the dining area is in the corner of the kitchen, or is a full blown formal affair, complete with chandeliers. Don't simply stick some tables and chairs in a room or corner; think about your dining area and make it as interesting and inspired as the rest of your home. A sure sign that you have got it right is when family or visitors tend to linger there long after the meal is over, rather than look around hopefully in search of a more comfortable place to relax!

CHECKPOINTS

Before planning a dining area, think about how the space will be used, following the points listed here.

► How many people will use the room regularly?

► What is the maximum number of people you would like to entertain?

► Is there also a dining space in the kitchen for snacks, etc?

► Will the dining area be used only for the main meal in the evening, or will you also serve breakfast and lunch there?

The answers to the questions below will give you an idea of the size of table and number of chairs needed. If space is short, a round folding or extending table takes up a smaller area than a square or rectangular model. Folding chairs can help too, but be sure that there really is enough room for the table when it is opened out and for all the chairs. Check too, that the chairs are comfortable. On some fold-away designs the back can seem too far forward so that it is impossible to sit at ease with just the right amount of back support. Others are not very stable if occupied by anyone of generous proportions.

Dining tables come in all sorts of shapes and sizes. The basic rule is to allow around 2 feet, 3 inches per diner sitting on an armless chair. For chairs with arms add another 2 inches. There should also be enough space for people to get in and out easily without disturbing their immediate neighbor.

Tables come in many different materials. Most wooden and veneer tables have been

Below: *My own dining area is at the end of the living room. When it isn't being used for eating, the table doubles as a desk, sewing area and hobby space. It is also used for displaying plants and flowers.*

Left: *This simple modern dining room is an addition. Smooth wooden flooring adds to the uncluttered, airy feel, and is a good play surface for children. The table has been positioned so that it is framed by the entrance to the room.*

Left: *Farmhouse style at its best, with simple rustic furniture, gently lit by candles and recessed downlighters. The carved, upholstered chair and picture add a touch of softness to the scene. As there are no carpets or curtains, the room would look bare without these little extras.*

Left: *Shining marble, starkly modern furniture and an abundance of glass make a stunning setting. If you want to achieve this sort of look, it is important to keep everything in style. Adding a rug, for instance, might make the floor more comfortable to walk on but would completely ruin the feel and style of the room.*

treated so that they are heatproof. If you have small children, a wipe-clean lacquered or laminate table would be a practical choice.

Flooring needs to be practical, especially if you have children who may spill food on the carpet. Vinyl, ceramic or quarry tiles and wooden flooring look attractive and are easy-to-clean.

Lighting should be soft but bright enough for people to see what they are eating. A rise-and-fall pendant light gives just the right level of illumination and can be run from a dimmer switch when you want a soft background light to complement the glow of candles. The sideboard, hutch or serving area should be lit by wall lights.

The style of your dining area depends on personal taste if it is a separate room, and on the other furniture if it is part of a kitchen or living area. Eating should be a pleasurable experience and a good way to achieve the right feeling of relaxation and comfort is to think about restaurants you particularly like and adapt the look to suit your home.

Traditional style: Combine a fine old polished-wood table with matching chairs and sideboard, richly swathed curtains or drapes, dark warm colors, parquet flooring and an oriental rug. This style works well in a separate, high-ceilinged dining room, or in a living room where upholstered furniture is equally formal.

Farmhouse style: Best combined with a big pine kitchen. Look for a large scrubbed table (preferably old and original), a hutch and wheelback chairs. Terracotta or ceramic tile flooring and cottage prints are the perfect partners for this easy-to-live-with style. Can be combined with a living room if there is enough space for the table and the upholstered furniture has chintz or cottage print covers.

Colonial classic: A good idea if you want style on a budget as wicker dining furniture is sensibly priced and looks wonderful with a stripped pine or woodblock floor, Indian rug, white walls and plenty of lush green plants. This look goes particularly well with simple, modern furniture.

High tech: Lovers of the dramatic can choose a stark black dining table and matching chairs; the more conventional will like the clean looks of blonde ash or oak. The table could also be a trestle style, with a glass top and brightly colored legs. This clean, uncluttered look is good for a small room, or for a dining alcove off a modern living room.

DUAL-PURPOSE DINING ROOMS

In a home where space is valuable, you will need to make maximum use of every inch, including the dining room. Rule number one is not to have the traditional table surrounded by chairs. Look instead for a table which can be pulled away from the wall (where it can be used as a desk or for hobbies), and with extra leaves so that it can be extended for entertaining. Instead of the traditional sideboard, opt for shelving with cupboard or drawer bases. Some cabinets have a fold down desk section which will save cluttering the table with books – and having to clear everything away when you want to eat. It is a good idea to keep homework or hobby equipment on a wheeled cart that can stand beside you as you work and be whisked away when the room is needed for meals.

In a large dining room, you can set up a hobby or homework corner and hide it with a folding screen when serving meals. Where there is enough space, a sofa bed is a useful addition, especially for guests who don't want to drive home after a leisurely, delicious meal – or rather too much to drink. Using the dining room as a spare bedroom for more than one or two nights is not a very comfortable arrangement for your guests.

You'll find a cart is a very useful addition in a dining room where shelving or base cabinets mean that there is no space for a sideboard to use as a shelving area. Choose a well-made, solid cart that pushes easily.

What to do with dining chairs can be a problem. You will need at least two in the room for the times when it is being used for hobbies or study. Folding chairs are best as they can be stored in a cupboard or hung on the wall when not in use. Heaving solid dining chairs from various locations in the house every time you want to eat is an activity which will soon pall.

Don't forget about lighting for your home office or hobby area. If you are using the main table, a rise-and-fall pendant will be fine. A floor-standing light, clip-on spot or angled table lamp is best if you have sectioned-off a corner for privacy and neatness.

MAKING A DINING ALCOVE

A dining alcove in a living room is the best way to separate the two areas without building a wall. You may be lucky enough to have a natural alcove, in the bay of a window, the short arm of an L or the recess beside a chim-

ney breast. If you have, capitalize on this and tuck your dining table and chairs as far back into it as you can (making sure people can still get in and out of their seats with ease). A bamboo screen would help to seal off the area from the rest of the room. An area like this provides many interesting decorative opportunities. If there is space, you could line the walls of the alcove with narrow bookshelves, or cover them floor-to-ceiling with a collection of plates or pictures. Stenciling around the outside edges of the alcove, or adding a dado rail painted to contrast or complement the walls will have the effect of setting your alcove in a frame. The walls can be painted in a paler or darker shade than the rest of the room, covered in a patterned wallpaper if the rest of the room is plain, or plain if it is patterned.

A good way to save space in a narrow alcove is to build padded benches against the wall instead of using chairs. All that is needed is a simple wooden frame which can then be covered with tongue and groove boarding or kitchen cabinet doors, stained to look like panels. Add a lift-up lid (the space beneath the bench can be used for storage) and a comfortable padded cushion upholstered in fabric to match or complement seating in the main part of the room.

One of the prettiest alcoves I have ever seen was screened with lavish pinch pleated drapes, plain on one side, patterned on the other and tied back with a braided rope of the two fabrics. Inside was a lovely oval walnut table, with padded benches covered to match the curtains built around the wall. The effect was lavish and wonderfully Edwardian, rather like a box at the theater, or a private restaurant room in an old hotel in England.

The alcove will need its own lighting. A rise-and-fall pendant is best but may be awkward in such a small space. Recessed ceiling downlighters controlled by dimmers and corner-mounted spotlights which can be directed onto the table are a good combination. On special occasions, add a touch of romance with candles or a couple of old-fashioned oil lamps at each end of the table. While you are eating, lighting in the main part of the room can be reduced to a minimum, to give an increased feeling of intimacy.

Where there isn't an alcove, it is possible to create one by building a platform at one end of the room, or making the divide with low shelving or trellis. A collection of big indoor plants and a change of flooring from carpet to tiles or parquet is a simpler way to do the same thing.

ONE ROOM, THREE USES

Knocking a living room, dining area and kitchen into one is a bold step, but one big room cleverly divided by screens, plants, seating, shelving and furniture can often work better than three small rooms.

Not all houses are suitable for this sort of treatment. The ideal is a house from the 1930s, 1940s or 1950s, where the three rooms were often arranged either in a row or L-shaped with the kitchen forming the short leg of the L.

There must be natural light at both ends of the room. Don't be ruled by convention; the kitchen need not go at the backyard end but can be at the front of the house if you would rather plan your seating area where you can relax and look out at the greenery instead of the street.

If there is a hall running down the side of the kitchen and dining room, incorporating it can add even more space and light. I have seen a small row house transformed from dark and drab to light and spacious simply by removing the long hallway and knocking down the wall between the old living room and kitchen/diner. The kitchen was fitted into the space under the stairs, hidden from the main part of the room by a latticework screen.

When you open up rooms in this way, remember to plan doorways. In a kitchen/living/dining room combination, you will need an access door into the room (unless you have removed the hallway) and a door from the kitchen to the outside if you live on the ground floor or have a balcony.

ORGANIZING THE SPACE

Plan the kitchen first. It should be at one end of the room, not in the middle where it would act as a divider and destroy the open-plan atmosphere you hoped to achieve. The amount of space you use for the kitchen should not be more than one third of the room. Position base cabinets or shelves to mark a division between the kitchen area and the rest of the room. If space is limited, this divider can be used instead of a dining table.

A large, open plan room looks best if the same flooring is used throughout. Vinyl or sealed cork tiles are both good choices as they are hard wearing and easy to clean. Then, all you need do is leave the floor uncovered in the kitchen and use rugs in the dining and living areas.

Make sure that the kitchen is well ventilated so that cooking smells don't gather in

Left: *Try to engineer a smooth transition between the kitchen, with its necessarily functional look, and the softer lines of the living and dining areas. Repeating colors and decorative themes like the brown tones and wood trim in the picture helps to give a uniform effect.*

Left: *Give each area its own form of lighting, so that when one is in use, the other two can be effectively shut off by leaving them dark.*

Right: *This large, open plan area is broken up by the staircase running at a dramatic diagonal across the room.*

the living section. If you really hate being watched as you cook, attach some pull-down blinds to the ceiling above the counter facing into the rest of the room. The blinds can be brought into action when you don't want an audience. Alternatively, a row of trailing green plants on a shelf attached above the counter about 18 inches from the ceiling is a lighter way to screen your activities and will add color and life to the room. But bear in mind that while lots of houseplants positively flourish in a steamy atmosphere, none of them are at all partial to gas – so if you cook by this method you could find yourself replacing the greenery from time to time. Ivies tend to be pretty resilient however, and come in an extraordinary range of leaf-shape, size and shades of green, cream and

bronze-red.

Remember to keep the same decorative theme throughout. Paint, rather than patterned wallpaper, is the best choice for walls, because it can be given the occasional sponging down – kitchen walls tend to lose their pristine state rather sooner than other rooms do. Also, of course, paper can come apart at the seams in the sometimes steamy atmosphere. Choose kitchen tiles to complement the color.

Major pieces of furniture as well as co-ordinated accessories used in the kitchen and living/areas need to be from the same color group. If, for instance, you have chosen pale blue lamps for the living area it is a good idea to reflect the blue with pots, pans, china and accessories in the kitchen.

LIGHTING

Lighting is very important in this sort of room, as you will need a different light for each function.

All over the room: Ceiling recessed downlighters, individually controlled by dimmer switches.

In the living area: Table lamps or uplighters to provide pools of warm light around the seating area and create a relaxing atmosphere.

In the dining area: A rise and fall pendant light over the dining table.

In the kitchen: Under-cabinet strip lights to shine down on counters.

A ROOM FOR ALL REASONS

"Living room" is a more than accurate description of the most important area of the home. The kitchen, bedrooms, bathroom and dining room all have their own specific functions which help you to decide how to plan and arrange the space. Making living room furnishing and decorating decisions is harder. Watching TV, listening to music, reading, knitting, homework, play, board games, entertaining, eating and simply relaxing are just some of the ways in which the average family uses its living room. It is the room visitors see most of, too, so furnishing must combine stylishness with practicality.

Before you buy any furniture or begin do-it-yourself work, think carefully about the way the room is used. Style is a matter of taste, but for a harmonious effect, decide on the overall look you want and stick to it. Mixing styles can work well, or can be a disaster. The secret is that every object must be attractive in itself. If, for example, you own a stripped pine sideboard and decide to use it in the living room with a cheap black leather sofa, garish rug and imitation teak coffee table, you'll have the essential elements of seating, storage and warm floor covering but the effect will be neither attractive nor comfortable. Replace the garish rug with an Indian dhurrie in soft colors, the teak coffee table with a wicker chest and throw a colorful shawl or two and some pretty cushions over the cheap sofa and you'll have an attractive, welcoming setting.

The architectural style of the building may inspire you toward a living room look. High-ceilinged rooms can work well furnished in country house style, with warm, glowing woods, chintz and traditional rugs, or can look equally effective with sanded and sealed wood flooring and a minimum of stylish modern furniture.

Left: *If your living room has a good architectural feature, such as these lovely windows, try to make it a focal point. The simple curtains used here screen the windows at night but do nothing to detract from their attractive proportions during the day.*

Above: *The country house look relies on use of traditional pattern, polished wood, soft colors and comfort.*

If you are replanning an existing living room, make a list of the furnishings you like and want to keep. Don't write off upholstered furniture because the covering is worn or does not suit your new color plans. Recovering, even by professionals, is cheaper than buying new furniture. It may be possible to strip an unattractive finish from wooden furniture, if the wood is solid, not veneer. Once stripped, the piece can be sanded and left natural, colored with a stain or painted. Even the most unpromising piece can look lovely marbled or sponged and stenciled (please see *pages 60-65* for details of these techniques) to match upholstery or the pattern of your chosen wallcovering.

Remember that everyone, from the family cat upward, has a stake in the living room. It helps to make a list of the ways in which the room will be used as this will help to suggest furnishings and space arrangement. Comfort is the prime consideration and people, not furniture, should come first. Plan the color first, then the furnishings, then the extras for a scheme which is harmonious without being in any sense contrived.

A FRESH START

An empty room, completely free of furniture or decorative style, is an interior designer's dream. Planning and furnishing a living room from scratch is a golden opportunity, free from the usual constraints such as an existing carpet or sofa in a difficult color or furniture which must be kept because the budget won't stretch to replacement.

Think of the room as an empty box, ready for you to fill with all the things you like best. This is your chance to plan a room which is exactly right for you. Begin by making a floor plan of the room and a list of any features you dislike. If, for instance, there is an ugly fireplace, it can be removed and replaced with a simple "hole in the wall" design. Small windows can be made bigger (depending on local planning or zoning regulations); the position of doorways can be changed or the room itself made larger.

Make a list of the things you will need to buy. Paint or wallpaper, fabric for curtains or blinds, something to cover the floor, comfortable seating and some storage furniture are the essentials. Armed with the list, you can work out roughly how much you can afford to spend on each item and economize where necessary. Never be tempted to economize on seating; somewhere comfortable to sit is far more important than expensive curtains or wall-to-wall carpeting. You can save by buying a large rug in place of wall-to-wall carpet, putting up shelves instead of custom-built storage furniture, or by looking for second-hand bargains. Steer clear of stopgaps. It is far better to use a wicker chest or a piece of smoked glass on some bricks as an occasional table than to waste money on a cheap, nasty compromise which will spoil your scheme and be an eyesore until the day you can afford to replace it.

LOOKING AT SHAPE

Construction work must be done before decorating starts. Alterations will, of course, depend on your budget, but it is worth finding the funds to have work done in the beginning to save upheaval and redecoration later.

If the room is very small, it may be possible to increase the space by removing a dividing wall. Changing an awkward shape is more difficult to achieve with construction work.

Badly placed doorways can often be moved and small windows enlarged to bring more light into the room. Look at the position of electrical outlets. If you like pools of indirect light from table lamps, there may not be enough outlets for your needs. It is worth installing more if you plan to have a lamp on a low table next to a sofa or chair as it will save trailing the cord across the floor or under the carpet but, of course, you will then need to know pretty much how you want the furniture arranged.

The shape and size of the room, and the amount of natural light available will affect your color scheme. If the room is small and dark, pale colors and textures rather than patterns are the best choice. Add warmth with a deeper shade on curtains or upholstery, and contrast with a few bright cushions or accessories. Warm colors will make a big, empty room seem warmer. Use color to make the most of interesting features by picking them out in a darker shade. Paneled doors look effective if the molding is in a deeper shade than the main part of the door, as do other features such as particularly attractive ceiling cornices and roses.

Left: *Decorating a room in several shades of one color can work very well. Here, green was the color choice, used in a sage tone on the walls above the dado and on the ceiling and in willow below the dado. White adds a touch of freshness.*

Right: *When covering upholstered furniture in a patterned fabric, pick out the strongest colors for accessories and the paler shades for the walls. A paint technique like the one shown here allows you to use several colors from the same shade group.*

FURNISHING IN STAGES

A tight budget may mean that complete furnishing of the living room is impossible all at once, but by clever planning and buying, the room can look as good at the start of your furnishing plan as it does at the end. You may even discover that you prefer this minimalist look. It can be very restful.

STAGE 1

An interesting color treatment on walls is an instant and inexpensive way to make an empty room seem more welcoming. Sponging in two or three colors is an easy and effective way to do this, or you could paint the walls in a plain, pale shade and add a splash of color and warmth by hanging an oriental rug or Indian dhurrie on the longest wall – simply attach one end to a piece of doweling or a piece of wood that, in turn, can be attached to the wall.

The floor is important too. If the floor is wooden and you can't afford wall-to-wall carpeting, strip the boards using a rented floor sander. The result will be warm, honey-colored wood that you can seal with several coats of clear polyurethane. Alternatively, stain the boards, either in a wood shade or a color. Add an inexpensive rug for comfort. If you have a steady hand, stencil the area of bare boarding around the rug and pick up the design on the walls or around the doorways or window frames.

Concrete floors are more difficult to deal with. One possibility is to cover the floor with cork tiles and add a rug on top. Cork tiles are warm, quiet, inexpensive and easy to lay.

It is a good idea to invest in the best seating you can afford, at this stage. If your plan is to have a sofa and two armchairs, or two sofas, you can economize by buying just one thing and adding others later. If your budget is very tight, it is better to buy a battered but comfortable second-hand sofa and cover it with a bright throw of fabric than to buy cheap director's chairs, or floorcushions which always look cozy but are agony to sit on for more than an hour.

Think carefully about your lifestyle when buying upholstered furniture. If you have small children, or plan to have a baby in the near future, or if you have pets, avoid very pale fabrics, covers which can only be dry cleaned and loosely woven fabrics which will catch on claws or shoe buckles. Upholstery with zip-on washable slipcovers comes in many different styles and colors and is well suited to family life.

Take a scale plan of the room with you when you go to buy seating; the sofa and chairs which look a reasonable size in the shop may well be far too large for your living room. On the other hand, less expensive lines may be a little on the small side so that, for example, a so-called two-seater unit may be rather cramped if occupied by two adults and eventually be used as a large single armchair – wasting space and money. If you plan to add to the seating later, ask how long the line will continue to be available, and remember to allow sufficient space for the extra furniture on your plan.

Try the seating before you buy. Good upholstered furniture is firm, but not hard, and gives good, all around support. Very low or soft seating is difficult to get in and out of (especially for the elderly) and can quickly become uncomfortable. It can also have a devastating effect on both your posture and your clothing.

Lighting is another must. A couple of attractive table lamps or a corner uplighter will do for a start. Don't be tempted to rely on just the overhead light; bright, overall illumination is tiring and will make an empty room seem even emptier.

You'll need a small table or two for drinks, magazines, etc., and somewhere for television, stereo and books. Simple shelving will solve most storage needs and is inexpensive to build. A wooden chest painted or stenciled to match the walls makes a good occasional table and has the added benefit of storage capacity.

Good, well made drapes are expensive. You can compromise by draping swathes of inexpensive voile over a pole with a roller blind to cover the glass. The voile can be made up into drapes at a later stage and the roller blind used elsewhere.

Accessories are a luxury touch which you probably won't be able to afford at this stage. It is, however, worth buying one or two big green plants as they never fail to make a room attractive and welcoming.

STAGE 2

When there is more money to spare, replace the rug with wall-to-wall carpeting. The rug can be used on top of the carpet, or elsewhere in the house. You might, at this stage, add more seating by buying a second sofa to go with the first, or an armchair. If you can afford it now, invest in full-length lined drapes. As well as looking good, they will help to reduce your heating bills. The original voile can be turned into festoon blinds, or made into curtains to hang close to the windows for privacy in the daytime when the heavier drapes are drawn back.

STAGE 3

Now is the time to finish your seating plan and invest in well-planned, custom-built storage for TV and stereo, books and records. Add a couple of side tables and lamps to use at either side of the sofa or armchairs. Complete the scheme with paintings and accessories.

IMPROVING WHAT YOU HAVE

Starting from scratch is a luxury; most homeowners are faced with improving an existing, unsatisfactory room, or trying to work round furniture, carpets and drapes that must be kept.

Look at each item in the room. If the carpet is worn in patches, the threadbare parts can be hidden with rugs. If it is badly stained or you hate the color or pattern, you will probably be happier with stripped boards or cork tiles and a new rug. The carpet can be recut and used in a spare bedroom or the attic, where it won't be seen so often.

Drab, dull curtains can easily be given a new lease on life. If the curtains are plain, add a border of complementary fabric to the bottom, and make tie-backs to match. If they are patterned, the tie-backs and border can be in plain fabric. New track and heading can make a big difference too. Curtain poles are more interesting than plain white tracking and most existing heading tapes can be used with curtain rings. Long curtains could be permanently looped back to the wall with braided silk cords or tie-backs and a voile festoon blind or a complementary fabric roller or Roman blind hung at the windows. If the room is big and light, remove the curtains and replace them with louvered wooden shutters. Wooden louver doors are perfect for this purpose and cost very little.

FINDING A FOCAL POINT

A living room without a focal point will always seem dull and lacking in character. Adding this important centerpiece, or making the most of any possible focal point already in the room is one of the first things to consider.

Without a focal point, it is very difficult to devise a successful living room scheme. A fireplace is the natural choice, but many modern homes have no hearth or chimney. Some homes have gas or electric wall heaters in place of the traditional fireplace. There are now some very realistic gas flame-effect fireplaces available, far removed from the depressing arrangement of artificial logs illuminated by a red light bulb, so it may be worth considering replacing a conventional gas heater with one of these. Although electric log and coal effects are available, they are not as attractive or effective as the gas versions.

In a room where all the heating comes from radiators, it is tempting to turn to the TV set as a replacement for the flickering fire, but unless everyone wants to watch TV, this can

be intrusive as the focal point of a room. Conversation is automatically ruled out.

Picture windows or patio doors can become the heart of a room without a fireplace. If you are lucky enough to have a lovely view, place seating where everyone can enjoy it. Position flowering plants so that they can be seen during the spring and summer. A bird feeder will make the view more interesting during the winter months. Frame the window with interesting drapes tied back to make the most of the scene outside.

Where the view is dull, or the windows are small, a coffee table arranged with a selection of interesting objects, books or magazines

makes a center point for the seating arrangement. A big, low table is better than a narrow, spindly design. A table lamp will show off your display to best advantage. There is no need for anything elaborate or contrived; just a few favorite books, some colored stones in a glass bowl, a wicker tray filled with low-growing plants.

Warm pools of light, achieved by using ceiling downlighters or table lamps, will highlight interesting corners or displays and add character to your room.

If upholstery is in good condition but looks dull, adding a few cushions in the predominant shade used in the pattern, or in a com-

Far left: *Dull, plain upholstery can be brightened up by the addition of a few patterned cushions, and an ugly old table will be transformed into an asset if draped with designer fabric.*

Left: *Every room needs a focal point. Here, furniture has been arranged around an attractive wicker table. A grouping of potted plants adds further interest.*

plementary or contrasting color if the fabric is plain, will give instant interest. Carry the theme through to curtains or a blind. Many wallcoverings come with matching fabrics so if you have plain upholstery, look for a wallcovering to complement it; then you can coordinate walls, cushions and curtains at very little expense. Pale-colored plain slipcovers can be dyed a different color if the fabric is suitable. Test the color on a scrap of fabric first.

Worn close or slipcovered furniture can be transformed with new covers. Now that there are paper patterns to suit most styles of furniture, slipcovers are reasonably easy to

make at home. If you are unsure of your sewing abilities and cannot afford to have the covers professionally made, you can achieve a good effect by throwing fabric over the furniture and adding a few cushions.

Look at small points. If the doors have odd or ugly handles, replace them. Handsome polished brass handles and knobs come in both traditional and modern styles and you can usually find new light switch plates in the same line. Think about replacing old or discolored electrical plugs with pastel or plain versions fitted with cable to match.

Plain, flush doors can be given a paneled look with strips of beading. Old, scruffy

paneled doors may look better stripped and sealed or stained. A few accessories such as two or three new lamps, an attractive picture or print, or a couple of small round tables covered with floor-length cloths to match curtains or cushions, some lush plants in attractive planters or a stylish rug – a Kelim, perhaps – can be as effective as a major change of furniture and decor.

Bear in mind that, as well as making wonderfully colorful floor-coverings, Kelims make very striking wall-hangings and they come in a wide range of sizes so you should have no problem finding one to suit your needs.

A FAMILY LIVING ROOM

For those whose lifestyle is well-established and planned, organizing a living room is a fairly straightforward business of choosing furniture and accessories that appeal, and arranging them in a pleasing way. It is when children, pets and the trappings of family life enter the scene that planning becomes difficult. It is impossible to maintain a glossy magazine-look living room when toddlers, a boisterous dog or teenage children also share the room, and often surroundings which were once comfortable and attractive may all too quickly degenerate into a welter of clutter and discomfort.

The secret of success is to plan the room around the family. You may love the idea of a pale cream carpet and soft pink seating, a room with a minimum of furniture or packed with treasured antiques, but such schemes are impossible to maintain when that same room is being used for play, homework, snacks, watching TV (and playing ball games when you aren't looking!)

Decoration isn't too difficult; most paints and wallcoverings are hard wearing, washable and inexpensive to replace. Floor-covering is more important. Wall-to-wall carpeting is warm and comfortable and cushions inevitable toddler falls. If you want a pale color, choose a berber, as the flecked effect won't show stains as badly as an all-over shade. The carpet must be one designated for use in hard-wear areas. Cheap carpeting is a false economy in a living room as it will quickly show signs of wear. A combination of 80 percent wool and 20 percent nylon is perfect for living rooms. Wool is naturally stain resistant. Spills won't sink into the fabric of the carpet for several minutes, so if the accident is dealt with quickly, the stain will be minimal. The nylon content adds strength to the carpet.

The way the carpet is woven will also affect wear. Short pile is the hardest wearing carpet of all. Loop pile carpet is a better buy than cut pile for family use, as the loops don't flatten or pull easily. Sculptured pile, where the pile is a combination of loop and cut to give a three dimensional effect, is not a good buy for families, as crumbs and spills collect in the lower parts of the design.

Shag pile should be avoided as it flattens quickly and is awkward to clean. Adding a rug at hard wear areas around seating or doorways will prolong the life of the carpet.

Modular seating, where the pieces can be moved around and arranged in different ways, is a good buy for a family room. Most lines are available for several years, so you

can add on as the family grows. If the seating is of good quality, it should last long enough for teenage children to transfer pieces to bedrooms when they want to entertain friends away from the family. Loose slipcovers will keep the furniture in good condition until children reach the age when sticky fingers and muddy shoes are no longer a hazard or until you have bought all the units you want and they can then all age gracefully and uniformly. Make sure the slipcovers are made from a washable material.

Look for furniture with a good, strong framework. A patterned, smooth covering won't show dirt as much as a plain, loosely woven one. Spray the fabric with a stain repellent, such as Scotchgard. Arm caps (slip-on covers which fit over the arms of upholstered sofas and chairs) will protect these vulnerable areas of furniture from grease marks and fraying. Many manufacturers supply caps with the furniture.

Ring marks made by hot cups or wet glasses are a hazard if you have polished wooden

Above: *Removing walls can open up interesting possibilities and may allow you to set aside a corner of the living room for reading or hobbies. In this room, seating has been arranged around the walls of the alcove created by removing walls. Shelves above house books and are safely out of the reach of children.*

Left: *When you are working on a tight budget, choose bright, inexpensive furniture to make the maximum visual impact. These shelves were made using colored laminated chipboard and form an effective divider from the dining section of the room. A low-cost tubular chair upholstered in sunny yellow provides comfortable, modern seating.*

furniture so protect it with sheets of glass, cut to fit. The edges and corners should be smoothed so that they are safe. Most modern wooden furniture is treated with a polyurethane lacquer and is heat- and spill-resistant. Avoid glass-topped tables when children are small. The glass used in such dining and coffee tables is normally very strong but won't stand the onslaught of a determined toddler armed with a heavy toy and will show every smudge and fingermark. Small round tables covered with a long cloth look delightful but are a great temptation to a small child or playful cat. A few tugs (or perhaps only one) will pull the cloth down, along with anything on it, resulting in casualties.

Clutter is the curse of the family living room. Toys, games, books and magazines left lying around will quickly make the room depressingly untidy. Good storage facilities are essential. Wheeled boxes which will fit inside low cupboards make clearing up quick and easy as the jumble can be loaded into the

boxes and pushed out of sight in minutes. A box labeled with each child's name and a reward scheme for the tidiest child will help to reduce your workload. A big wicker basket with a lid can double as an occasional table and hiding place for magazines, newspapers and odds and ends.

Family living need not mean a bare, barrack-like room. Pretty or precious accessories will be safe on high shelves and TV and stereo can be housed in specially built storage for safety from small fingers (*see pages 114-117* for details on these units). Arrange lighting so that there is no danger of cords being pulled or tripped over. While children are very small, wall lights are safer than table lamps. Keep hardback and paperback books on high shelves, leaving lower levels for games and the children's own books.

Plan your living room to take account of the ways it is used and the room will work well. Seating works best in groups because people will naturally gather together to talk. It should be easy to rearrange, so that a com-

fortable chair can be moved away from the main area if someone wants to read or sew, and so that television can be watched by just one or two. Try to locate the television in a space where it does not dominate the room, so that people can watch if they wish, or play games, write or read without its intrusive presence. Try to arrange seating around a focal point, such as a fireplace, display of pictures or a low table.

Seating can be arranged to make a dividing line between the various areas of the room. A sofa, for instance, placed so that the back is toward a desk or dining table, will effectively fence this part of the room off from the relaxation area. Open shelving can be used in the same way.

Arrange furniture so that it does not cross main pathways through the room from door to door, or to seating, frequently used storage or the TV set. Children will appreciate a clear floor area for play, or a folding table which can be tucked away out of sight when the game is finished.

MINIATURE LIVING

The obvious way to deal with a small living room is to make it bigger with structural work. Taking down partition walls, blocking up, or changing the position of doors and windows, or adding part of an adjacent hall or corridor to your living room are all possibilities. You'll find more information and ideas on structural solutions on *pages 18-21*. But, sometimes the room cannot be enlarged, particularly if the property is rented, or in the case of many old homes, built on a small, difficult-to-expand scale. The answer is to think creatively and use a color scheme and furnishings that both draw attention away from the lack of space and make the room comfortable and convenient.

Aim for a clear, uncluttered floor area as this will make the room easy to move around in and will visually increase its dimensions.

Built-in furniture in the form of seating units positioned along a wall take up far less space than free-standing furniture. Building the units is a simple job, well within the scope of the average do-it-yourself enthusiast. Decide on a comfortable height and width for the seating, then build a wooden framework. The front can be covered with tongue and groove paneling, or with plain wood that can be painted, stained or paneled later. Use chipboard for the top and hinge each section so that you can use the storage space beneath. "Piano" hinges will give the best result. For cushions, either buy ready-made feather-filled ones to fit (available from good upholstery shops), or cut blocks of thick foam to size and cover them in fabric. Use the same cushions at the back or, for a neater look, make wall-hung cushions.

To make wall-hung cushions, select a curtain rod the same length as the base unit and attach it to the wall by the mounting brackets provided with the rod. If the rod is very

Above: *In a small room, open shelving takes up less space and is usually less bulky than modular storage units. An adjustable system, like the one shown here, allows you to move the shelves up and down to accommodate objects of different sizes.*

long, you may need a couple of extra brackets. Subtract 6 inches from the length of the rod and divide the remaining amount by the number of cushions you want. Use foam at least 3 inches thick and cover in fabric to match the seat cushions. Make fabric loops, fastened with Velcro or snaps to attach the cushions to the rod.

If the room has any recesses or alcoves, build seating or shelving into the space to leave more floor area free. Use as much transparent and fold-up furniture as possible. A work surface hinged against a wall can be used for eating, writing or sewing. A see-through table will visually take up much less space than one made from a solid material.

Keep clutter to a minimum in a small room and incorporate as much storage as you can. Narrow shelves just deep enough for books won't take up too much space and the strong horizontal lines will make short walls seem longer. Special wall brackets are available for a television, a neater, smaller solution than a floor-standing set. Most brackets allow the set to be angled for comfortable viewing.

Choice of color and pattern needs careful thought, as both can help to visually enlarge a small room. Use pale colors, and give the ceiling, walls and floor the same overall treatment to encourage a feeling of space. Plan perspective so that the eye is drawn into the distance. Using mirrors behind a group of plants, a lamp, shelves or inside the reveal of a deep window or on doors and cupboards is a simple way to increase the amount of space visually. You will find more ways to use mirrors on *pages 57-58*. Directional lines on the floor or wall are a great help, especially pale diagonals on a darker ground. Vertical or Venetian blinds used at the windows are another effective way to play the perspective trick.

Using a pale color against white will give a three-dimensional effect. Trellis patterns are best; use them on upholstery in conjunction with white walls, cover walls with trellis wallpaper, or use white garden trellis with a pale color behind.

Garden trellis is equally useful if you need to divide a dining or study area off from the main room. Use trellis floor-to-ceiling height to make a partition which comes just under halfway across the room, or build a double partition to half height with a shelf on top for plants. A trellis archway is more ambitious but looks wonderful if French windows or a patio door can be seen beyond, leading the eye out of the confines of the room, into the garden. Trellis and flourishing green plants

have a natural affinity and will add to the airy, spacious feel so sought after in a small room.

Good, well-planned lighting is important in a living room of any size, and in a small room can play a secondary role of helping to give an impression of space. Position spotlights to highlight architectural details, groups of plants or an alcove. Washing the walls with light from uplighters will soften solid lines but a bright, overhead light will make the room seem solid and box-like.

Above: *This attic living room has a low, sloping ceiling, a difficult feature which is minimized by using the same color scheme on the walls. In a small room, keep furniture pushed back against the walls and leave the central floor area clear.*

WELL-PLANNED STORAGE

Housing and storing all the things you may want to use in the living room can be a problem. From children's paraphernalia to all your latest video and stereo equipment, a home must be found for everything. The best plan is to invest in some versatile storage.

Technical equipment can be a particular problem when all the component parts have to work together in harmony. Most of it also needs to be kept still and level for best results, yet be easily accessible and visible. Another point to remember if you are building shelves or cabinets to house electrical equipment is the position and capacity of electrical sockets and the perpetual problem of trailing wires.

Central heating can have very deleterious effects on your sound system unless you provide protection with a humidifier which puts the moisture back into the air. Don't put anything made of wood near a radiator or in direct sunlight; audio and video cassettes can be badly affected by excess heat and light.

MEASURING UP

You can hide your latest electronic wizardry in an armoire, stripped-pine cupboard or rosewood cabinet, but before you buy anything, take the measurements of all the pieces of equipment that you need to store. Measure the depth of the TV (with aerial), as well as the height required for raising the lid of the turntable. Shelves will have to be set at the right height and any furniture used to house a color television will normally need to be at least 19 inches deep. Unless you invest in a custom-built piece, you will have to drill holes for the wires to pass through.

BEFORE YOU BUY

Good modern storage for video and stereo equipment is now available in many lines – but some have design limitations, so consider exactly what you need before you make your purchase. Make sure that cabinets for television and video have sufficient space for tapes and cassettes. Bear in mind that collections tend to grow and rarely diminish – so if the storage size is just sufficient when you buy it then you will soon be looking to replace it with something larger.

Once you have examined your requirements, look at the storage systems available. You can choose from free-standing furniture, built-in cabinets and modular systems.

Left: *Custom built storage will keep stereo and video equipment neat and in good condition.*

Right: *A small, boxy room can benefit from a bold color treatment and some clever storage. These units help to alter the shape of the room by adding a diagonal across one corner. The salmon pink and chrome yellow color scheme may not be to everyone's taste but it does make this cramped space into a talking point.*

Bottom right: *This kind of cluttered display gives a cozy, lived-in feel to a living room but is not very practical. Each time a book is needed some of the ornaments must be moved out of the way.*

Free-standing furniture includes mobile bookcases, cupboards and chests, whereas built-in cabinets are in place for good. These do save space and are ideal for awkward and unused spaces but they are expensive.

Modular systems include shelving and cupboards that can be added on to as and when you need the extra storage space (and can afford them). These units can be bought in knock-down packs for do-it-yourself assembly or custom-built for you. Or you may even prefer to design and build your own.

SHELVING

Shelving is really the staple form of storage. It comes in endless shapes and sizes, with varying adjustability. You can choose from metal, wood, even plastic in a variety of finishes, widths and lengths. The best place to look for shelves is the home improvement stores.

In older homes, alcoves on either side of the chimney breast can be fitted with shelves.

MODULAR STORAGE

These units can be added to as you go along, they are easily arranged and very mobile, so you can move them from room to room quite easily. Perhaps the simplest form is a cube system, based on simple wooden or plastic boxes which can be either open or shelved. The contents can then be concealed behind fronts and drawers or left on display. Open cubes can make a versatile and attractive form of storage for TV and stereo. They can also provide an appealing focal point to a room or act as a room divider. In this case take care that an unsightly array of trailing cords don't spoil the desired effect – or worse, become a hazard.

Many different combinations are possible. Some lines offer a wide selection of base units including cabinets with transparent or opaque doors, adjustable shelves, drawer units and open-down tops. Quality units that are properly made should be well finished at the backs so that you can place them at right angles and use them as room dividers. If you can only afford cheaper modular furniture, this can be dramatically improved by applying a couple of coats of paint or by replacing the door handles with something superior or more original. Interior details are very important. Many options are available, so, look for drawers, shelves, wire trays, cassette racks and tape boxes if you know you are going to use them.

Below: *Simple stacking cubes are available ready made with a number of different interior fittings, or you can build your own using laminate-coated chipboard.*

Above: *Encourage children to keep their toys tidy by providing brightly colored plastic storage boxes or a wicker chest for quick, easy clearing away at the end of the day. The boxes can be stored inside living room cupboards.*

CHILDREN'S PARAPHERNALIA

Remember that anything that stores toys and games for children must be placed at a lower height if it is going to be accessible to them. If you keep everything out of reach you will spend your whole time being asked to get things down for them.

As children get older they often become fascinated by minutiae. Compartmentalized storage, such as tins, small wicker baskets, glass jars and narrow shelves are perfect for when they get to this age. Otherwise just use a little imagination to adapt conventional forms of storage to their needs.

Shelving: Adjustable shelving is a wise choice for coping with the constant build-up of children's toys and general clutter. Giant low-level shelves can be used as seating as well as providing a place to store toys and later books and games. Low-level cupboards with an assortment of boxes placed inside them can be used to contain all sorts of things from puzzles to marbles. The higher shelves can be used to display anything you don't want the children to get their hands on!

Boxes: Perhaps the most fun idea for storage is to use large primary-colored plastic boxes that can be stacked. These are wipeable – an important consideration. Or use a pine blanket box to store children's things in – these can be bought new from furniture shops or picked up quite cheaply from junk shops. If you can fit them with castors it will be much easier to move them from one room to another. Even a rough plank chest can be resuscitated by sanding and a good coat of pretty colored paint, but make sure that you don't leave any nasty splinters to catch on little hands. If you have time and inspiration you could paint them with your child's favorite storybook character or animal. Stencils are another nice idea – and perhaps more fitting if you are going to keep the box in the living room. Another idea is to keep an old picnic basket or other large wicker basket in which to scoop up children's toys, or even an old-fashioned metal steamer trunk. These can be painted in lively colors.

Carts: A form of mobile storage, carts are a good idea for storing children's things as they can be brought out during the day when the children are playing in the living room and wheeled back into the bedroom at bedtime – or when unexpected visitors arrive. In summer you'll even be able to wheel them out into the garden.

ALTERNATIVES

Ask yourself what kind of look you want to create and whether you need mobility. A good alternative to traditional storage is office-type storage such as filing cabinets, revolving racks, peg boards and even wire mesh merchandise baskets. If used imaginatively they can be used to create an unusual and inexpensive chic.

Other alternative display systems include lazy Susans, carts on castors and swivel shelves. Some manufacturers offer shelving on a pivot base so that the television can be turned to face the wall when not in use. Carts allow the TV to be wheeled away and transported to another room; both high-tech tubular steel models and wooden country-look designs are available.

CREATING A CORNER

With the living room becoming more and more the undisputed center of the home, design and furnishing of that room has become an increasingly complicated business. To cope with various demands, the room can be separated into different activity areas. Perhaps one of the best ideas is to create a private corner of your own. You need not use a "corner" as such, but you can create a sense of privacy by using different ways of isolating yourself from the rest of the room. Use furniture, lighting, an interesting focal point, decor, color or some type of screen to create your special area.

You should plan carefully first, with a view to having comfortable, attractive seating, the right lighting for your needs, and furniture and decor which reflect the mood you wish to create. Try to keep this corner as individual as possible.

ERECTING A BARRIER

Probably the most effective way to create a private area is by using a spatial barrier. Hanging Venetian, fabric or cane blinds can effectively separate off your corner in an attractive way, or you could erect a screen for the same purpose. Screens are definitely back in style. Today's designs are sleek, elegant and versatile. Folding panels screen off a corner while still letting in light, or fold back to allow through passage. Lace or a sheer fabric stretched across a wooden frame looks less solid than a wood screen and when the lights are on at night the effect can be very romantic. A trellis frame or open grid screen can be used very successfully. These can be free-standing on metal feet with adjustable glides or free-wheeling castors. Try to find something that is easily moved around or rolled up for added versatility. Miniblinds are another idea; you can choose a color to coordinate with existing window blinds, while vertical blinds are ideal for really shutting yourself off to get away from it all. Some screens even offer built-in compartments and drawers – useful if you are short of storage space. Open shelving can be used in a similar way.

FURNITURE

The type of furniture that you choose will depend on what you are going to use your corner for. If your main activity is going to be relaxing and reading, you need to invest in a

comfortable sofa or armchair at least. Plenty of comfy cushions are also a good idea. If you are lucky enough to have a window seat this is a perfect place to pile up cushions and relax with a good book in the sun. You may need little more furniture than a table and chair, a coffee table for larger pictorial books and perhaps some shelving for a library of smaller books, such as paperbacks.

If you are going to spend a lot of time writing or typing, then you will need to choose a good desk to work at. Make sure that it is the right height for you and that the chair is comfortable (especially if you are going to spend many an hour there). Try to find a desk that is in keeping with the style of the room. A glass and chrome table will look good with a primary color background and modernistic metal chair, but if the style of the room is very country, a pine desk with a cut-glass inkwell and brass desk lamp would look much better. It is not a good idea to change the style of furniture within one room; you should be able to isolate your corner quite successfully simply by giving due thought to the careful placement of the pieces alone.

It may be best to resist heavy, large furniture and choose instead something small and light that can perhaps be swiveled or moved to accommodate change. Make sure that your corner is out of the way of "traffic routes," or you will be continually disturbed, and ensure that you immerse yourself in the things you will need most – whether it be books, cassettes, records or video tapes.

LIGHTING

Adopting different lighting styles can help to distance the corner from the rest of the room. You can create a quiet, relaxed mood by using table lamps with soft colored shades or use bright spots and a desk light that can be adjusted to whatever angle is appropriate if you need to read or work. Concealed lighting above a window seat or set in an alcove can look very attractive. Whatever form you choose, the lighting should be independent from that in the rest of the room; because this will help to maintain an air of individuality in your special corner.

Left: *In a small home, space for a hobby room may be difficult to find but you can create your own corner in the living room. This simple sewing area works well because the worktable faces away from the main part of the room.*

Right: *Latticed screens divide the space to make small, intimate areas but don't restrict light.*

WINDOWS

Cleverly used windows can really enhance a cozy corner. Always remember to choose curtaining that hangs well and is a delight to look at. Silk taffeta is gorgeous, if you can afford it. Try to make a feature of the window by using an unusual treatment, perhaps even beautifully draped festoon blinds or swagged curtains. The style of the windows themselves should influence the decor of your corner; café curtains, for instance, look attractive if combined with a window seat.

If you have rather awkward windows on either side of the corner, try to unify them with the curtain treatment. Position your desk across the corner so that when you are seated at it, you will have your back to the center of the room and will be facing toward the windows, particularly if you have an attractive view over a garden; this way you leave the hustle and bustle of the room literally behind you. If the windows have no view or you don't want to be distracted by it you can still turn the furniture away from the room and put up roller blinds – with an interesting pattern or painted with their own "view" if you are something of an artist. If you need the windows as a source of light in your corner, hang a blind that rolls up from the bottom, a sheer roller blind, a lace panel or sheer vertical blinds.

FOCAL POINTS

Creating a focal point in your corner will help to give it a character of its own – and therefore make it easier to isolate. If you can incorporate a fireplace into your corner then this will make it a very attractive nook in which to hide yourself away. A fireplace always becomes a focal point and can be surrounded by plants in summer.

If you are fond of greenery but not lucky enough to be overlooking a garden, you can create one of your own by grouping pots and plants in profusion. Light them artificially in the corner or have a huge arrangement of dried and fresh flowers set against a feature

Left: *A corner by a window is ideal for a home office or a place for hobbies. Make the corner as comfortable and relaxing as possible, and ensure that it is well lit, either from an overhead spot or a table lamp. This is especially important if you use a type of curtaining that will reduce light from the window.*

Above: *A mini home office, well stocked with shelves and equipment, will be used by all the family in turn. If the corner has a television, supply headphones so that noise won't disturb people in other parts of the room.*

mirror for dramatic impact. The mirror effect will also create the illusion of making your corner appear bigger.

For alternative focal points group a gallery of drawings and paintings on the wall at either side of the corner. Take time choosing what you want to hang and build up your collection gradually – adding only items that appeal to you personally – for a really individual effect. Again these can be spotlit for a more dramatic look. For collectors of particular objects, a private corner would be the perfect place to display them. Pebbles, boxes, decoy ducks, fine glass, jugs and fans would look good displayed on open shelving or in a display cabinet. If you decide you have room for open shelving you could position them as a screen to isolate your corner further from the main area of the room.

An architectural feature in your living room could be incorporated into your "corner." Having the area positioned behind a graceful arch or pair of ionic pillars would be very spectacular as well as further enhancing your privacy.

DECOR AND COLOR

It would be unwise to create something so different from the scheme in the rest of the living room that your corner looks out of place. On the other hand, you could try something unusual that complements the existing scheme, and something different enough to give the corner a look of its own. Using an interesting paint effect is a possibility.

Color is very important, as it makes a visual impact and creates mood, whereas the patterns you choose define the style. Red imparts vitality and energy, so would be a good choice if you want to work in your corner, but you may tire of it quickly. Orange, rose and peach tones are warm and relaxing and would be more appropriate for reading and putting your feet up. Yellow is best for making artificial sunshine and would therefore be perfect if your corner is rather cut off from the light or far from the nearest window. Green is refreshing and can give an appearance of space in a rather cramped corner, while blue is peaceful, but rather cold unless warmed with violet or lilac hues.

Light, neutral colors can be the perfect background to your corner, especially if you intend to mount a display. They are relaxing too, and can be brightened up by your choice of accessories or other details that you may need for working or resting.

THE HALL STORY

The entry hall is the introduction to the rest of the house, a buffer state between you and the outside world. It may not seem an important room, but the way in which visitors see your home is colored by that vital first impression made as the door is opened. A warm, welcoming, pleasant foyer is good to come home to, less depressing after a hard or difficult day than opening the front door to meet a dark, dull space, strewn with schoolbags, shoes, sports equipment and bicycles. Making a good impression can be as simple as painting the walls in a warming color, or covering the floor with a rich Oriental rug. If you live in an apartment building, the hallway is the ideal spot to mark the difference between the communal space outside and your home, a welcome relief from faceless brick and featureless corridors.

THE PRACTICALITIES

Unless you have a front porch, the foyer flooring will bear the brunt of wet and dirty feet so it must be practical, hard wearing and easy to clean. Terracotta or ceramic tiles are the traditional choice but are cold and hard underfoot. Adding a rug will warm tiling. If the tiles are patterned, choose a rug in a complementary plain color. If they are plain, look for a patterned rug. If the hall runs through to a living room, using the same carpet throughout will give a unified look. Choose a carpet that is marked as being suitable for hard wear areas. A combination of 80 percent wool and 20 percent nylon is tough, stain-resistant and easy to clean. Protect the carpet with doormats just outside and inside the front door. If you live in the country, old-fashioned boot scrapers installed just outside the main door, back and front, will remove mud before it finds its way onto the floor. Use the same carpeting on the staircase. If the floor is tiled, install carpet to complement the tiles.

A wooden floor will look effective if stripped and sanded, then stained or sealed, with a warm, colorful rug to add a touch of comfort and deaden the sound of footsteps. Polished parquet looks beautiful providing that it is kept in good condition. Modern parquet tiles are an inexpensive way to re-create the look of original woodblock flooring. The tiles are ready sealed with a protective coat of clear polyurethane. For safety's sake, never polish parquet beneath a rug, and as an extra precaution it would be advisable to put grippers at either end of the underside of the carpet.

Most hallways in older homes have several doors, which will look best if all the handles and the paintwork match. Stripped doors look good with a matching stripped floor or with terracotta tiles. If the hall is very dark, glazed doors will allow light through from the other rooms. Install safety glass if you have children under ten.

Because the foyer is the first room you or visitors enter, it should be warm and welcoming when the weather is cold or wet. Heat can be controlled to switch on in the morning, when people pass through the hall as they come downstairs or from an adjoining bedroom, and in late afternoon or early evening as the family returns from school or work. Weatherstripping around the front door, and a mail slot with a draft excluder will help to keep wind and weather out if the house is in an exposed situation.

Above: *The hall gives visitors their first impression of your home, so make it comfortable and welcoming. Here, a glowing oriental rug adds color to the gentle pastel scheme.*

There's a great temptation to turn the hallway into a dumping ground. You can combat this by providing either a hall tree or a built-in closet for coats, bags and umbrellas. If the hall is attractive as a room in its own right, people will be less inclined to treat it as a dumping ground for possessions. It is inevitable that mail, circulars, newspapers and the like will collect, so provide a hall table for them. If the hall is too narrow for a table, consider a shelf. Lack of space may mean that there is no alternative but to leave the baby's stroller or a bicycle in the hall. Think about this when you buy the stroller or bike. Most modern strollers will fold and can be tucked away in a hall closet. The bicycle will take up less space and look better padlocked to the wall outside. An alarm will deter thieves and a waterproof cover will keep the bike dry. If you cannot leave the bike outside, it might be worth looking at folding bicycles – at least they will fit into a cupboard.

THE HALL IS A ROOM TOO

How you furnish and decorate the hall depends very much on the style of the rest of the reception rooms. The hall is an introduction, and should lead naturally to the rooms just off it. Light is a major factor in the decorative scheme. If the hall is dark, choose a pale color, such as pale primrose, apple green, pale peach or any of the natural white shades. The exception to the rule comes in an older home, where you may want to create a dark, cozy atmosphere with warm terracotta, deep rose, plums and tawny colors.

A high-ceilinged hall will seem more welcoming if you reduce the visual height of the walls with a dado rail halfway up. Use pattern below the dado and plain above and paint or stain the rail to match the doors and woodwork. Painting the ceiling, coving and baseboards in a darker color than the rest of the walls is another height reducing trick worth trying.

A narrow hallway can be made to appear wider by covering one wall with a mirror, or with a series of mirror archways or strips to give the illusion of a room beyond. The same trick can be used to make a small, boxy hall seem longer, but this time position the mirror on the end wall opposite the front door.

A mirror is a must in the hallway. It allows you to check your appearance as you leave the house, and visitors to check theirs as they come in. Attach a mirror to the wall just above a small table and add a picture light above for maximum visibility. If your decorative scheme is traditional, look around for an old-fashioned hall tree with a mirror. Most are lovely pieces of furniture in their own right and include a useful drawer, shoe rack, place for umbrellas and hanging pegs for outdoor clothing as well as the mirror.

Choose hall furniture carefully. It is, after all, there to be seen. An old pine settee, packed with cushions in natural-colored, textured covers, always looks welcoming. If a telephone is in the hall, you'll need somewhere warm and comfortable to sit while you take calls, with a notepad and a steady surface on which to take messages. If there is enough space, a small bureau or desk, complete with a lamp and comfortable chair, will double as a center for family correspondence.

In a home with a staircase, use the space under the stairs for a telephone niche. There will probably be enough space for a small round table to house the phone and a lamp, plus a comfortable chair. If space is really short, a shelf and stool are better than mounting the telephone on the wall and taking calls standing up.

If you have a wide enough hall, the space could be used for a dining table. Position the table in a corner, with seating built around the L-shape of the walls and a rise-and-fall pendant light above. Hall and staircase walls are the time-honored place to display pictures and memorabilia. Favorite family photographs, menus, theater programs, a collection of plates, straw hats, tapestries, samplers, dried-flower pictures, prints and cards are just some of many ideas. Collections unsuitable for wall hanging can be displayed on narrow shelves. If there is space, you can line the walls with bookshelves. Use odd corners, windowsills and ledges for plants or attractive pieces of china or sculpture. In a small hall, paint the walls white or in a pale color and display just one stunning picture or object.

Most hallways suffer from lack of natural light. A lace or opaque roller blind will let the light in but effectively screen a typical small hall window. If you are lucky enough to have long, gracious windows, make maximum use of them with a pair of sweeping, full drapes, hooked back to the wall with braided silk or fabric tie-backs to match or contrast with the drapes themselves.

Left: *Formerly dark green and depressing, this hallway was given a new lease on life with primrose yellow and pale green wallcovering. Sanding the parquet floor (originally molasses colored) revealed glowing golden wood.*

LIGHTING

The first essential is a two-way switch, so that general lighting can be switched on as you come into the hall and off as you enter the living room. General lighting can come from recessed ceiling spots or downlighters. These look neater than the traditional hanging pendant and provide a good basic level of light. Spotlights on a track are a cheaper alternative and can be angled to light pictures or wall-mounted displays. A lamp on the hall table or shelf will add a cozy glow and looks especially effective if overhead lighting can be dimmed so the area around the lamp is bathed in a golden pool of light. Hiding strip lighting behind a cornice is expensive but effective as the light bounces off the ceiling and washes down the walls. Wall lights are another way to create the "washed" effect.

Left: *Don't forget the space under the stairs. If the staircase is steeply pitched, you will be able to fit in ready-made shelving, as shown here. Made-to-measure shelves can be used in lower spaces.*

Right: *A roomy hallway can become a miniature study, a reading room or simply a place for extra cupboard space. This narrow desk unit fits neatly under the sloped wall and the chair tucks away into the kneehole. Alternatively, use a folding chair.*

CHANGING THE SPACE

It was fashionable during the 1960s to knock the hall and adjacent living room into one, an uncomfortable idea as visitors, welcome or not, step straight in from the street. From a security point of view, getting rid of the "buffer state" between the living area and the street is unwise as callers can quickly see whether there is something worth stealing if the front door opens straight into the main reception room. But if you are desperate for living room space and incorporating the hall would provide it, add a porch as a shield between you and callers. A cheaper alternative would be to install a semicircle of drapery track to the ceiling just inside the door and hang a drape there to match those at the windows. This is a good way to exclude wintery drafts, too.

Cutting an archway through the hall wall will make the living room seem bigger but preserve your privacy.

If the hall is tall and narrow, it may be possible to install a loft, either for use as a storage space, or as a spare bedroom if there is enough headroom to sit up. An architect will be able to advise on the best design for the intended purpose.

THE STAIRCASE

Although it may be tempting to think of replacing your staircase with a sweeping, *Gone with the Wind*-style model, or a modern open-plan design, the end result is not usually worth the cost. Replacement is only worthwhile if the old staircase is beyond repair, or if the staircase is part of the dividing wall between two small rooms which would work better as one big space. A spiral staircase occupies only a small amount of space but is unsuitable and unsafe for small children and the elderly. Some fit adults find spirals unnerving to use which might cause difficulties should you want to sell the property in the future. Carrying even a cup of coffee up a spiral is difficult, and moving large pieces of furniture up or down the stairs is impossible.

Staircase safety is important. Stairs must be well lit and the carpet should be securely affixed. If you have small children, a folding gate, which can be installed across the top or bottom of the stairs, will stop them from going up or down alone. It makes decorative sense to match the hall and staircase color schemes. If you have used the hall walls to display pictures, carry the display on up the stairs. Take the geometry of the staircase into account by stepping the pictures to match the rise of the stairs. Long, horizontal lines of pictures, diminishing as the stairs rise, will work better than a vertical display. Add a picture light at the top of each display, or beam spotlights down from the landing to show the pictures to best advantage. Lighting for a staircase should be arranged so that it illuminates the treads (not the risers) and there should be a light fixture at every landing or wherever the stairs change direction. Arrange for two-way switches here, too, so that lights can be turned on and off progressively as you go up (or down) the stairs.

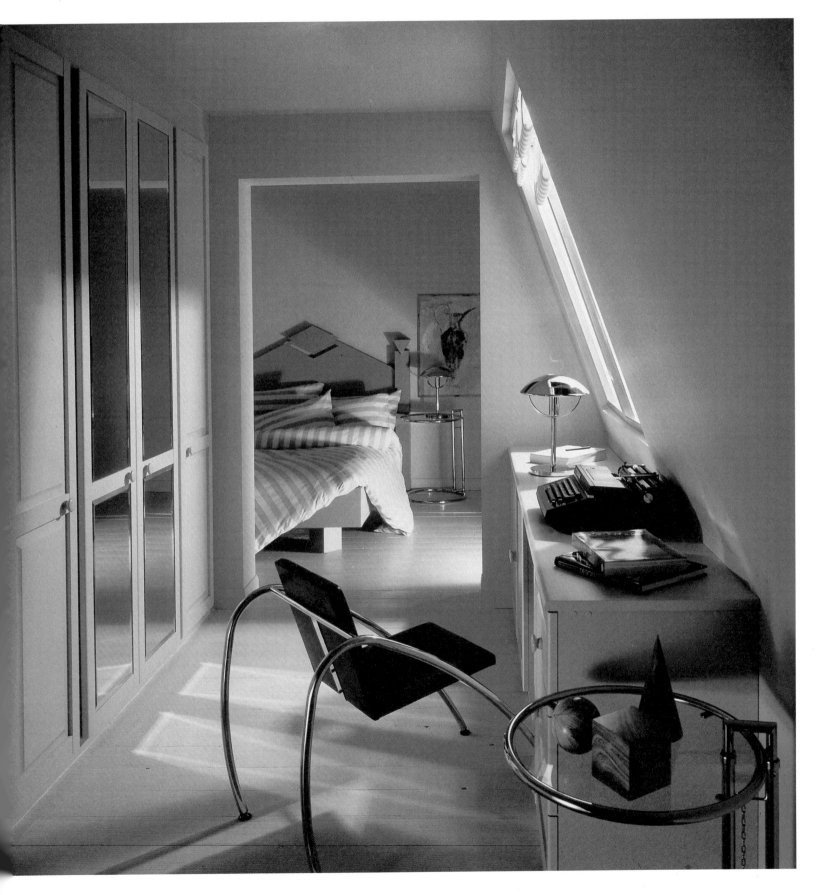

SPLASHING OUT

The bathroom should be one of the most comfortable rooms in your home; a combination of warmth and luxury with the practical attributes of easy-to-clean fixtures and splashproof walls and floor.

Lounging in a hot bath at the end of the day or enjoying an invigorating shower at its start are both wonderful ways to unwind and pamper yourself, but a chilly, unattractive bathroom is no place to linger. Often, a coat of paint, a fluffy foam-backed carpet, plenty of good, thick towels and the installation of a heated towel rail can make the difference between spartan discomfort and welcoming warmth.

For problem bathrooms, where the fixtures are in poor condition, an unappealing color or badly placed, or the plumbing is faulty or the space hopelessly disorganized, more radical improvements are needed.

Before you begin your bathroom improvement program, it will help to make a checklist of what is wrong with the existing room, and what you need.

BATHROOM CHECKLIST

Make your list following these guidelines:

► How many bathrooms, showers, toilets do you really need? If the children have left home, would you be better off with a master suite and a separate half bath, for instance?

► Is your present bathroom in the right position? In some homes, the bathroom was built downstairs – an inconvenient arrangement worth changing if at all possible.

► Does your present system provide enough hot water for your needs?

► Do you have a heated towel rail?

► Who will use the bathroom? Do you need to make special safety provisions for small children or elderly people?

► Are the fixtures in good condition? If they need replacing, now is the time to think about colors and send for manufacturers' color samples.

► Is now the time to add a bidet to the system?

► How much can you afford to spend on improving the bathroom?

► Is the bathroom warm enough or would it benefit from some extra heating?

Left: *An ideal bathroom combines comfort, practicality, warmth and good fixtures.*

Right: *For those who hate ruffles and flounces, a clinical, high-tech look may appeal.*

BATHROOM SAFETY

Although it is unlikely that children under five will use the bathroom alone, fives to tens have a strong sense of independence and won't welcome constant supervision from parents.

Follow these simple rules to make the bathroom safe for children to use on their own.

▶ If there is a shower, it must be thermostatically controlled so that there won't be a surge of either very hot or very cold water. A temperature control that can be pre-set by an adult is best, as children can't change the heat of the water themselves.

▶ Children love to splash water around, so cover the floor with a material which is non-slip when wet. Avoid ceramic tiles; they can be dangerously slippery and are very hard to fall down on.

▶ If the bathroom has a heated towel rail or radiator, set it on a low heat. Small children have sensitive skin and can easily burn themselves on a hot radiator.

▶ Keep medicines, razor blades and cleaning materials out of reach or in a locked cabinet. Do not leave the key the lock!

▶ Make sure that the bathroom door can be opened from the outside. Children are experts at locking themselves in.
    While children are small, it is easier to remove the lock and replace it with a bolt positioned above child height, so that adults can enjoy privacy in the bathroom .

▶ Put a non-slip mat in the bottom of the bath or shower.

▶ Put a box by the bath, or build a platform so that small children can get in and out without the danger of falling on a hard surface.

Before you begin any bathroom improvement work collect together as many manufacturers' brochures as you can find. Although many of the rooms shown take up a larger space than the average bathroom, you will see plenty of good ideas on how fixtures can be arranged, and ingenious ways of adding storage which may never have occurred to you. Some manufacturers include a free planning kit in their literature.

If you can, it is worth visiting some specialty bathroom shops. Here you will find tubs, basins, bidets and toilets in many different shapes and colors. Specialty shops are a good source of non-standard size baths, such as the continental sit-up models, and showers. You will also see unusual finishes, such as fake marble and pearlized effects. Many specialty shops also sell the latest "environmental enclosures" complete with soft rain effects and sweet music, faucets, tiles, towels, flooring and matching accessories, so it is possible to do all your shopping under one roof.

When looking at brochures, remember that color printing can be deceptive. Most bath and fixture manufacturers will supply color samples that you can then match up with tiles, wallcovering and flooring. Always take the color sample with you when choosing tiles and wallcovering, and ask at the shop if it is possible to compare the colors in natural light as fluorescent lights can change tones dramatically.

If you are unsure how the changes you would like to make might affect plumbing – and whether or not plumbing restrictions would make your plans possible – it is worth asking a plumber to come and make a preliminary survey before you buy any expensive equipment. A skilled plumber who is a member of a trade organization will be able to give you informed and impartial advice. And if you're looking for someone reliable to carry out the work, this is a good way of "interviewing" a prospective candidate without commitment.

Most homeowners have to cope with a bathroom in a space which is really too small to meet the needs of a family. In this chapter, you'll find ideas on planning and outfitting a new bathroom, and if money is tight and improvements have to be limited, on making the best of what you already have.

STARTING FROM SCRATCH

Installing a brand-new bathroom is a golden opportunity. Starting from scratch with new fixtures – plus new flooring, lighting, heating and decor – gives you the chance to plan the room to suit both your tastes and your lifestyle. There is an enormous choice of fixtures available for home use, including pale and deep shades, baths in many different shapes and sizes and with whirlpool or spa effects, coordinating tiles, wallcoverings and fabrics, and custom-built installed cabinets.

ASSESS THE POSSIBILITIES

Start your bathroom improvement plan by measuring the room.
As well as the length, width and height of the room, you will also need to note the positions of all the following:

▶ The location of the door and the direction in which it opens.

▶ Size and position of windows.

▶ Pipes for hot and cold water supplies.

▶ Waste pipes from bath, basin and shower.

▶ Position of toilet sewer pipe.

▶ Linen closet or laundry hamper (if located in bathroom).

▶ Radiator or heated towel rail.

▶ Electrical fittings.

▶ Any features you want to keep.

Once you have recorded all the measurements, transfer them to graph paper. A good ratio is to allow every small square on the paper to represent ½ foot of space in your bathroom plan.

The next stage is to think about how the bathroom is used at the moment . . . and how you would like it to be used in the future. List the drawbacks and the features you would like to install. Starting from scratch is your chance to get things right. If shortage of space means you can't have some of the features you would like to include, think about the following: If the bathroom and toilet are separate, you could knock them into one, giv-

ing more room for fixtures and storage. Can an adjoining bedroom wall be moved to give extra space in the bathroom? Remember that moving the bathroom can be expensive if it involves changing the position of the main toilet outlet and plumbing.

If you do decide to relocate the bathroom, establish the position of the main toilet outlet first. Unless the new bathroom is in a master suite, it should be positioned so that it can be reached without the need to walk through another room. Replace the door with a pocket door to free the wall space behind it. Install an opaque glass door to give an impression of light and space – (use safety glass). Reduce the size of the window to give more usable wall space. If the window is in an awkward position, consider moving it. If the linen closet is in the bathroom, consider moving it into an adjoining room, where it can be concealed in a run of closets, or in a hallway.

MAKING A PLAN

Before you can make a plan, you will need to know the size and the shape of fixtures. Collect as many bathroom manufacturers' brochures as you can and make a shortlist of fixtures which appeal to your taste. Think about the kind of effect you want to create. If the house is modern in style, clean, geometric lines and pastel colors would be a good choice. Softer, rounded lines are more suitable for a traditional home.

Choose a selection of basin, bath, toilet, bidet and shower tray sizes and move them around your plan until you find a combination that works well. Remember that fixtures need to be linked to the main sewer line. The easiest and cheapest way to do this is to line bath, basin, bidet and toilet up along one wall. Alternatively, plumbing can be ducted away behind paneling, giving you the opportunity to create a low dividing wall between the bath and shower and the bidet and toilet, or to create a separate area for the children, with basins at a lower height and their own shower cubicle.

Floor space around fixtures is important. Allow sufficient floor area around the fixture for it to be used comfortably. There should be enough floor area at the side of the bath to allow the user to get in and out easily and dry himself. Give at least 2½ feet of standing space at the front of the washbasin, toilet and bidet and about 8 inches at the sides. If there is a separate shower cubicle, access should be clear of obstruction. Activity areas can

overlap if fixtures are placed side by side. The standard size bath measures 29 to 32 inches wide and 5 feet long, but smaller and larger versions and different shapes can be found. The material from which the bath is made governs both the price and the shape.

Enameled cast iron: The traditional and usually most expensive choice. Cast iron baths are receptive to color, stable and hard wearing but are very heavy and cold to touch.

Pressed steel: Has many of the qualities of cast iron but is cheaper and lighter.

Acrylic: Warm, light material which can be molded into different shapes. It scratches easily and will "move" and creak when installed unless supported by a rigid cradle. Available in many different colors.

Fiberglass: Similar to acrylic but less inclined to move around. Fiberglass baths come in many different shapes and are available in pearlized, metal, marble and other exotic effects.

A standard-sized bath will be suitable for most bathrooms. If you have a lavish amount of space, make the most of it with a luxurious two seater or a sunken marble effect tub. Where space is restricted, a corner-mounted bath or a stall shower will prove useful. If your budget will allow it, whirlpool, Jacuzzi and spa systems can be installed in domestic baths, or you could add a redwood hot tub to the bathroom.

The usual site for the tub is with one side and one or both ends hard up against the wall, but if space and plumbing permit, it is possible to achieve a more interesting layout by centering the bath along a wall, or in the middle of the floor. If the bath is centered in the middle of a long wall, you can build a plumbing partition duct along the end and put the washbasins and toilet on the other side of it to give a built-in look. Another idea is to add a floor-to-ceiling tiled partition at either end of the bath, with the toilet at one side and the bidet or a shower cubicle at the other. Run a curtain rail along the ceiling above the bath and use it to hang ruffled curtains with a waterproof lining and tie-backs. Use the curtains as a coordination point for towels and accessories for a look both individual and luxurious. You can achieve a similar effect by curtaining off a bath where one short end and the side are hard up against a wall, or for a more modern effect, build open shelving partitions.

Other bathroom fixtures are normally made

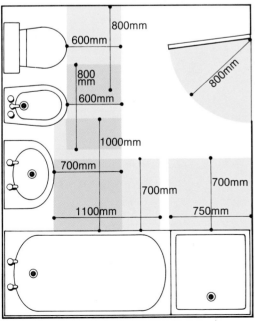

Above: *This spacious modern bathroom features attractive fixtures in gray with maroon trim. Towels and accessories have been chosen to blend in with this color scheme.*

Left: *Wood paneling has given this small bathroom a touch of class. Gold taps and hanging plants complete the effect.*

Far left: *When designing a bathroom make sure you allow sufficient space for everything – including the door. Our plan shows the recommended spaces for each piece of equipment.*

Right: *A bold color scheme is a quick way to revamp a bathroom. Here costs are kept to a minimum as only one row of tiles is used with the rest of the walls sponged in a low-cost paint.*

in ceramic ware in colors to match the bath.

Washbasins come as wall-mounted, pedestal or vanity designs. In a small bathroom, a wall-mounted or vanity model looks neater and plumbing can be hidden in a panel behind which will also serve as a shelf. A vanity model is always useful because a cabinet built around it adds storage space. There are various size basins, ranging from tiny corner-mounted shapes suitable for a powder room or bedroom, to one big enough to double as a baby bath.

Toilets and bidets are available either free standing or wall mounted. In a freestanding model, the unit is screwed to the floor. The wall-mounted version is neater because the unit is mounted on a bracket hidden inside a partition (known as a duct). The water and waste connections and the toilet tank are also concealed behind the duct, giving a neat, space-saving finish. If you install a recess above the duct, it can be used for storage or to make a focal point for the room.

Toilets are also available in water-saving models. These toilets use about $3\frac{1}{2}$ gallons per flush, as opposed to 5 gallons for a standard toilet. Other special toilets include low-profile, extra-gusset and corner models.

Think carefully about who will be using the bathroom when choosing fixtures, especially if there are small children or an elderly or disabled person in the family. A step up to the bath will make climbing in and out easier for toddlers and adds an interesting feature. A separate shower cubicle means that children can wash safely, unattended, but the shower must be a thermostatically controlled type with a preset temperature a child can't easily alter. Thermostatic control prevents a rush of hot or cold water if a tap is turned on elsewhere in the house. A non-slip shower mat fitted in the base of the bath and shower is another safety precaution – and a must in the case of children, the elderly and the infirm.

Installing two basins is sensible if you have children of any age as it eases the strain at peak times. You could set one basin at a lower level, or provide a stool.

As children have a habit of locking themselves in the bathroom or toilet, install a lock that can be opened with a screwdriver from the outside.

It is easy to adapt a domestic bathroom for use by a disabled or infirm person. Install grab handles on the wall beside the bath and toilet and inside the shower cubicle and make sure all floors are non-slip. The elderly, or anyone suffering from rheumatism,

arthritis or the effects of a stroke may find ordinary twist faucets difficult to operate, so install levers instead. Most bathroom manufacturers now include lever taps in their brassware range. If a member of the family is wheelchair bound and cannot use the bath, install a shower with a built-in seat, grab handles and an entrance wide enough to admit the chair. Many bathroom manufacturers now offer shower cubicles designed for the disabled.

PLANNED STORAGE

Organizing bathroom storage can be a real headache, partly because most bathrooms are short on space, and because of the variety of things the average family uses in the bathroom. Toiletries, soaps, medicines, shaving equipment, tissues, cotton, makeup and bath toys can quickly clutter basin and bath surrounds, so organized storage is a must.

The ever-inventive Germans have a ready-made answer with built-in bathroom furniture, a natural development from the kitchen. Cabinets are planned and installed around fixtures and include heated areas for towels, locking sections for medicines, pull-out baskets for dirty linen and many other features. If your budget won't stretch to custom-built storage, installing shelves above the bath and setting the washbasin into a vanity cabinet can help. Putting a skirt of fabric around a

wall-hung basin is a quick and inexpensive way to make a hiding place for cleaning materials, but has drawbacks as the materials will quickly become wet and dirty. Think about setting a basin into a chest of drawers or an old-fashioned marble-topped washstand as an original way to add storage space. If the bathroom is big enough, an old-fashioned pine wardrobe or a dresser will look good and hold towels, toiletries and toys. A corner cupboard is useful because it does not occupy much space but will accommodate a surprising number of bottles, jars and boxes.

At a simpler level, a tier of wire baskets on wheels is a convenient way to house toiletries or you could erect industrial shelving brackets with wire baskets as shelves for a high-tech look. A stacking tier of plastic vegetable storage boxes is useful for bath toys. A couple of hooks or rods near the hand basin will cope with towels and robes. But for safety's sake you should never fit hooks on the inside of a door.

COLOR SCHEMING

Color can affect the overall look of your bathroom as much as shape. Most bathroom manufacturers provide accurate color samples so that you can match fixture shades to wallcoverings and flooring. If the room is small, then an all-around pale color scheme will help to give a feeling of space. Avoid

Left: *Kitchen cabinet doors were used to build this vanity around the washbasin. Cabinet doors come in many different finishes and styles and can be painted, stenciled or stained.*

dark-colored fixures and busy patterns, as both of these will make a small room seem even smaller. Keep the color scheme simple by coordinating colors with one another and making use of shades of the same color, rather than adding a disturbing element with contrast.

Add interest to a pale scheme with one strong color from your chosen shade, such as a vibrant pink or turquoise, then combine with subtle variations bordering on white. A relaxing scheme will always work better in a small bathroom than one designed with impact in mind. Keep patterns small and to a minimum. If you do decide to have more than one pattern in a bathroom, choose from a mix and match range designed to coordinate. Remember that simplicity is the key when the room is small.

A large bathroom can feel chilly and unwelcoming, particularly if the ceiling is high. Use deep colors in shades of terracotta, rose, apricot, maroon and ochre to make the room seem warmer and avoid large areas of plain, pale coloring. If you don't like deep shades, marbled wallpaper in rose or apricot has a warming effect. It is easy to visually lower the ceiling with paper and paint. Painting the ceiling in a deeper shade than the walls is the simplest approach, or you can carry the paint down the walls to a depth of around 1 foot, then finish off with a wallpaper border or a dado rail. Cutting high walls in half with a dado rail and applying pattern below the rail and plain paint above it has a similar effect.

Look for warmth and depth in textures, with deep pile carpet and luxurious towels to counteract a chilly feeling. Soft lighting is a better choice than the harsh glow of a fluorescent tube.

LIGHTING, HEATING AND VENTILATION

There's nothing more uncomfortable than a bathroom which is chilly and dripping with condensation. The bathroom should be a warm, comfortable, even luxurious room – qualities impossible to achieve in a cold, damp atmosphere.

Condensation is caused when warm, moisture-laden air meets a cold surface. Boxing in cold pipes will remove a major cause of the problem, as will the more expensive business of installing double glazing. Make sure that the room is well ventilated, either by opening the window or installing a fan. Heating can be

supplied by a heated towel rail, a radiator or a wall-mounted electric heater or a combination of all three.

Good lighting is essential in a bathroom, to facilitate the daily activities of shaving and applying makeup. Boost general light, ideally from recessed ceiling lights or spotlights on a track with direct mirror lighting. The light should shine on the sides of your face, not

straight into the mirror. Hollywood-style dressing room bulb strips make perfect mirror lights, or you can buy a mirror which comes with fluorescent tubes mounted at the side.

Avoid a mirror with lights at the top as they will shine onto the glass and cause glare. They are not exactly flattering either so why spoil your day by installing them!

Far left: *A suspended ceiling can turn a cold, boxy bathroom into a cozy retreat. Adding clip-on spotlights and hanging green plants enhances the effect.*

Left: *Comfort is important in the bathroom. This relaxing setting contains all the elements needed for bathtime luxury. The color scheme is warm and relaxing, the flooring soft and comfortable. Pipes are hidden behind ducting and there is plenty of natural light.*

a flat, featureless wall. Plan your design on graph paper first. If the room is small, use 4 inch or smaller tiles, as the larger 6 inch design is difficult to plan in a small area. Matching floor tiles help to give an uncluttered look in a small bathroom.

Walls must be clean, dry and level before tiling. Tiles can be applied over existing tiles, a good idea if you are unsure of the condition of the walls beneath the old tiles. In addition to planning the tile design, you should work out in advance where cuts will fall. When a wall is divided by a door or window, make it your focal point by surrounding it with whole tiles and working outward. On a whole wall, cut tiles should be positioned at the top and bottom at the ceiling and baseboard. If the wall is to be half covered, have the cut tiles at the bottom. When working within a window recess, put the cut tiles next to the frame and whole tiles at the edge.

Tongue and groove paneling can be used to create a Scandinavian look but can be confining in a small bathroom. Plain paneling can be painted and is an easy and attractive way to cover an uneven ceiling or a wall that is in poor condition. Laminate-faced white tongue and groove is easy to clean. The paneling is attached to wooden strips with clips or screws. Plain wood paneling should be sealed with clear polyurethane varnish to protect it from steam and water. Apply at least three coats, allowing each one to dry thoroughly and then lightly abrade with fine sandpaper before applying the next coat, to ensure a good adhesion.

The bathroom floor comes in for more than its fair share of punishment. Water spills are inevitable and can quickly damage many floorings. A waterproof, easy-to-clean, nonslip, comfortable material is a must.

Cork tiles are warm underfoot and are not slippery when wet. For bathroom use, you must buy presealed tiles; otherwise water will soak into the cork. Tiles come in various finishes and can be laid on any sound, dry subfloor using recommended adhesive.

Vinyl tiles are water resistant, easy-to-clean and reasonably comfortable underfoot. They can, however, be dangerously slippery when wet. Tiles are available in plain colors, marble effects, stone and ceramic looks. They can be laid on any sound, asphalt-free subfloor. Bear in mind that ceramic and stone floor tiles are extremely heavy and the subfloor must be very sound if it is to bear their weight. If in any doubt, check this out with a qualified builder. If a solid floor is uneven, you will need to apply leveling compound be-

WALLS AND FLOORS

Bathroom wallcovering must be hard wearing and resistant to steam. Paint is the cheapest choice and can look as interesting as a patterned wallcovering or tiles if you use a paint technique such as sponging or rag rolling. Walls and woodwork must be well prepared before the paint is applied. Wash the walls and woodwork down with TSP or a similar product and rub woodwork down lightly with fine sandpaper to provide a key for the new paint. Seal knot holes on new wood or the resin will leak through the paintwork. Use either flat or semigloss latex paint on walls and gloss on woodwork.

Wallcovering is available in hundreds of different colors and patterns, some as part of a collection to coordinate with curtains, towels and tiles. Choose a washable or vinyl wallcovering for bathroom use. Make sure the walls are sound before you hang the paper. If the walls have been replastered, you may have to wait for the plaster to dry out before hanging paper. Use an adhesive containing fungicide to prevent mold from growing behind the paper in the steamy bathroom

atmosphere. Using wallcovering on just one wall, or combining it with tiles or paint, can look more attractive than papering all four walls. You can add a designer touch by making fake panels along the bath side and on vanity cabinet and room doors using doweling, and wallpapering the area inside the panels. Paint the walls in a coordinating color and add a wallpaper border, either at dado rail level or about 1 foot from the ceiling. If the wallpaper line includes fabric, add the final touch by appliquéing part of the pattern onto towels.

Tiles are the traditional bathroom choice and are ideally suited to a warm, steamy atmosphere. Ceramic tiles come in hundreds of patterns and finishes, from simple plains and transfer-printed patterns to expensive handpainted designs. Tiles can be used to bring unity to the small bathroom by presenting an overall finish. The bath panel and windowsill can be tiled to match the walls. Designs that come with a border tile allow you to create interesting effects, by running a border along the edge of the bath panel, for instance, then repeating it halfway up the wall. Panels of patterned tile mixed with plains will liven up

Left: *Fitted bathroom furniture is a good way to organise storage and keep a family bathroom tidy. Many kitchen manufacturers now have bathroom ranges in finishes varying from ultra-modern to country style wood.*

fore installing the tiles. Floorboards should be covered with hardboard (rough side up), screwed or nailed to the floor at 6 inches intervals and attached firmly at edges. Before laying hardboard, it should be thoroughly dampened with water and left to dry in the room where it is to be used. If you can wait a couple of days before nailing it down, so much the better. This process will prevent the hardboard from buckling at a later stage and unsettling the tiles laid on top. When laying the hardboard panels, start at the center of the room and stagger the seams in each row – don't line them up. Gaps must be sealed using a filling compound.

Vinyl tiles should not be laid over asphalt, or on vapor barrier membranes based on bituminous compounds, or on a floor that has been treated with silicone-based sealer. In any of these instances, the floor should be treated with latex screeding first.

Before laying the tiles, measure each wall in the room and find its midpoint. "Snap" a chalked string across the floor between the midpoints so that it leaves two lines. The two lines should cross at right angles at the center of the room, showing the starting point. Loose lay a row of tiles along each line and adjust the crossover point so that the cut in tiles at each end of the lines will be about the same size.

Self-adhesive vinyl tiles are the easiest to lay. Lay the first tile in the angle of the crossed lines, then continue laying the tiles, working from the first tile until you reach the edges of the room. To give an accurate fit at the baseboard, place a single full tile over the last whole tile laid, then place another single tile against the baseboard, overlapping the first. Draw a pencil line along the first loose tile where the second overlaps it. Cut the first tile with a craft knife along the line and press into position.

To fit around doorways, moldings and other difficult shapes, use a profile gauge or make a cardboard cutting guide and draw around the outline on a tile before cutting the tile to shape.

Carpet is warm and adds a touch of luxury to the bathroom but must have a waterproof backing. Ordinary carpet will shrink, hold water and begin to smell. Carpet is not the ideal choice for a bathroom regularly used by small children as it will quickly become grubby from splashing and spills and small boys who aren't always as careful as they might be when using the toilet. If the bath-

room is part of a master suite, carry the same carpet through. Many bedroom carpets are also available in bathroom grade. Rubber-backed carpet tiles are, however, a good choice. Buy more than you need so that damaged tiles can be replaced and so that there is cover when dirty tiles are being cleaned. An extra tile can serve as a footmat in front of the basin or toilet.

Ceramic tiles look wonderful but are unpleasantly cold, hard and slippery underfoot unless combined with a large, thick bathmat. Ceramic tiles can be laid on a sound subfloor but should be installed by an expert. Remember that anything dropped on the floor is not only liable to break but may damage the tiles as well – and repair is a job for a professional tile installer. Bear in mind also that while a boldly patterned tile may at first seem striking and adventurous, it is going to fall when you long for a change of decor and are restricted by the flooring.

Sheet vinyl flooring is inexpensive, warm, easy to clean and lay but can be slippery when wet. The drawback in laying sheet vinyl is that you need a space large enough in which to unroll the flooring and enough room to cut it around doors, baseboards and moldings. Studded rubber flooring presents similar problems. It is harder underfoot than vinyl and non-slippery when wet. The industrial look of rubber flooring makes it a good buy for a high-tech style bathroom.

Left: *Vinyl tiles are warm and comfortable underfoot, easy to clean and non-slip when wet. They are a safer choice for the bathroom than ceramic tiling as it can be dangerously slippery when wet and is cold and hard. Vinyls are available in many ceramic style designs, like this attractive marble look.*

THE FAMILY-SIZE BATHROOM

Left: A family bathroom should be bright and cheerful, with no frills or fuss. Wipe-clean walls and floor could turn out to be a bonus, especially if your family is large and mostly under the age of five!

If you are lucky enough to have a large space for a bathroom, there is plenty of scope both for using the room efficiently and for making family life easier. Musts are a separate bath and shower cubicle, dressing area, ample storage, a double basin, a bidet and a really roomy heated towel rail. You can allow for the room to be used by more than one person at a time without loss of privacy by screening areas off. You could, for instance, install the bathtub with the faucet against a waist-height plumbing partition. Put a bidet, toilet and basin on the other side and build open shelving from the top of the plumbing partition to the ceiling so that the bath can be used in privacy even if the other part of the room is occupied. Screening off the bath with an opaque folding or sliding shower door is a possibility if plumbing does not allow a dividing wall.

A separate shower cubicle is another way to ensure that more than one person can use the bathroom at a time, but be sure water pressure is adequate. Two small children can shower together, in half the time and in half the amount of water as in a bath.

ORGANIZING THE FAMILY

Children from about four to sixteen seem by nature untidy. Given free rein, they will festoon the bathroom with damp towels and dirty linen, flood the floor, leave the sink with a liberal coating of mud and the bath with a ring. A bathroom to be used by the whole family must be practical and easy to clean, with plenty of storage space for toys, toiletries and cleaning materials.

Reorganizing a typically messy family bathroom is sometimes possible with a minimum of fuss. You'll see an instant improvement if you cover the walls with practical, easy-to-clean tiles. Bathroom wallpapers look pretty and are resistant to water but will soon begin to peel when faced with constant splashing by small children using the bath or shower. A shower door looks better than curtains – and will keep the water safely inside the tub. A separate shower is better still if you have the space.

Have individual cups, washcloths, etc – children are much more inclined to be careful and tidy with personal possessions than they are with things used by the whole family. Choose a range of coordinated towels and either initial them in embroidery, or appliqué the child's favorite character. Matching colored hooks for each towel will encourage tidiness. A nice touch is to stencil each child's name beneath the hook. Put hooks near but not on the door for bathrobes and beside the sink for washcloths.

You can add the same personal touch with colored soaps and by painting initials or a pattern on the handles of toothbrushes and on cups.

Storage for bath toys is a must. Children are more likely to put things away if storage is easily accessible, so a wheeled wire cart or a big hamper or basket are both ideal. Although drawers and cupboards probably won't be used by smaller members of the family, try to include as many as possible, including one specially reserved for medicines (this section must lock and be out of reach of small children), cleaning materials and toiletries. You can buy specially designed bathroom cabinets from many major kitchen manufacturers, or build your own with a wooden framework and ready made louver or solid doors. If there is space, a series of kitchen wall cabinets around and above the basin can provide an amazing amount of storage capacity. Ensure that even the tallest adult in the household will have ample headroom above the basin.

Wet towels quickly become smelly so try to provide as much towel drying space as possible, with a double, heated towel rail, or a long radiator with a rail from side to side.

Although carpet is warm, comfortable and looks attractive, it is not the ideal choice in a family bathroom where children may tramp in with muddy feet, and will splash water at bathtime. Choose easy-to-clean (and mop) sheet vinyl or vinyl tiles instead. Add a thick bathmat for grown-up comfort. The mat can be lifted when children are using the bath. Ceramic tiles are waterproof and easy to clean but can be dangerously slippery to small children. If you want to put ceramic tiles on the floor, then try to make your choice from the ridged, non-slip type like those used at public swimming pools.

DUAL-PURPOSE BATHROOMS

A big bathroom is an area packed with space potential. The business of bathing takes up very few hours in the average family week. Adding another role makes sense in a family home where space is at a premium. Combining bath and utility rooms is a logical, commonsense move. Dirty clothes can go straight from their wearer to the washing machine and you will free space for more

cabinets in the kitchen. The neatest way to plan a washing machine, tumble dryer and hamper in the bathroom is to install the machines in built-in cupboards with washbasins set into a counter alongside. The equipment should be plugged in outside the bathroom, or connected to a fused switch which, for safety reasons, cannot be unplugged. If you have a machine that is capable of taking a trim kit (panel specially made to fit the appliance and match surrounding doors), it will be easy to achieve a sleek, built-in look. Alternatively, you can build your own cupboards. Make a framework slightly wider than the back-to-front measurement of the machines so that they can be hidden behind the doors. Bi-fold or sliding doors will help to save space. You can incorporate a clothes hamper into the cupboards by making one

section with a hinged top to take dirty clothes.

A large bathroom can include a small home gymnasium. Install wooden exercise rails along one wall (they can double up for towels). If there is enough space, put a home sauna in a corner. A spa bath or sports "power" shower with several different sprays is a must in this sort of room. Other equipment to consider is a small exercise bike, multi gym or set of weights. Invest in a proper beam balance scale, or one of the latest digital readout memory models for a completely professional look. Keep the decor stark and modern; pine paneling combined with white tiling, mirrors, plenty of light and white or primary-colored towels is a simple but successful scheme.

Turning the bathroom into a miniature library/study may seem an odd idea but can

When closet space is short, a big bathroom can double as a dressing room. Install closets with the tub or sinks in the center. Most professional closet companies will design something suitable, or you could ask a carpenter to do the job for you. Install a well-lit mirror to give a clear top-to-toe view.

ADDING A CHILDREN'S BATHROOM

A second bathroom, especially for use by younger members of the family, makes life much easier to organize in a household of Mom, Dad and two or three children of varying ages. The second bathroom will come into its own during the school-to-teenage years and will save a lot of angry banging on the door at peak periods.

If there is no space for a second bathroom, think about finding space for facilities in the child's room. Providing there is a water supply nearby, and somewhere to run the waste pipes, you can install a basin, shower or a bidet. A bidet is useful during the baby and toddler years. While the child is a baby, it can be used for rinsing diapers and soiled clothing.

When the child reaches school age, the bidet can be replaced with either a basin or a thermostatically controlled shower. A shower is more useful and takes up approximately the same amount of space as a sink. A shower cubicle can be located in a corner or hidden in a run of wardrobes. Some manufacturers sell space-saving models that fold flat against the wall when not in use.

When there is room for a second bathroom, try to locate it near the child's room. A suite arrangement with a door from the bedroom is best. Consider partitioning off a section of a big bedroom, or knocking a door through to an adjacent room as ways to find the space.

Fixtures should be practical and easy to clean. Children love to splash water around, so choose vinyl or sealed cork floorcovering and tiles or paint for the walls. Provide plenty of hanging space for towels, a heated towel rail and a laundry hamper. Storage for bath toys is a must if the children are small. Stacking plastic vegetable bins or a wheeled tier of wire baskets will house battleships, ducks and soaps.

It may seem sensible to choose dark-colored bathroom fixtures, but the paler shades are better at concealing water splashes and soap marks.

Left: *If space is short in the kitchen, the washer and dryer can sometimes be housed in the bathroom. Check with an electrician for safety requirements.*

Above: *A stool or box will allow toddlers to reach the washbasin easily.*

work well if the toilet is separate or if there is another toilet elsewhere in the house and your books are not so precious and/or valuable that you would not subject them to a steamy atmosphere. You can introduce a wonderfully Edwardian air with floor to ceiling bookshelves in dark mahogany, matching paneling around the bath and basin, a rich Oriental rug on the floor and a *chaise longue* or armchair divided from the "business end" of the bathroom by a screen, somewhere to sit and relax or read after a bath.

SHOWER POWER

A shower is invigorating, economical and fast, well worth including either within the tub or in place of the bath where space is short. Showers can range from a simple diverter run from the bath faucet, to a complex "environmental enclosure" that will reproduce the sensations of soft mist, gentle rain, bubbling champagne or a cold shower, all to the sound of your favorite music!

As the average separate shower enclosure takes up an area of about 3 feet square, there's plenty of opportunity to add extra bathing facilities around the house. Stalls can be installed in the attic, in the basement or under the stairs, provided that there is sufficient headroom, a suitable water supply and a means of draining dirty water away. But check your local building code for restrictions. The average shower uses about one fifth of the hot water needed for a bath, so in a family of four or more, you should see energy savings.

There are several different types of showers:

THE BATH MIXER

A bath mixer is a hot and cold mixer faucet with a lever or pull knob in the center. When the lever is moved, the water is diverted upward to a shower head mounted on the wall above the bath instead of downward through the faucet. A bath mixer is easy to install and economical to run, as it uses water from the existing system, but there are drawbacks. If you buy a mixer without thermostatic control, the water temperature will change if someone switches on a water faucet elsewhere in the house when the shower is in use. This can cause a dangerous surge of hot water or an unpleasant surge of cold water. Thermostatically controlled bath mixers are available but there is little price advantage over other, more controllable systems.

INSTANTANEOUS GAS OR ELECTRIC SHOWER

An instantaneous shower is connected directly into the cold water supply – which makes it the ideal solution for houses that have a "direct" plumbing system, in which all cold taps in the house are at main pressure. It is, however, more expensive to install than a standard shower.

An instantaneous shower can be mounted over the bath or, preferably, in a separate shower cubicle – the heater must be positioned so that it is not in the direct line of spray. Many instantaneous showers are fitted with thermostatic control (temperature stabilization) and some have a choice of power settings. The temperature control in fact alters the flow – the lower the flow of water, the higher the temperature – but it is difficult to get a forceful flow from an instantaneous shower unless it is fitted with a pump. An electric shower control needs its own separate circuit.

THERMOSTATIC MIXER

A separate thermostatic mixer is the most reliable and efficient type of shower. The mixer takes hot and cold water from the existing systems and mixes them together to a preselected temperature. Many mixers incorporate a pump for a high pressure shower, whatever the location. Installing a mixer with a pump means that you can install a special shower head. Special heads include sports spray (a fine, high-pressure needle-like spray), champagne (bubbly, frothy water), a massage head (soft brush on a perforated backing so water surges through the bristles) and impulse spray (fine sprays of water at different levels and at different forces and temperatures). Be sure you like the feel before buying. A thermostatic mixer can be installed over the bath but is more useful if housed in a separate shower enclosure.

LOCATING THE SHOWER

If you choose an above-the-bath shower, the walls should either be tiled from top to bottom at the shower end of the bath, or protected by a prefabricated tub-shower surround. A shower door is the neatest way to protect the rest of the bathroom from water. Shower curtains look good when new but quickly become untidy and unpleasantly slimy. Bath shower doors are made from safety glass, in clear, smoked, bronze or obscured finish. The door can be hinged to the wall at the faucet end so that it extends about halfway along the length of the bath, or you can choose a full-length model; either needs to be enclosed in a stall. You can build a tiled stall just by simply erecting two walls at right angles to the wall where the shower will be mounted, or by setting the shower into a recess. Install a shower floor in the bottom, tile the walls and ceiling and add a ready-made glazed door and your stall is complete. Always try to accommodate the largest shower floor possible. Some floors are large enough to use for bathing a small child. In this case, make sure that the floor is equipped with an overflow drain. Check the position of the drain outlet in the shower floor as it will save time and money if it is easy to connect to your drain system with a minimum of piping.

When building the shower cubicle, don't forget a shelf for soaps and shampoo and a hook for soap on a rope or shower gel. If there are small children in the family, position the shower so that the controls are out of reach. It should be possible to use the shower head in more than one position so that the shower can be used easily by everyone. A head that pivots or is attached to a flexible hose (telephone style) is ideal.

Ready-made shower enclosures come in all

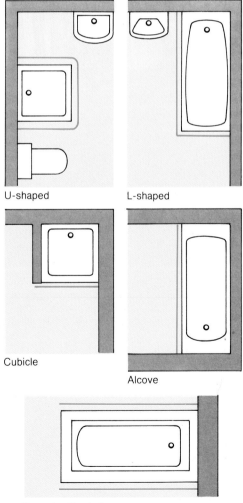

U-shaped

L-shaped

Cubicle

Alcove

Free-standing bath

Left: *Lined shower curtains can be installed in a variety of shapes and positions.*

Above: *A separate shower stall adds extra bathing facilities. The stall need not be in the bathroom. Often, it is possible to find a corner in a basement, or to convert a built-in cabinet.*

shapes and sizes and in a variety of materials. Those made from safety glass are the most attractive and versatile. The standard safety glass stall has a simple front-opening door, but where space is short, you can choose a corner-entry model or one with a sliding door. If sharp corners are impractical because there isn't sufficient space for people to pass without catching the edge, look for a rounded enclosure. It is also possible to buy an enclosure which will fold flat against the wall, and a pressed steel model to fit into a closet.

If you have the space for a separate shower room, a Scandinavian-style wet room would perhaps be a better choice than an enclosure.

A wet room is tiled on all surfaces, with the floor sloping toward a drain outlet either in the center or in one corner. The wet room is ideal if you want to install a sports-style shower with spray outlets at different levels. It can also accommodate twin shower heads.

This kind of functional arrangement would suit anyone who plays a lot of sport and needs to shower several times a day, but not those who value luxury when bathing.

THE SMALL BATHROOM

When the bathroom is very small, or you are searching your house for any available nooks and crannies with space to install a second bathroom, it may seem impossible to cram in all the necessary fittings. The answer is to look at the wide range of non-standard sizes available. Even the smallest, most difficult space can be equipped with a small corner bath, a tiny hand washbasin or a continental-style sit-up tub or a compact shower.

The secret of the successful small bathroom is to use every inch of space as economically as possible. Choose a smaller-than-standard size bath or a space-saving corner model. A continental sit-up bath takes about half the space of a standard bath and you can luxuriate up to your neck in water. Look for a model with a seat for maximum comfort. An elderly or disabled person will find a continental bath difficult to use.

Above: *Extreme circumstances call for extreme solutions, and here a bath, toilet and washbasin have been squeezed into a tiny cubbyhole barely larger than the width of the bath. This kind of arrangement is not built for comfort and would only really suit the fit, young and agile.*

If the bathroom is very small, think carefully about replacing the tub with a shower stall. A shower takes up approximately 1 square yard of floor space, can be installed in all sorts of odd corners and is faster and more economical to use than a bath. Shower enclosures are available with sliding, corner-entry or curved doors and can be sloped to fit under an attic ceiling or staircase recess. Replacing the tub with a shower may free enough space to have a double basin or to add a bidet. For a tiny space, steal an idea from Scandinavians and build a "wet room". The walls and ceiling are tiled and instead of a shower floor, the entire tiled floor slopes slightly toward the center so that water can drain away through a grille. The shower is mounted on the wall without partitions or drapes to take up valuable space. Most wet rooms contain a small corner-mounted washbasin and a toilet. To use the room, you simply walk in, close the waterproof glass door and switch on the shower. Because every surface is tiled, water drains away quickly. The wet room is an excellent way to hose down muddy children and dogs, as grubby foot- and handprints are washed away by the water. You can build a wet room, complete with corner basin, in a space only 4 feet square.

A vanity cabinet built around the washbasin, and a wall-hung toilet and bidet with pipes concealed behind panels will help to make a small bathroom look neater.

Mirrors are an infallible way to make a small bathroom look larger and lighter. A wall of mirrors at the end of the bathtub will make the room seem twice as long. Acrylic mirror won't steam up and will save you a lot of mopping and cleaning.

Avoid fussy detail and dark colors, as both will make a small room seem even smaller. Choose white or pastel-colored fixtures and a wallcovering that will reflect light. Expensive, shiny foil wallpaper can look stunning when used where it will catch natural light from the window. Install a neat glass shower door instead of untidy curtains.

Use odd spaces and corners for storage units. Narrow shelving doesn't occupy much space and can be concealed with sliding or bi-fold doors. Stick to white to achieve maximum effect.

Replacing the door into the room with a pocket model can free useful wall space for a basin, bidet or toilet. A towel rail mounted on the back of a conventional door is another way to save wall space, or you can hang the towels on the wall above the bathtub, where they are easily within reach.

Left: *Another compact bathroom using every inch of available space. A mirror has been used along the top of one wall to give the illusion of an extra dimension.*

MAKE DO AND MEND

The bathroom should be warm, comfortable, even luxurious; a place to relax and soak away the stresses and strains of the day. If you are starting from scratch, comfort can be your prime consideration when choosing fixtures and accessories. But what if you've inherited a chilly, uncomfortable bathroom, and you don't have the funds to replace the existing fixtures? If the plumbing is in good working order but the fixtures chipped or in a color you dislike, rescue is possible. Chips on a bath can be retouched with epoxy paint, or fixtures can be recolored by a specialty bath restoration company. Look in your local directory for the names of companies. Some can apply patterns and special metal or pearlized effects.

If the bath is an old-fashioned footed type and is not boxed in, painting the sides can give a bright new look. Stenciling is easy and adds an individual touch. Stencils can be bought from art and craft shops, or you can make your own designs by cutting shapes from stiff cardboard. Allow each section of the design to dry before applying the next color. Use an enamel paint for best results.

BOXING IN THE BATH

Boxing in an old bath can help to give the bathroom a built-in look. If you are retiling the walls, a tiled bath surround will give a built-in feel. It is better if you can move the surround out slightly from the sides of the bath so that there is a shelf all around. Build a framework first, then box it in with plywood or hardboard. If you are using a mix of plain and patterned tiles, run a line of pattern around the top edge of the bath surround. Louver doors or replacement kitchen cabinet doors or tongue and groove paneling is a good, inexpensive choice if you like the look and feel of wood. Buy plain louvers and stain or paint them the color you want. Wooden replacement kitchen cabinet doors can be stained to look like mahogany or pine, stenciled or given a treatment such as rag rolling, sponging or marbling. Seal pine tongue and groove paneling with clear polyurethane and match it with a pine towel rail, soap dish and toothbrush holder.

For a luxury feel, carry carpet up from the floor to cover the side of the tub. Alternatively, cover the bath panels with washable vinyl wallcovering. If the bath has a hardboard panel, paint it the color of your choice, then make fake panel sections with doweling. Wallpaper inside the paneled sections and paint the panel edging in a deeper

shade to match both the main paintwork and the predominant color in the wallcovering. You can extend this effect to a plain door. Hiding the bath behind a curtain is an economical, trouble-free solution. Hang a rail from wall to wall above the bath and use it to support swathes of filmy drapery, tied back in the center with wide satin ribbon or a circlet of silk flowers. Add a cane chair with some lace cushions, a deep pile carpet, some plants and pretty accessories for instant romance. A jungle of plumbing beneath the washbasin looks unattractive and makes the bathroom feel utilitarian. Boxing the basin in, with a countertop above and louver or replacement doors below, hides the pipes and makes storage space for toiletries and cleaning materials. Hanging a skirt of fabric below the washbasin is a pretty idea but not very practical as the fabric quickly becomes wet.

Changing the color or covering of the walls can provide an instant facelift for a shabby bathroom. If one or two tiles are damaged, they can be replaced, either with matching tiles if available, or with a contrasting or complementary tile in plain or pattern. Look around junk shops for Victorian and Edwardian tiles as their elaborate and colorful patterns look particularly good set into a wall of plain tiling. To remove a damaged ceramic tile, drill into the center using a drill bit recommended for masonry or ceramics. Wear goggles to protect your eyes as the tile may splinter. The tile will crack around the drilled hole. Insert a small screwdriver into the hole and use it to lever the old pieces of tile away from the wall. When the area is clear, remove any traces of old adhesive, then apply fresh tile adhesive and install the new tile.

If you dislike the color or pattern of tiles, it is possible to either paint or retile over the top. To paint tiles, wash well with TSP or a similar cleanser to remove all traces of grease and grime. When the tiles are dry, paint over with a coat of alkyd semigloss paint. Top with gloss. If the tiles are in a strong color, you may need to apply two or three coats of base paint before the gloss.

To tile over tiles, spread the old tiling with tile cement, using a ridged spreader to provide a "key", then apply the new tiles on top.

Make a feature of half a tiled wall by adding a band of doweling or a dado rail above the top row of tiles. Paint the wood and wallpaper or paint the wall above to complement the tiles. There is no rule that says tiles must match. A collection of individual Dutch, Victorian or Edwardian or Mexican tiles is

always effective, or you could experiment with different colored pastels, or a combination of white and one or two primaries in an interesting pattern. Sometimes, tile shops are willing to sell off odds and ends.

Plain painted walls can make a bathroom seem bare and chilly, even if the color scheme is in warm shades. Add interest with a dado rail halfway up, either made from wood or using a wallpaper border. If you look for a coordinated wallcovering range, you can use two different patterns and a dado border either in the middle or about a foot below the level of the ceiling with the second pattern starting immediately above the border and extending over the ceiling.

Less than perfect walls can be hidden by painting first then attaching white garden trellis mounted on slats. Or you could paint the walls and cover them with a display of pictures, framed photographs, china plates, menus or memorabilia. If the bathroom is big enough to stand it, a dramatic color scheme is an inexpensive way to add an individual touch. Try painting the walls glossy black or red, with matching and contrasting towels and accessories. Bathrooms in older homes are often dull and dark. The answer is to paint everything white and cover the floor in either a textured white Indian rug or vinyl tiles. Use cane accessories, mirrors positioned to catch available light and a mass of leafy green

Far left: *Leafy plants and pine accessories provide a cheap and easy facelift for any bathroom.*

Left: *Old-fashioned fittings are given a new lease on life with a pretty color scheme and traditional mosaic flooring. The walls were painted in soft beige flat latex paint with the ceiling in white. The bath was paneled in, using tongue and groove paneling, then painted to match the walls.*

plants for an airy colonial feel. Stenciling is a simple way to add interest. You could stencil a garland of leaves and flowers around the door or window and along the edge of the bath, or cheat and use wallpaper border instead.

Many modern bathrooms are functional and clean but lacking in character. A few little touches can make all the difference. Add a couple of shelves for books, pretty bottles or colored soaps, bath salts and cotton balls in jars. Buy a quilted box to hold tissues, or make one yourself. A small basket lined with fabric is an attractive way to store toiletries and you can add matching borders to towels. If you are good at needlework, embroider posies of flowers on towels, washcloths and bathrobes. Most needlework shops sell transfers. Look for interesting Victorian or Edwardian bathroom accessories, such as a pitcher and a basin set, a shaving bowl or a pair of china candlesticks. If your taste is modern, a few stunning, brightly framed prints or a crackle glaze or spattered vase will help to add the personal touch.

Plants give an instant facelift and add character and most thrive in warm, humid bathroom conditions. Plants need good light so if the bathroom is dark, you must keep the lights on for part of the day. A lush fern will thrive hanging from the ceiling above the tub, as rising steam creates ideal conditions for this plant.

BEDROOM BASICS

Above: *Choose a soft color scheme for your bedroom and make it as comfortable and relaxing as possible. Pale blue is a favorite bedroom choice because it is a color associated with tranquillity. Bold colors, such as red and yellow, have the opposite effect.*

The way any bedroom is planned and decorated depends on the lifestyle of those who use it. But, with the exception of babies and children, we all need the same basic ingredients if we are to enjoy comfort, relaxation and restful sleep.

A bed is the most important ingredient. A good night's sleep is vital for health and energy. Restful sleep is impossible on a bed which is lumpy, uncomfortable or too small, so it is worth buying the best bed you can afford. A good bed will give around 15 years of comfort; a poor quality bed will last for about a third of this time.

The type of bed you buy depends on your individual needs and preferences. You will see beds described as "orthopedic" – but as any orthopedic surgeon will tell you, there is no such thing. A bed described as orthopedic simply means that it has a firm mat-

tress and base. This is not necessarily good for someone suffering from back problems or arthritis or rheumatism; check with your doctor before buying a new bed.

The comfort factor of a bed depends on the mattress being able to hold the spine in its normal position. If the bed is too hard, the body will slide downward; if it is too soft, the heavier parts of your body will sink into the mattress.

The only way to see if a new bed is comfortable is to try before you buy. Look for a bed at least 6 inches longer than the tallest person who will sleep in it. Lie on the bed for at least ten minutes. Sitting on the edge gives no indication of how the bed will feel when you sleep in it. Don't be embarassed about trying the bed. If the store objects, go elsewhere. A bed is a big, expensive buy and a mistake can be uncomfortable as well as costly.

TYPES OF BEDS

Beds come in all shapes and sizes. The size depends on whether one or two people are to sleep in it, and on the dimensions of the room. Measure the bedroom before you go to buy a new bed and mark possible positions on a floorplan. If space is really tight, go to a store specializing in space-saving beds which will fold into a wall or convert to a sofa.

All beds are composed of two parts; the base and the mattress. The way each is constructed affects the price and the comfort. In general, you get what you pay for.

Traditional springing: The traditional spring base on an iron or brass frame is now only seen on antique and reproduction beds. A wire web is stretched across the frame and a mattress used on top. In the past, this would be of feather or flocking encased in ticking. Today, it is more likely to be a modern sprung interior design. Provided the mattress is new and of good quality, a brass or antique bed can be just as comfortable as a bed with a sprung base.

Firm-edge box spring: The firm-edge base has springing inside a wooden framework and gives extra support to the mattress on top. Better-quality beds are made in this way.

Sprung-edge box spring: The springs inside the base are lashed together at the edge so that the sleeping area offers the same support right across the bed. This system offers good support to the mattress above and is usually only found on good quality beds.

Wooden base: Pine and some other wooden beds are made with a slatted wooden base, headboard, footboard and legs all joined together. If you buy a wooden bed, make sure that it is firm around the joints. Avoid self-assembly beds held together by screws or clamps as the frame can become uncomfortably wobbly with use. Custom models with storage drawers in the base or simple platforms are also available and are popular in contemporary-style rooms.

Water beds: Water beds enjoyed popularity in the '60s but the problems of maintenance and keeping the bed filled to the right tension meant they quickly lost their appeal.

Folding beds: Folding canvas and Z beds are a one-night-only solution. If lack of space means you must have a folding bed, buy a good-quality sprung sofa bed. Cheap canvas or metal frame folding beds are uncomfortable and do not support the spine.

Futon: The Japanese futon is a natural fiber stuffed mattress on a folding slatted wooden base. Sleeping on a futon may suit the spartan minded but is too hard and unyielding a surface for most people.

Left: *A mattress and box spring are the favorite bedding choice. Comfort depends on the way the mattress is sprung. Beds are available with storage drawers in the base.*

Left: *A Japanese futon can be used as a sofa, or unfolded to make a bed. Sleeping on a futon is an acquired taste. A futon sofa bed is not as easy to fold away as a sofa bed.*

The mattress which goes on top of the base is the most important part of the bed. The way in which the mattress is made affects both the level of comfort you can obtain from it and the price of the bed.

If you buy a sprung-edge or sprung-base box spring, the mattress will usually come with it. If possible, avoid those with synthetic covers, which can make the bed uncomfortably hot in warm weather. If you buy a wooden or brass bed, you will have to choose and pay for the mattress separately.

The traditional or innerspring mattress has rows of springs joined at the top and bottom by a continuous small spring. The more expensive pocket-sprung mattress has nearly three times as many springs. Each spring is sewn into a fabric pocket attached to burlap. As the springs can move independently, this type of mattress offers good support to the recumbent form.

Continuous springing is a single web of steel wire, rather like the old-fashioned, often uncomfortable iron-frame bed.

Foam is sometimes used in conjunction with springs to make bunk bed matresses. Mattresses made entirely from foam can be hot and uncomfortable unless the foam is layered to provide you with support where it is needed most.

BEDLINEN

The color and pattern of bedlinen depends on the way the room is decorated, but before you choose sheets and covers, you will need to make the decision between having a comforter or sheets and blankets.

There's no doubt that a comforter is more comfortable, attractive and less trouble than sheets and blankets. Covers can be changed to suit the room, are easy to wash and bed-making takes a matter of seconds.

The size of the comforter and the filling are the two most important points to consider when buying. Measure the bed before you go shopping; the comforter should be 18 to 20 inches wider than the bed.

A comforter can have either a natural or synthetic filling. The higher the loft, the warmer the comforter will be.

Natural fillings are down or a mixture of feather and down from waterfowl. Pure down is the most expensive filling. Down and feather comes next, then feather and down. Fillings described as curled feather come from poultry and are not as warm and light as those of waterfowl.

The cover of a naturally filled quilt is usually made from cambric stitched into channels which hold the feathers. Naturally filled comforters cannot be washed; they need specialized dry cleaning.

Man-made fillings have improved greatly over the last few years. Look for a filling with a brand name and avoid comforters with slippery nylon covers and a generic filling. Good quality synthetic-filled comforters have the filling anchored at intervals, rather like quilting. Synthetic filled comforters are machine-washable and suitable for those allergic to feathers.

Whatever your color scheme, you are sure to be able to find sheets and quilt covers to match. Some lines include curtains, cushions, lampshades and wallcoverings. Most bedlinen is made from a mixture of polyester and cotton, a combination which is washable, permanent press and crease resistant. It is still possible to buy pure cotton, linen or even satin sheets – at a price. Cotton blends can go straight from the tumble dryer to the bed; but pure cotton and linen will both need ironing if they are to look their best.

FLOORING

Bedroom flooring can be of almost any material you like, from ceramic tiles to thick pile carpet, so long as there is something warm and comfortable by the bed to cushion feet on chilly mornings. Bedroom carpet need not be of the same hard-wearing quality as that used in a living room. A thick, colorful rug on a stripped pine floor can look just as good as wall-to-wall carpet – and will cost considerably less. Also, if you feel like a change you can swap it over with another rug from elsewhere in the house.

LIGHTING

Bedroom lighting needs to be a combination of general light and directional light for reading, making up, dressing or writing. Make sure that there is an electrical outlet by the bed, and others near the dressing and make up areas. Dual controls for general lighting are a good idea as you can switch on as you enter the room, then switch off by the bed or dressing table when other lamps are lit.

Bedside lamps should be tall enough to shine onto a book, but not to the other side of the bed where your partner may be trying to sleep. Small lamps which can be angled or dimmed are worth considering if one of you is a dedicated late night reader.

If there is a chair in the room, a table lamp on a side table, or a floor-standing light behind the chair provides the right level of illumination for relaxing, reading or sewing.

Light for dressing can come from overhead recessed ceiling bulbs. These are at their most useful if equipped with a dimmer as the light level can be increased when you want to see how you look, and decreased when all that is needed is a soft, overall glow.

Applying makeup in a bad light usually has disastrous results, so make sure that there is a fixture near the mirror that will throw light onto your face. The ideal is a film star-style row of bulbs at either side of the mirror. If this isn't possible, install a downlighter above the dressing table, and boost it with lights from either side so that your face is not in shadow when you are making yourself up.

Left: *Pretty bedlinen comes in hundreds of different colors and patterns, many designed to mix and match, as shown here. Some bedlinen collections include curtains, blinds and wallcoverings.*

Right: *The country cottage look is tailor made for a bedroom with a sloping ceiling. Look for a traditional iron bed, but replace the old flocking mattress with a modern innerspring model.*

149

THE MASTER BEDROOM

Old fashioned and sexist though it sounds, master bedroom is the best way to describe the place where you or you and your partner sleep. It is your own private space, a haven from pets, children and the pressures of family life.

It is worth spending time and effort in making this most important room comfortable and pleasant. The main functions of the room will obviously be sleeping and dressing, but by adding a comfortable chair and a portable television, a shelf of favorite books, a desk or a hobby table, you can make better use of the space – and provide yourself with an escape hatch to use at any time of the day.

Think first about the style of the room and if you have a partner, decide on a look that both of you find comfortable. If one wants a frilly, pastel-colored room and the other a sternly spartan setting, find a middle ground for the sake of harmony. Although it is a design rule that reception and living rooms should be unified in color and style, the bedroom is the place to let your imagination run riot. Formula "looks" can lead to a stilted, artificial effect, so use our style guidelines as a starting point.

The country cottage look: Essential elements are mellow pine furniture, a stripped, stained floor with a traditional rug or a dhurrie, walls, bedlinen and curtains or drapes in a combination of soft colors and cottage prints, pretty knickknacks, dried flowers, potpourri and old china. Works well in a bedroom with a sloping ceiling and small windows.

The English country house look: Essential elements are a wooden bed, possibly a four poster, chintz curtains or drapes and bedlinen, comfortable traditional rugs on the floor, a skirted dressing table with silver-backed brushes and family photographs in silver frames, freestanding mahogany or rosewood wardrobes, a chest and brass light fixtures. This look works best in a high-ceilinged, well-proportioned room.

The boudoir: Hollywood-inspired, lavish with oyster or cream-colored satin throw, pillows and quilting. Look to the 1930s for inspiration. Essentials include a shell-shaped or corona headboard, thick white carpet, voile curtains (drapes), Lalique lamps and perfume bottles, art deco silver picture frames.

Full of Eastern promise: If you see yourself as Scheherazade, the tented ceiling, moody Eastern colors, Kelim rugs and Turkish cush-

ions which make up this look are for you. Bear in mind that this is a style which can make a small room seem even smaller. Tented ceilings are difficult to maintain and attract dust.

Last days of the Raj: Cane furniture, cool, leafy greens, muslin drapes or wooden shutters, stripped floor with an Indian dhurrie and white walls. Inexpensive, attractive and a good way to add style and the illusion of greater space to a small room.

American country classic: Essential elements are a wooden four-poster, naive paintings, embroidered samplers, traditional quilting, polished wood and rag rugs, lace curtains, large comfortable chairs, baskets of flowers and books. A comfortable, easy-to-live-with style for larger rooms.

Cool and modern: This is a good compromise style, pretty enough to appeal to those who want a soft, attractive look, but with simple elements for those who prefer uncluttered style. Essentials are blonde wood or pale gray furniture with simple, straight lines, plain wall-to-wall carpet, Venetian or Roman blinds, subtle lighting and a soft gray, blue, pink or apricot scheme.

For those on a strict budget, achieving any of the styles above will probably be a project for the future. Given that you have been able to buy a bed and a carpet, and have decorated the room, adding a touch of individuality can seem impossible but a few clever, inexpensive accessories can make all the difference to a basic bedroom.

Above and right: *Two looks for the master bedroom. The soft, pretty style, lavishly draped with fabric and frills, won't appeal to most men but is comfortable and relaxing. A darker, moody combination of cobalt blues and sumptuous florals is Romany-inspired and, as shown right, is an effective compromise.*

MORE DASH THAN CASH

► Add a designer touch with simple bought or homemade round tables by the bed. Cover with a floor-length ruffled cloth to coordinate with bedlinen. A piece of old lace or an antique lace-trimmed fabric over a plain or patterned cloth looks charming. Add bedside lamps, framed pictures or a small collection.

► Pile the headboard with throw pillows to match or complement the bedcover.

► Make a headboard by hanging looped cushions from a curtain rod mounted on the wall. Make curtains and a bedcover to match.

► Look around junk shops for a pretty cane or wooden chair. Cane can be repainted and wood stripped and sealed. Add a pile of cushions.

► Give curtains a facelift with tie-backs and a valance in a plain or patterned fabric. If curtains don't quite meet in the middle, make a ruffle for the edges.

► A paper or stenciled border will give plain walls a lift. Make your own stencil or buy one precut.

► Hang a colorful quilt or rug on the longest, plainest wall in the room.

► Give the bed a touch of opulence by draping muslin or voile over three lengths of curtain rod. Attach one at each side, roughly 3 feet above the bed, and another in the center, close to the ceiling.

Right: *When cash is short, add a touch of originality with inspired decoration. Stenciling is easy to do using precut stencils and always looks wonderful. Choose a simple stencil for your first attempt.*

USING SPACE WISELY

The ideal bedroom has well-planned storage for clothes, a desk and a comfortable chair, bookshelves, bathing facilities, TV and stereo for private viewing and listening and enough space for exercise machines, sewing and hobby equipment. In reality, many bedrooms are too small to house much more than a bed, bedside tables and clothes storage. Well-planned modular furniture which can be built into awkward spaces and a bed with storage drawers beneath is a start toward making the best use of limited space. Two or three small three-drawer chests along one wall can double as storage, desk space and a dressing table.

When there isn't enough space for a comfortable chair, a window seat is a good alternative. Another option is an old-fashioned ottoman with a padded lid. The space inside can be used to store bedlinen or clothing. Make use of alcoves for shelving or workspace. Having closets built up to the ceiling makes maximum use of the full height of the room. Installing mirrored wardrobe doors will make the room look larger and give you a good full-length view when dressing.

In a generously sized room, you will be able to divide the relaxing or hobby area from the sleeping area. Simple low shelves, or open shelving from floor to ceiling just under halfway across the room will mark the divide without visually reducing the space. Screens, two or three low chests pushed together or a sofa with its back to the bed are other ways to make a simple division. Gear the relaxing space to the way you want to use it. An exercise area needs plain wood flooring, a large mirror, wall bars and good light. A hobby area needs a roomy worktop, storage and good light; a mini library can be soothing, with soft light, and comfortable seating.

If you like to watch TV in bed, a low, wide shelving unit at the foot of the bed will hold the set (turned to face you), magazines and books. Shelves built between the bed and the walls running at right angles are a space-saving alternative to bedside tables.

Two adults sharing a bedroom can cause conflict, especially if one partner is tidy and the other lackadaisical, or one likes to read late into the night when the other wants to sleep. Men and women have different storage needs. Half the space in a full-size wardrobe is wasted if the rail only holds trousers and shirts. Add a second rail halfway down and hang jackets and trousers at the top, shirts below. Put wire baskets in the bottom for sweaters and socks, or use this area for shoes. Women's clothes need full-length hanging space to prevent them creasing.

152

Left: *If you can't enjoy a bath or shower in peace – or worse still – can never get into the bathroom because it is constantly occupied by teenagers, a shower cubicle in the corner of the master bedroom will give you privacy and relieve the pressure on the main bathroom.*

Individual bedside lamps which can be angled so that one side of the bed remains in semi-darkness will help to prevent arguments about late reading. If one person want to watch TV or listen to the radio in bed, a set of headphones will keep the peace.

LITTLE TOUCHES

A comfortable bed, warm flooring and balanced heating and ventilation are obviously important but anyone who has ever visited a top hotel will know what a difference it makes to find a room equipped with a jug of fresh water and a glass on the bedside table, tissues and cotton, a wastepaper basket and

a mixture of soft and strong lighting. All of this is easy to copy at home. Hotel rooms are cleaned by chambermaids; at home the job falls to you so make it easier by providing a basket or hamper for dirty clothes. Another hotel tip is to make sure that drapes or blinds are easy to close, meet in the middle and exclude light.

ADDING BATHING FACILITIES

There is nothing quite so luxurious as an *en suite* bathroom. In a busy family home, it is an indulgent touch with a practical side, relieving pressure on the main bathroom. If the main bedroom is large, it may be possible to

partition a section off for use as a bathroom. Using a shower instead of a tub will reduce the amount of space needed. Another possibility for you to consider is to knock through into an adjoining room.

If a full-scale bathroom proves impossible, you will probably be able to find space for a shower, but check your local building code first. The average stall takes up only 3 square feet of floor space and can stand in a corner. If the bedroom already has a washbasin, replace it with a shower.

However you plan or design the master bedroom, remember that it is your space. Once children and pets are allowed to wander in and out at will, you will lose your retreat, so be firm from the start.

A ROOM OF MY OWN

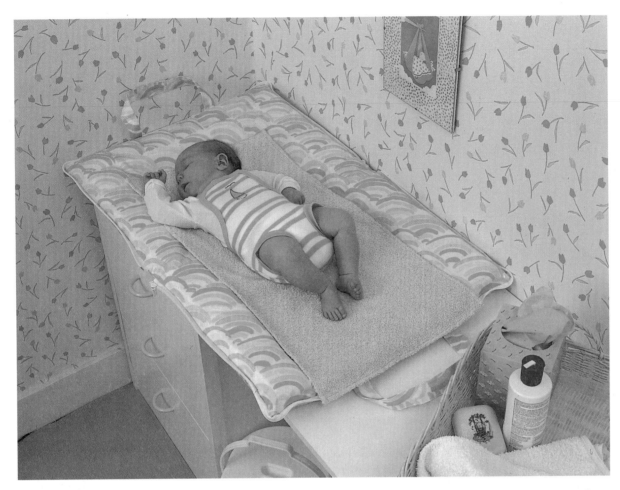

A bright and simple flower-design wallpaper like this will have a far longer life in the baby's room than a nursery rhyme pattern. Today's diaper changing area can become tomorrow's space for school work if you plan ahead when buying furniture.

It's very tempting when you have your first baby to indulge in a fairy-tale nursery, complete with voile-draped crib, flounces, ruffles and flopsy bunny wallcovering. Any parent who has succumbed will tell you that the Hollywood-style nursery has a short life. Small babies can be sick (or worse) all over your pretty crib and will make short work of ruffles once they reach the grabbing stage. By the time the average child is two, that once-charming nursery will be chaos.

Adopting a "look to the future" approach when planning a nursery doesn't mean that you can't create a fun room. The trick is to be sensible with furniture and decoration and as uninhibited as you like with accessories and soft furnishings as these won't cost too much to replace when the child is older.

While the child is small, the room should be within hearing distance of Mom and Dad. It should also be in a quiet spot, preferably away from street noise and certainly not next door to a bathroom or above the living room. Older children will prefer to be farther away, out of earshot, in an attic bedroom or even a separate apartment if there is space.

YOUR FIRST NURSERY

Think about the basics of the room before you decorate or plan. Heating is a must. If you don't have central heating, install a wall heater. Radiators are a safe way to heat a child's room but make sure that the fixture has no sharp corners (lethal when the baby reaches the crawling stage), and that it can be thermostatically controlled so that the room is warm but the surface of the radiator is not hot enough to burn tender skin. You will need good general lighting to give a clear view when changing or dressing the baby and a soft night light. A dimmer switch gives you the option of both from one light source. Electrical outlets will be needed for a plug-in night light, bottle warmer and for car-racing games and other electrical toys when the child is older. Be sure to fit sockets with safety covers.

Flooring should be warm, non-slip and easy to clean. Cork tiles or soft, cushioned vinyl combined with a rug are both better choices than carpet for very small children as cleaning the inevitable spills and stains is

then made much easier and more successful.

The windows will need thick curtains or blinds to block light when the baby is asleep. There is no need to use a heavy, dull fabric. Bright or pale curtains will do the same job if lined with plain white fabric.

Keep decoration simple. Pale paintwork is easy and inexpensive to change. The idea of nursery motif wallcovering may appeal and is safe enough when the child is a baby and has no definite likes and dislikes but it will dictate the color and styles of other accessories. Plain paintwork or a wallcovering with an unobtrusive pattern allows more scope for colorful soft furnishings and nursery mobiles.

Furniture should be sturdy and have a wipe-clean finish. There is no need for a closet for a baby, as infant clothing can be folded and stored in drawers. Scaled-down nursery furniture will quickly outlive its usefulness and charm. Two plain white or pastel-colored three-drawer chests will provide enough space for clothes, diapers, creams and lotions. Position the chests about 4 feet and rest a length of white, pastel or primary-colored worktop across them to use as a changing table. Don't leave the baby un-supervised on the table after the age of two to three months as an active child can easily roll off the edge. Add a padded waterproof mat for extra comfort. A set of wire baskets on wheels is a convenient way to keep creams, lotions and other essentials on hand and can be pushed under the worksurface when not in use. Nursery specialists sell custom-made changing tables – not a good buy, as their use is quickly outgrown. The homemade chang-ing table can become a desk or play area when the child is older.

Open shelving is useful for toys and games and should be positioned where the baby can see bright colors from the crib. When he reaches the crawling stage, toys can be moved to big plastic boxes or bright baskets stored on the floor.

Although a cradle is pretty when the baby is small, it is another item that the child will quickly outgrow. A traditional drop-sided crib is a better investment, as it can be used until the child is two or three. Look for a crib with a selection of base heights, as this will save you bending when the baby is small. Lower the height once he or she is active to thwart escape bids.

Most cribs are in plain wood, or are white, but you can add a touch of individuality with quilted "bumpers" to cover the sides. As well as bringing color to the nursery, the bumpers protect an active baby from contact with hard woodwork.

To make crib bumpers, measure the sides of the crib. Add 2 inches to the top, bottom and sides of each measurement and buy two pieces of quilted fabric and one piece of bat-ting for each side.

Stitch the quilted fabric pieces for each side with right sides together, to make an en-velope. Catch-stitch batting to one side of the envelope, then turn the bumper right side out. Catch-stitch the open edges. Attach rib-bons or pieces of tape at the top and bottom edge of each bumper. Position bumper inside the crib and tie in place. If you are good at sewing, insert a piece of see-through fabric across the center of one of the side bumpers so that the baby can see out. For a coordi-nated look, use the same quilted fabric to make a crib quilt, then add curtains, cushions and lined straw baskets in a complementary color or pattern.

Both parents will probably spend a lot of time in the nursery, cuddling or feeding the baby, so add a comfortable chair with good back support. Make sure the chair is easy to get out of when holding the baby.

Above: *Pretty stencils make a charming addition to this plain, rather sophisticated room, making it as suitable for guests as its toddler occupant.*

Left: *A good, solid chest of drawers is a worthwhile investment, and works well in a more traditional nursery setting. A colorful frieze adds a sense of fun.*

THE TODDLER STAGE

Unlike small babies, toddlers don't stay where they are put, have a strong sense of curiosity and can be devastatingly destructive. All of this is natural and inevitable, but rather wearing on parents and property. Most toddlers can't bear to let Mom or Dad out of their sight, so the tide of destruction tends to spread through the house. If the nursery is adapted to be a playroom and you spend some time each day playing there, your toddler will eventually find it a more appealing spot for games than the living room or kitchen. At least then you will have half a chance of containing the tide of havoc in one area. You will probably find all of the following ideas helpful.

Writing on walls is a firm favorite with most two- to four-year-olds. Cater to the urge by covering the nursery walls and door with blackboard to adult waist height and supply a container full of bright, thick chalks. If there is enough space, add a roll of paper and some poster paint or nontoxic crayons. As scribbling on a blackboard is far more satisfactory than trying to make an impression on paint or wallpaper, your junior artist will soon come to prefer the blackboard to the living room walls.

An adult-size single bed, fitted with safety rails, is the best and safest replacement for a crib. Bunks are not safe for use by small children, but you could buy a set and store the top bunk elsewhere. You will need to add a chair, so that the child can use the work-surface for scribbling and games. For storage, add more shelves, but make sure that they are really secure. The best way to store toys is in big baskets, or in wheeled boxes which can be pushed out of sight under the bed. This sort of storage makes clearing up quick and easy and keeps toys within safe reach of small hands.

The original cushioned vinyl or cork floor is still the best choice – and is the ideal surface for toy cars and pull alongs. Add a couple of big floor cushions for sleepy afternoons.

Toddlers enjoy looking at nursery rhyme characters and will have their own favorites. Do try to avoid the temptation to buy novelty wallcovering, as it will dictate the entire color scheme and furnishings – and become a source of irritation when Snow White or Mickey Mouse are no longer popular with your youngster. Nursery friezes which can be attached at waist or ceiling height, posters, mobiles and a bulletin board of pictures are easier to change.

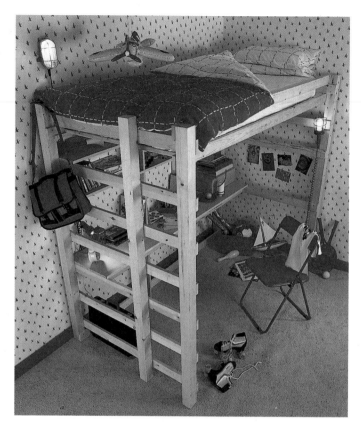

Paint is still the best choice for walls. It can be wiped clean, is easy to retouch, provides a neutral background for posters, toys and games and has no loose edges to attract small fingers.

Safety is vitally important once your child is active. The bedroom window should lock, and you may want to install bars on the inside. The bars should be close together to prevent the child from trying to push his or her head through them. The same applies to safety rails on the sides of beds. Several small children have choked to death when their heads became lodged beneath a bed safety rail. A bed with a solid side is the best and safest choice.

If the child's room is upstairs, fit a safety gate across the door for the times he or she is in the room unsupervised. A fall down a flight of steep stairs can be fatal. Make sure that light fixtures are out of reach and that electrical outlets have safety covers to ward off inquisitive small fingers. If there is a radiator in the room, keep it on a low setting, or use a radiator shield.

By planning the nursery with the future in mind, the only extras you will need to buy when the child reaches toddler stage are a few new accessories. These new purchases will last until the teenage years.

Left: *What child could resist this bedroom-cum-adventure playground? Shelves and a desk fit neatly underneath the platform bed.*

OFF TO SCHOOL

Schooldays mean a dramatic expansion in interests. These are the collecting years when you'll need to find homes for postage stamps, picture albums, marbles, cars, assorted livestock and all the other paraphernalia dear to the average five- to ten-year-old heart. Children of this age love boxes, tins and compartments, colorful and inexpensive ways to meet their new storage needs. You can remove blackboards from the walls at this stage, and replace them with bulletin boards and low-level shelving. By the time a child is six, he or she can use a bunk bed with safety. If only one child uses the room, it may be worth either buying or building a platform bed with storage and work space below. A bed like this will last well into the teenage years, although if money is tight the child should be able to make do with the original single bed with its safety rails removed. A desk and chair will become increasingly important as the child gets older. Add a good clip-on desk light to avoid eye strain.

If your child has a computer, a desk which allows the monitor and keyboard to be at different levels will be appreciated. The nursery arrangement of two three-drawer chests with a work surface on top can be adapted as a

Left: *A rustic atmosphere prevails in this delightful child's bedroom. Its clever high shelf enables things to be tucked away, literally out of sight, out of mind.*

computer table by putting the chests against a wall and adding a shelf at eye level for the monitor and disk drive.

Allow the child some say in the choice of paint or wallcovering, but resist pressure to buy a Batman comforter or Superman wallpaper. Children are notoriously fickle when it comes to heroes. Suggest posters instead – and make sure the wallcovering is hard wearing enough to cope with frequent changes. At this stage, you can safely replace vinyl or cork flooring with carpet.

At this age, children often have to share the room with a younger sibling. To avoid arguments, it is best to give each child his own space. There's no need to build walls – the division can be marked by something as simple as different colored bedlinen or shelving. A low bookcase, a folding screen or a curtain can be used if a more definite division is needed. To avoid battles, make sure both children have the same sort of furniture. If an older child has to share with a toddler, provide locking cupboards to keep treasured possessions away from small hands.

Left: *This ingenious room divider can be used for storage, display and hanging up clothes.*

THE TEENAGE YEARS

Teenagers crave privacy and independence. Sharing is no longer a workable proposition and the bedroom/playroom will need to change to cope with study, entertaining, hobbies, music and sleeping. A living room cum bedroom is the ideal. To find the space, you may have to convert the attic or consider an addition. If it is possible to add bathing facilities, the room can be completely self-contained. There is space in most rooms to add a shower stall but even a washbasin will help to ease strain on the main bathroom. You'll find more ideas on *page 139.*

As the room will double as a living area, it is worth replacing a conventional bed with a sofa bed or sleeping platform with storage or study space beneath. A folding bed is a useful addition – teenagers enjoy having friends stay overnight. Big floor cushions or bean bags are an inexpensive and colorful way to add seating.

Noise is an inevitable part of teenage life. You can reduce both the racket and the level of complaint from the rest of the family by covering the walls with insulating board and that the floor with a thick carpet and making sure the door shuts securely (add weather stripping if necessary).

Plain paint makes a good, easy-to-repair background for posters. Cover the back of doors with cork so that the space can be used as a bulletin board – and for you to position important reminders where they can't possibly be missed.

At this stage, shelves of varying depths and plenty of space to hang clothes are the most

Below: *The ideal teenage girl's room. There is plenty of bed space for friends to stay overnight, or use as a seating area during the day. The walls are plain to accommodate changing tastes in posters, and there is a pretty chest of drawers, which doubles as a dressing table.*

important types of storage. Provide wide shelves for records and narrow ones for cassettes and computer disks. If closet space is a problem, think carefully about the future of the room before you add a custom-built closet system. Teenagers eventually leave home and those expensive closets will be extraneous. A wheeled hanging rail is a sensible, cost-conscious solution. Girls will appreciate a well-lit makeup mirror. Once again, two of the three-drawer chests and worktop bought for the nursery can come into play, this time as a makeup table. Both sexes will need a full-length mirror.

A desk or big work surface for study is an essential. Add a clip-on light, office filing trays and some containers for pens and pencils. You may need to add electrical outlets for extra lighting, computer, stereo and tele-vision. For safety's sake, make sure there is an outlet for each appliance. Adaptors can be dangerous if too many are used. Lighting should be flexible. Recessed ceiling spots controlled by a dimmer switch will take care of general light. Add clip-on flexible lamps around work and dressing areas and by the bed for night reading.

Most teenagers will have strong views on how the room should be decorated and will appreciate being allowed to choose color schemes and upholstery. Remember that this is your child's private space and listen to ideas – within reason. It can be tempting to give in for the sake of peace – but you as parents will have to pay for materials and cope with repair and redecorating when the fad for all-black walls or a giant mural of the current pop favorite has passed.

Above: *A boy's room can be modern and functional, especially if it is to combine a hobby or homework area as here. Crisp, clean lines in bright yellow and dove gray give an uncluttered, high-tech look.*

ROOM FOR ONE MORE

Almost everyone enjoys having friends and family to stay, but in many homes, finding the space for a guest room means that those who live there all the time are more crowded than is necessary.

Unless you have the luxury of space to spare, a room which is used only a few times a year is a waste of resources. Think of the many ways in which the room could become part of everyday life, for hobbies, homework, as an extra den, or a play area. This doesn't mean friends and family can't come to visit; with clever planning, the guest room can quickly change roles from family space to extra bedroom.

A convertable sofa will make the room more adaptable than a conventional bed. Choose a good-quality model with a good, thick sprung mattress. The bed should be easy to open and close – test it out in the store first. If the room is to double as a work space, choose furniture which has space for storage

of clothes and a worksurface. The simplest way is to position two three-drawer chests about 3 feet apart from each other, then place a laminate or wooden worksurface across the top. The worksurface can be used as a dressing table when friends visit – simply add a free-standing mirror.

Guests will need somewhere to hang their clothes – and you will find the extra closet space useful. There is no need to go to the expense of a custom-built closet system. It is easier, and cheaper, to partition off part of the room with louver or mirror doors and position a shelf and hanging rail inside. A space as small as 6 inches wide is perfectly adequate.

My own guest room, once a sort of dumping ground that had to be hastily cleared when friends were expected, has recently been converted to a bedroom/study and is now used daily for computer games, work, homework and relaxation. The room is small,

Below: *The ideal guest bedroom has ample closet and cabinet space plus a big, comfortable bed. The addition of a small table means that some meals can be taken in the room, giving a luxurious degree of privacy.*

Top and bottom right: *Investing in a sofa bed means tired dinner party guests can stay the night with a minimum of fuss. The sofa bed folds down, and, the table is pushed against the door for privacy.*

around 12 feet by 9½ feet, with windows along one short wall and a door and closet on the other. We planned floor-to-ceiling cabinet storage for one long wall, incorporating a small closet, a computer desk and shelving, then carried the shelving around under the window, spaced out with drawers and another work area. A sofa bed, bedside chest and lamp occupy the second long wall. This easy-to-copy idea can be adapted to almost any space big enough to house a folding bed. We made the cabinets from laminate-faced chipboard but it is possible to buy similar designs ready built.

Although you will probably read suggestions that guests can be accommodated on a sofa bed in the living room, dining room or hall, most people find this sort of arrangement absolutely apalling for any more than one night, and completely lacking in privacy. If you want to have people stay, do try and find a private space for them, safe from the early morning attentions of your dog, cat or boisterous children.

If you entertain regularly, it may be worth having the attic space converted, or adding a ground floor bedroom/study with its own bathroom. Both these rooms will be useful to the family when the visitors have gone.

Try to make the guest room as comfortable as possible. Take a tip from the top hotels and provide a carafe of water and a glass, tea- and coffee-making equipment, a bowl of fruit and some crackers and a selection of magazines and books. Line the drawers with pretty paper and hang scented sachets in the closet. Add some plastic bags for dirty clothes, a needle and a selection of thread, cotton balls, tissues, soap and thick, warm towels; they will all be appreciated. Don't forget a waste basket, and a clock that tells the time accurately. Make sure that the curtains or blinds are easy-to-pull and will meet in the middle. Check the efficiency of the heating or air conditioning in the guest room too. This kind of hospitality is a compliment to your guests that will never go out of fashion.

BATHING FACILITIES

A separate guest bathroom is a luxury which comes low on the list of home priorities but a shower cubicle hidden behind a closet door, or tucked into a corner is easy to install if there is a water supply nearby. If space is really limited, a corner-mounted basin will provide enough space for brushing teeth, shaving , washing hands, etc.

A PLACE TO PLAY

Growing teenagers need space for entertainment, stereo, computer, games and the sort of noisy fun the rest of the family can find irritating. The owners of the home pictured here decided that the garage would make an ideal recreation room; a simple, inexpensive way for the house to grow from within.

Conversion was a simple matter of replacing the solid garage door with a glazed door and panels, painting the brick walls and adding lighting. The brick floor was covered with insulating board, then topped with hard-wearing cord carpeting. Heating comes from a radiator added onto the main central heating system.

The result is a spacious room with a sitting area, a work corner and a sauna. When the sofa is pushed to one side, there is enough room for a ping pong table which can double as a dining table for entertaining. There is space next to the sauna to store the table when not in use, and the sofa is a convertible so friends can stay overnight.

The furniture was selected with flexibility in mind. Everything is lightweight, fitted with castors and easy to move. The chairs can be folded and stacked when not in use.

Left: *The window wall was previously the garage door. The color combination of hot pink and bright white helps to make the room seem much lighter.*

Right: *With the sofa pushed out of the way, there's space for a game of ping pong. The folding chairs stand in the narrow area on the right, next to the sauna. The same space is used for the folding ping pong table when it is not in use. The sofa has been moved into the work alcove.*

Below: *The ping pong table doubles as a dining table for entertaining.*

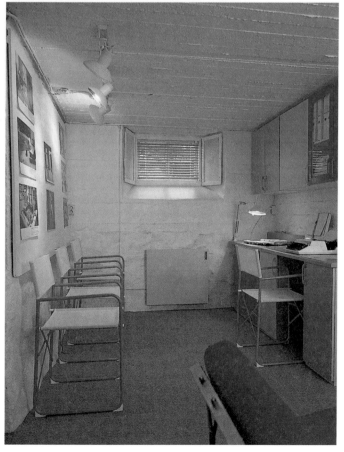

Left: *The home office is furnished with simple kitchen cupboards, a working counter, folding chairs and a bulletin board. The cupboards were painted with car lacquer, the only paint available in this shade of pink.*

163

Right: *A garage or a disused basement or cellar often has excellent scope for converting into an office or den. Furniture can be kept very basic in this type of room.*

The rumpus room or den is a long-established fact of family life, and there are many precedents for converting the garage, basement or attic to this use.

If you have children, the recreation room can grow with them, starting life as a playroom, adapting and changing as the children grow. When they finally leave home, the space can be converted to a library, a study, hobby room – or go back to being a playroom when grandchildren begin to come along.

Most basements, garages and cellars need little structural alteration. Heating and lighting are the most important factors in conversion, especially if the room is chilly or tends to be damp. Covering bare concrete walls and floors with insulating board will make the room warmer, combat the dampness and cut down echoes. Most wall and floor dampness is caused by condensation, when warm air meets cold stone. In an old building, damp air in a cellar or basement can be caused by lack

of a vapor barrier, the vapor barrier being bridged outside the building or in the wrong position. This sort of dampness usually shows itself as dark, stained patches, unlike the surface wetness of condensation. Call in an expert to deal with the problem. If you want to use the cellar to store wine, cold conditions are ideal, so don't install insulation.

Most basements and cellars have very little natural light, so artificial light must be well planned. Ceiling-mounted spotlights are the simplest to install and can be directed where needed. Combine the spots with localized lighting around work or seating areas. Painting the walls in a pale, glossy color will help to reflect the light.

Natural light can be brought into a garage be removing the solid door and replacing it with a glazed model and some glass panels. It is worth installing an opaque blind for use on sunny days; otherwise the garage can become unbearably hot.

Radiators or other central heating can usually be added to the main system. Install individual controls so that the heating can be switched on and off as required.

The way your basement, attic or garage den is furnished depends on who will use it. Small children need soft, easy-to-clean flooring, low shelving, a work surface, a blackboard or wall-mounted roll of paper for artwork and plenty of big bins or wicker hampers for toy storage. School-age juniors will need more shelving, their own TV, space for a computer, some comfortable seating and a higher, bigger work surface. What teenagers

want depends on their interests, but make sure there is storage for a TV, stereo, computer, records and tapes, plenty of furniture for lounging, a sofa bed for overnight guests, a shower or washbasin, or even a mini-bathroom if there is enough space, a well-lit work area for study, ample shelving, a refrigerator for drinks and food, and a table.

Outfitting an attic, basement or garage as a hobby room gives you the space to enjoy your particular pastime, and the freedom to leave equipment on hand for the next time it is needed. A big workbench with storage cabinets and drawers beneath, plenty of shelving, a comfortable floorcovering and good lighting and heating are basics which can be adapted to most interests. Cellars have been used as an amateur radio shack, as a mini-engineering shop, complete with lathes, for dressmaking, pottery, painting and weaving, all with a minimum of conversion costs. Whatever your plans, make sure that access to the basement or attic is safe and easy. A well-lit staircase with a handrail is best. Rickety ladders and dark flights of steep

stairs should be replaced for safety's sake. You will find a garage room more useful if there is an entrance from the house. Making a doorway from an adjoining room is usually easy and inexpensive.

Where local planning regulations and your personal finances allow, it can be possible to convert a garage to a two-story recreation room by building on top of the existing structure and adding a staircase inside. A conservatory built on top of a garage, with access by spiral staircase from below and by door from the second floor of the house, gives a multi-purpose home leisure center, with space for children or teenagers at ground level and a sun room for adults above.

If your home does not have a cellar or basement, adding one big enough to use as a room will be impossibly expensive. If, however, you yearn for a wine cellar, it is possible to buy a round, prefabricated model which can be sunk into the garage floor or a similar location. As most wines can be stored in any cool, dark room, this piece of storage is only for the serious collector.

Left: *A recreation room strictly for the kids frees bedrooms and living rooms from the clutter of toys and games.*

ROOM DOWNSTAIRS

If you are lucky enough to own a house with even a small basement or cellar you can use it in any number of ways. Traditionally, wine, beer and bottled preserves have been stored in cool, dark places such as cellars, and you may find this an ideal way to free your kitchen cupboards of vast quantities of bottles and jars, provided, of course, there is no problem with dampness.

If there are teenagers in the house they may want to use the cellar as a miniature disco. Decor can be kept to a bare minimum when the cellar is used for this purpose. All that is needed is the transference of stereo equipment from upstairs, and perhaps a couple of sofas and large mirrors and posters on the walls. Bare, stone cellar floors are ideal for dancing on. Giving teenagers their

own space downstairs will have the added bonus of freeing overcrowded living/rooms of extra bodies and cutting down on squabbles over which TV program to watch!

Hobbies can cause clutter, especially the type which need a lot of equipment, such as woodwork, photographic developing, pottery, machine knitting or computers. One way to reduce the mess and free space in the house is to find a self-contained place for the hobby, where equipment can be left lying around indefinitely without getting in everyone else's way.

If your house has a basement or cellar, it can easily be converted into a hobby area or home office. Basements with a window are not too difficult to convert and are usually connected to the main house by a conven-

tional staircase. Cellars in older homes are more difficult, as they are dark, often damp and badly ventilated and only accessible via a ladder or open-sided steps. If you want to convert a cellar, it is worth asking an architect for advice on heating, ventilation, lighting and safe access.

Heating: It may be possible to extend the main central heating system from the house into the cellar. If not, use individual electric heaters. Gas wall heaters are not usually suitable as there is no outside wall for the flue.

Lighting: The cellar must be well lit, especially around the work area. General lighting can come from fluorescent tubes with additional light from spotlights mounted where they are most needed. It is most important to illuminate the staircase.

Ventilation: A wall fan may be needed if the cellar does not have windows or other ventilation. Good ventilation is especially necessary if the cellar will be used for photography, model making or any other hobby involving chemicals.

Flooring: Choose a flooring which is easy to clean but warm and comfortable underfoot. Cushioned sheet vinyl is good.

Storage and workspace: Only the person who has the hobby will know exactly what sort of storage and workspace is needed, but as a general guide you will need a large, clear, flat area and plenty of shelving.

Access: The cellar will be under-used if the only access is via a precarious flight of steps. An architect or builder will advise on installing a safe staircase with a handrail. The staircase must be well lit and you should be able to switch the light on and off from the top of the stairs.

Adding a cellar to an existing house is not worthwhile, as it involves complex and expensive construction work. An outside addition is a far better idea in this case.

CELLAR AND BASEMENT SAFETY

► Install an intercom or an alarm button so that anyone using the cellar can make contact with the main part of the house if there is an accident.

► Some hobbies can be dangerous so install fire extinguishers and make sure that everyone in the family knows how to use them.

► Make sure there is sufficient ventilation if the room is to be used for model making, photography or any other hobby involving chemicals or strong adhesive.

► Hang a first aid kit.

► Make sure that the stairs are safe for anyone carrying equipment up and down, and that they are properly lit.

► If you have small children, the cellar or basement door must lock. A small child can easily fall down a flight of stairs, or be injured by sharp woodworking tools or photographic chemicals.

Another possible location for a hobby room is in the garage, but only if it is connected to the main house by a door and can be heated and ventilated properly.

Left: *A basement hobby room needs a minimum of furnishings. Roughcast walls like these look good left plain and painted white.*

ONE-ROOM LIVING

The days when one-room living more often than not meant a dingy, badly furnished box with shared bathroom and a view of the local railroad yard are happily a bad memory. Today, one-room living is often a choice rather than necessity. Young singles prefer the easy maintenance of a well-designed studio; the more affluent are attracted by the chic character of a converted warehouse or attic and both teenagers and the elderly like the combination of freedom with help close at hand offered by a one-room apartment within the family home.

Property developers are conscious of the attractions of one-room living and there are many well-designed studio apartments and warehouse conversions on the market in most big cities. Furniture manufacturers have been quick to spot the trend and have responded with sofa beds in all shapes and sizes, folding chairs and adaptable storage systems that fit whatever space is available as though they were custom-built for the purpose.

This chapter looks at the practicalities of one-room living; how to cope with the essentials of a working kitchen and bathroom, lighting and heating; choosing furniture for a studio and coping with the very different problems that you may encounter in a loft or warehouse conversion.

Below and right: *A stylish warehouse conversion like this makes the most of one-room living. The introduction of different levels breaks up the space.*

OPEN SPACES

Above: *The kitchen is divided from the living and dining areas by pull-down blinds. The blinds are made from a see-through striped materials which closes the area off but does not restrict light or appear visually solid.*

Right: *Built-up planters at the living side of the kitchen and a change from stone flooring to carpet help to mark the divide without building a wall. The pillar is part of the original construction.*

This stylish one-room apartment was once a vast, empty space in a converted warehouse. Clever division, using blinds, plants, furniture and wooden sections, breaks up the space without destroying the wonderfully open, airy feel of the room.

Open-space living, often in big, airy spaces created by the conversion of individual floors in warehouses and other abandoned industrial buildings, is on the increase in the major cities of the west. A big area of open space, often expertly converted and combined with a stunning river view, is a property opportunity many find hard to resist.

Space is as much a problem as it is in a single room – but it is how to effectively divide and use such a vast area which presents difficulties. At first glance, a warehouse or industrial conversion is simply a large, open space, interspersed by support pillars, and it can be difficult to see how such an area could ever become home.

One of the most attractive points of an industrial conversion is that it is a big, airy space which it may seem a pity to divide, but the logistics of living, eating and sleeping mean that some screened areas are essential. Building simple wood and plasterboard walls is the easiest way to section off bathrooms and bedrooms, but if this seems too much like conventional living, you can use sliding Japanese-style screens for the bathroom, and simply hide the bedroom behind ordinary folding screens or pull-down blinds. Another option is to put the bedroom on a platform, providing the ceiling is high enough.

Different floorings can mark the change between areas, with ceramic tiles, vinyl, cork or wood for the kitchen and dining section, and carpeting in parts used for living and relaxing. Give the relaxing area a focal point, such as an open fireplace, an unusual low table, or a dramatically lit sculpture or painting and you will find it easy to group seating in a natural, comfortable way that will act as its own division from the rest of the room.

Lighting is important to the atmosphere in a big, open space, and can be used to create divisions by having different levels of light in the various sections of the room.

Spotlighting or recessed ceiling lights controlled by dimmers are useful for kitchens and bathrooms. Use freestanding uplighters to show off interesting corners, sculpture and paintings. In the living area, table lamps will cast a friendly glow. Each type of lighting should have its own controls, so that you can have most of the room in semi-darkness and just one section brightly lit if you wish.

Above left: *The apartment is full of interesting display areas. Here, uncompromisingly modern chairs and table are dramatically lit by an angled lamp and ceiling spotlights.*

Above right: *Looking from the living area toward the kitchen. A stunning glass table reflects the plants beyond.*

Right: *An open fireplace built into one of the old pillars provides a focal point for the seating and relaxing area.*

A comfortable level of heating is important. If the conversion does not have a satisfactory system, it will be worth calling in a heating consultant to design one for you. An ordinary domestic central heating system is not geared to this sort of space.

In a big space, you can afford to be bold with furniture. Seating can be large, dramatic and in an assertive color or pattern; comb junk shops and auctions for unusual pieces, or look to Italian design for bold, starkly modern tables, chairs and storage. You will probably find a couple of carts useful, for wheeling food or drinks from the kitchen to the living area, for instance, or for transferring clean clothes from the utility room to the closets. Cleverly planned storage furniture can be used to make "walls." Closets make effective dividers to screen the bedroom from the main area, especially if you install a double-sided design so that the cupboards face both ways. Open-shelving units will house TV, stereo, books and odds and ends – and serve the purpose of dividing space.

Use big, lush plants to add life, color and greenery to the room. They can be trained by support pillars, grouped in raised platform containers or used as screening. Most varieties will survive in a well-lit, reasonably warm environment.

THE ESSENTIALS

Whatever the size or shape of your one-room apartment, you will have to decide on how to plan cooking and washing facilities, heating and lighting. As space is usually limited, clever, well-organized planning is essential if everyday living is to be comfortable.

THE KITCHEN

The four kitchen essentials are cooking, refrigerated storage, preparation space and dishwashing. In a restricted area, it may be difficult to see how to find space for all four, so it is important to buy equipment of exactly the right size to suit your needs.

Cooking: Think carefully about the kind of foods you plan to cook before buying equipment. If you regularly eat out, or cook light meals for one most of the time, a multi-function microwave oven will suit, leaving space free for storage, preparation, etc. A multi-function microwave is one that incorporates hot air convection and a broiler, less limiting than a microwave-only oven. The microwave could be built under a counter, or beneath wall cupboards to leave the maximum amount of work surface free. As the microwave will boil liquids and cook vegetables, there is no need for you to install a separate cooktop.

If you intend to entertain at home, you will need a bigger oven and a cooktop. A single multi-function oven that combines convection, conventional heat and broiling is most useful. Build the oven under a counter with a cooktop above. This arrangement occupies less space than a tall oven housing. Think carefully about the cooktop; you may not need four cooktop burners. Two-burner models are available and take up only half as much space as a four-burner version.

There are so many small cooking gadgets available today that it is easy to be tempted into buying more than you need. When space is at a premium, curb your enthusiasm. Best buys to think about are a toaster, adjustable to take both thick and thin slices of bread, a food processor to make chopping, slicing, puréeing and blending easy (and cut down on the amount of space-eating equipment needed to do these jobs), a kettle and a coffee percolator. If you are elderly, suffer from rheumatism or arthritis or find it difficult to grip, an electric knife is another worthwhile buy that will soon justify its cost by making many cutting tasks a whole lot easier.

Preparation and storage space: Preparation space is important, whatever your culinary plans. An arrangement which runs oven and cooktop, workspace, drainer and sink (with dishwasher beneath drainer), counter, refrigerator and a storage cabinet is efficient. Install as many wall cabinets as possible for storage of pots, pans and non-perishable foods. If you are working under a strict budget, open shelving can be used. Midway shelves between the counter and wall cabinets make good use of normally wasted space and can be used for salt, pepper and herbs that need to be close at hand. Remember that sliding or tambour doors are easier to use in a confined space than the conventional outward opening type.

Some kitchen manufacturers offer all-in-one kitchens which include a sink, refrigerator and stove, planned into one big unit. Some are designed to fit inside a cupboard, others to be part of the room. Most specialists are happy to design a kitchen for a studio or one-room apartment, a good solution if the space is small or awkward.

WHERE TO PUT THE KITCHEN

However well planned and efficient your mini-kitchen is, there will be times when you won't want it on view. Most cooks hate being watched as they work and would rather guests didn't see what goes on behind the scenes. There are days too, when sheer tiredness means you would rather leave the dishes until morning and won't want to see the clutter as you attempt to relax.

Siting the kitchen depends on the shape of the room. An alcove, or the short leg of an L-shape are both good locations. In a long, narrow room, locate the kitchen at one end, and hide it with bi-fold or sliding doors, or a ceiling-mounted Venetian blind. If there is space, use open shelving three quarters of the way across the kitchen space, or build a narrow base cabinet with shelving or a collection of leafy green plants on top. Both of these ideas will add an interesting feature to the living side of the room.

VENTILATION AND LIGHTING

Good ventilation is vital if you cook, live, eat and sleep in the same room. If possible, locate the kitchen where there is an openable window. A ventilation system at the cooktop will clear cooking smells before they can linger. The system can either be an overhead hood, which sucks cooking fumes up and

Left: *This totally self-contained compact kitchen is ideal for small attics, studio apartments and offices.*

Right: *Storage space in the kitchen is of prime importance. Here, tall cabinets offer maximum space and the large refrigerator with built-under freezer and combination of microwave and combi-oven are perfectly placed.*

Food storage: Refrigeration is essential for healthy, hygienic storage of perishable foods. The size of refrigerator depends on your needs. If all you want to store is milk and the odd piece of cheese, then a small, apartment-size model is fine. If you want to store more, choose a larger one. Frozen foods are quick and convenient for students or working singles, so make sure the unit has ample freezer space for your needs. In tight kitchens, consider separate small under-counter refrigerator and freezer. However, if you rely heavily on frozen foods, at least during the working week, you may find it essential to have a refrigerator with a large freezer section. Collect as many manufacturers' brochures as you possibly can and then, having gotten a good idea of the range available, go to a large department store with a good choice of models, or an appliance showroom, and find a salesperson qualified to answer any remaining queries before you make a final choice. This is a purchase you are going to rely on a lot, so get it right!

You will also need a well-ventilated cupboard for the storage of vegetables and other foodstuffs. Cans and packages can go into wire baskets mounted on the inside of the cupboard door.

Dishwashing: If you can afford it, invest in a dishwasher. A space-saving dishwasher won't take up too much space will help you to keep the kitchen area tidy and free from clutter as dirty dishes can be put out of sight immediately. Otherwise there's a tendency to think it not worthwhile washing a few items, and they accumulate!

If a dishwasher is beyond your means, look for a good, deep sink and mount a drip rack above it. A double sink is a waste of space; look instead for a single-bowl model, possibly with a slide-over chopping board. A garbage disposer installed in the sink will prevent you from carrying bags of garbage through the apartment and down the stairs, and will help to keep the kitchen fresh smelling by getting rid of food remains instantly.

vents them outside, or a down-draft model, a low-profile system that draws the fumes down through the appliance body and then out.

The kitchen area needs a different type of lighting from the part of the room used for living. A ceiling-mounted spotlight track will allow you to beam bright light where it is needed. Small fluorescent strips fitted beneath wall cabinets or shelves can be used to light the worktop areas. Good lighting is an essential when you are working with sharp knives or pouring boiling liquids from one container into another. For safety's sake don't try to manage with just a single overhead light that casts shadows.

DECOR

Kitchen decor must, of course, be practical and easy to clean. As the kitchen is part of a larger room, the color schemes should complement one another. Wallcovering quickly becomes dirty in the steamy environment of the kitchen, so paint or tiles are a better choice. All-over tiling can make a small space look like a public lavatory, so compromise with tiles between counter and wall cabinets and paint in a complementary color elsewhere.

Simple white tiles always look good, and will live happily with changes of decor in the main room. You may be tempted to choose tiles in a very definite color or pattern because they match the wall treatment in the main part of the room, but this will restrict your choice of decor.

The flooring should be warm, comfortable and easy-to-clean. Carrying carpet through from the main part of the room is not a practical idea as it will quickly become shabby and stained by inevitable spillages. Cork or vinyl tiles or vinyl sheet flooring are all warm, quiet and easy-to-clean and will suit most styles of decoration.

A PLACE TO EAT

Although you will probably want a dining area in the main part of the room, it is useful to have an area for solo snacks and light meals in the kitchen. Using a base cabinet and countertop as a room divider creates a space that can be used as a breakfast bar if the divider is built so that there is room to tuck a stool beneath the top. Some kitchen cabinet manufacturers offer pull-out tables built into base cabinets, or you can build a folding flap table against the wall.

Left: *This versatile kitchen divider cabinet combines a variety of useful functions. Notice the slide-out breakfast bar, the shelves of different widths and heights and the storage cabinets, all stacked efficiently in the same unit.*

Above: *If your dining area is small, use mirror tiles on one wall to give the effect of an extra dimension. A glass-topped dining table creates a spacious effect too, as it appears to take up less space than a solid one would.*

THE BATHROOM

Most ready-built one-room apartments and studios have a small separate bathroom. It is more than likely that the bathroom provided with a studio or one-room apartment will be too small for anything more than the bare essentials. If it is your own space, there are various ways to make even a gloomy box cheerful and comfortable. Carpeting the floor is a good start. Use proper bathroom carpeting with a waterproof backing. Cover one wall with mirror, paint the others white and add some healthy green plants for instant light and an airy feel. Thick towels, a heated towel rail and a smart shower door instead of shabby shower curtains are quick and easy brighteners.

If you are converting former warehouse space into loft living quarters, you will probably have to create a bathroom from scratch. This affords you the opportunity to go to town (budget permitting) with separate tub and shower, generous storage and any multipurpose elements you desire. You will likely already have a small bathroom, with toilet and sink, which should form the basis of your new bathroom simply because rerouting the plumbing is a formidable expense. A space planner can offer invaluable advice.

Adding a new one-room apartment, either for use by teenagers, as a guest suite or a grandparent's apartment, gives you the opportunity to plan a bathroom designed to make the best of minimum space. Local building regulations will dictate the distance and number of doors required between the bathroom and kitchen/living area, so check these first before deciding on a convenient position for the bathroom.

The bathroom will need to be divided from the main part of the room by partition walling or a folding door. The amount of space you partition off depends on how big the room is, but it is possible to fit a lot of bathroom equipment into a remarkably small area – as you will see in our plan showing a bathroom only 5½ feet long by 4½ feet wide. Remember that a shower takes up much less space than a bath and enclosures come in curved shapes, with corner-entry and sliding doors or can be custom-built to fit under a sloped attic ceiling. If you feel that you can't live without a tub, a continental sit-up bath is a better choice than a short-length standard bath as it will allow you to wallow up to your chest in water in about half the amount of space. Add a shower attachment for hair washing and for the days when there isn't

Left: *Small bathrooms don't have to be dingy and unwelcoming. Glowing wood panels and imaginative lighting make this compact bathroom warm and cozy. Once again, mirror has been used on one wall to create a feeling of space.*

Right: *Sensitive lighting with the aid of uplighters and downlighters help create a good atmosphere in the living area of the apartment.*

time to soak. A sit-up bath is not always a good choice for the elderly who may find it difficult to get in and out of, although some may find it easier than a conventional bath.

When the only space available is an area just big enough to stand up in, a tiled "wet room," a sort of shower in a closet where the water drains through a hole in the middle of the floor, is a good solution. Equipped with a non-slip mat, grab rails and a thermostatically controlled shower, this arrangement is suitable for anyone elderly or infirm who may not be able to climb in and out of a bath. There will probably also be enough space for a recessed or corner-mounted basin.

White tiles and brightly colored recessed fixtures will make a small bathroom seem bigger without creating a cold, clinical atmosphere. Build a vanity cabinet around the washbasin, and position shelves on the walls above the bath for storage of toiletries and cleaning materials. Hide the plumbing behind the panels (called ducting) for a neat, streamlined look and for ease of access.

Ventilation is important in a small bathroom as a build-up of steam will cause condensation and dampness. A window with an opening vent is best, as it allows fresh air into the room. Failing this, install a ducted fan that operates when the light is switched on (in some areas, this is legal requirement in a bathroom without a window).

Flooring should be warm and waterproof. Carpet is comfortable underfoot and easy to install. Most bathroom carpeting can be lifted and machine washed when it is dirty. If you want a hard floor, sealed cork tiles or sheet or tile vinyl are both suitable and available in hundreds of patterns and colors. Ceramic tiles look attractive but are cold and can be dangerously slippery when wet.

LIGHTING AND HEATING

Good lighting and heating are important in the main part of the apartment. Heating may be run from a furnace designed for the whole building. If this is the case, make sure that there are sufficient vents or radiators for the size of the room and that they can be individually controlled, whatever the setting of the main furnace. The same system may also supply hot water. Again, make sure that there is enough to suit your needs. Where a one-room apartment is being added to a family home, it may be necessary to install a bigger furnace, or a larger water heater. A small plug-in convection heater will be useful when instant warmth is needed, but make sure it has a thermostat to reduce the danger from fire, and don't fall asleep with it on.

As well as specific light in the kitchen area, you will need a variety of lighting in the main part of the room. General light can come from ceiling-mounted recessed lights, controlled by a dimmer, so that their intensity can be varied from strong illumination to a gentle background glow. Back this up with table or freestanding lights near seating and work areas and a rise-and-fall pendant light above the dining table.

FURNISHING A STUDIO

Small-space living calls for furniture which can lead a double life. Before buying furniture for a studio or small one-room apartment, think carefully about what you need as there will be little space to spare for non-essentials.

Think first about how you will use the room. Sleeping is the most obvious function – and even a single bed can take up quite a lot of space. Fortunately with the number of good-quality, attractive sofa beds now available, this is an easy problem to solve. When buying a sofa bed, make sure that it is easy to open and close, even when your chosen bedding is *in situ*, and be sure there is adequate space in front to open it.

Eating comes next – *see page 86–87* on small kitchens for information. Do you need a place to study? Somewhere to store books or a large record collection? What about clothes? Where will friends sit when they come to visit?

If you already have some furniture, assess whether it will work in the confined space of a studio apartment. It may be tempting to try to make do, but life will become uncomfortable and irritating if you have to move large chairs or an awkwardly shaped table to get access to any particular area of the room.

Look at the location and number of electrical outlets before you move into the room. Bear in mind also that a dearth of outlets could indicate old wiring – in which case it would be dangerous simply to add more sockets and probably overload the system. Trailing cords can be dangerous in a confined space. Try to arrange lighting so that wires don't interfere with traffic patterns.

Building permanent partitions is not a good idea in a small room as it will make the space seem even more cramped, but if you feel you want to conceal a dressing area, or the kitchen, shop around for folding screens, or see if it is possible to mount a roller or Venetian blind on the ceiling.

Avoiding big or busy patterns on walls or floors is a design basic, but plain surfaces need not be boring. Walls can be rag rolled, sponged, stippled or stenciled to add depth and interest and carpet can be plain in the center, but have an interesting border. In a ground floor room, where echoing footsteps won't disturb anyone below, a wooden floor could be stripped and stenciled, then dressed up with a colorful rug to pick up one or more colors used for the stencil. If it is a patterned rug, it should, of course echo the stencil pattern, or the result will be too busy in a confined area.

Comfortable seating is important, both for

Left: *Owned by a busy illustrator, this studio apartment has limited space, so work and relaxing have to share the same area. A sofa bed is an absolute essential.*

Above: *Built-in drawing boards are a special feature.*

Top: *After the day's work is done the drawing boards become ordinary domestic worktops and the sofa bed folds down. The clip-on spotlight becomes a bedside light.*

personal relaxation, and for friends when they visit. A good-quality sofa bed will accommodate two to three, but if this is beyond your means, a convenient day bed can be made to look like seating. Push the bed against the wall, add a tailored cover, then pile with cushions for an opulent, semi-eastern look. A day bed with storage drawers in the base is doubly useful. Floorcushions are inexpensive, but they do take up a lot of space. Upright folding canvas director's chairs are a better option, as they are comfortable, space-saving and can double up as dining furniture. On the minus side, they can quite quickly begin to sag if constantly occupied by a fairly heavy person. You can, of course, replace the canvas when this happens. If both space and money are short, upright folding beach chairs are another alternative, at least as a stopgap until you can afford something rather more substantial, comfortable and enduring.

When choosing a table, remember that a glass top is visually smaller than one made from a solid material. A folding model, or a flap hinged against the wall are other possibilities but check that there really is enough room to use the table full out without moving other furniture. A round table takes up less space than a square or rectangular one and there are no sharp corners to bump into – an important consideration if the room is for an elderly person.

Built-in closets are the best way to store clothes, but unless the room already has these, finding sufficient space may be tricky. Closets can be installed in an alcove or recess without eating into the main area of the room, but if built against a flat wall, will occupy around 3 feet.

If you can't afford the space, think about a hanging rail on castors, or hooks on the wall hidden by a screen. Brightly colored sweaters and other foldable clothes can become part of the decorative scheme if stored on open shelving with shoes, bags and hats. Some furnishing specialists stock lightweight wheeled units, specially designed for clothes, with sections for hanging, shelves and a rack for shoes and boots.

For the sake of comfortable living, do try to keep the room tidy and free from clutter. Fold the bed back every day, throw away old newspapers and magazines, make sure there is a good circulation of fresh air (especially if you smoke) and provide a few delicate touches such as bowls of fruit or fresh flowers, and however small, your studio will always be a bright and welcoming place.

UP THE GARDEN PATH

When all of the ways to capitalize on space have been exhausted, one solution to the problem may be to look outdoors.

The Victorian idea of building a gaslit, ferny retreat at the end of the garden and calling it a summer house is a romantic notion easily adapted to suit today's needs. We all need somewhere to escape to from time to time, and a quiet spot reached via the garden path might prove itself sufficiently removed from the trials and traumas of the household to enable you to do just that. As a place to work, gossip or pursue a gentle interest such as painting or sewing, a summer house is ideal. It need not be large, or over-furnished – just a couple of wicker chairs and a table, plus lots of plants, are all that are necessary.

If a lack of storage space is your main bug-bear, a less romantic structure may be the answer. The garage has always been used for the overflow of household junk, but if you have a car that needs housing as well, space is bound to be limited.

Both the do-it-yourself expert and the budding gardener need a storage for the selection of tools and equipment vital to building and horticultural activities, and there are few structures to beat the ubiquitous wooden shed. It's attractive and useful in any garden and the ideal protection for a host of items. These days, kits make self-assembly so easy. If you want to extend your growing season, or to concentrate on raising more exotic blooms, you'll need a greenhouse. But you don't have to resort to buying the frequently expensive modern metal types; building your own design from wood isn't complicated. A wooden shed could solve all your storage problems. They are available in a range of sizes to suit all gardens and are no problem to build.

Far left: *A summer house or folly at the bottom of the garden may seem like a frivolous idea, but if space inside the house has been stretched to the limits it could be the only way to find your own private space.*

Above: *This garden shed has the pleasant feature of louver windows. It would make an ideal workshop or hobby room.*

Right: *This type of basic shed is just right for storing outdoor equipment not needed on a daily basis.*

Far right: *A slightly larger construction can be used as a base for outdoor relaxing and entertaining.*

A garden shed is always useful as a place to lock away your garden tools and equipment, bikes and deckchairs, as well as a place to pot plants and store them over winter. A larger shed with good window light and lots of headroom can even be used as a small workshop if you so wish.

Most garden buildings are wooden, but you can also get metal sheds and sheds with concrete panel walls. Metal sheds will last a lifetime, but they are utilitarian and, unlike the more natural-looking wooden sheds, are out of place in most gardens. Concrete panel sheds are really an alternative to building in brick and are considerably more expensive to erect than a wooden building.

CHOOSING A SIZE

The most popular size for a shed is just over $6\frac{1}{2}$ feet deep by about 5 feet wide. This gives plenty of storage space and room for a narrow waist-height shelf or a fold-away workbench. If you want a shed just for storage, or if space is very tight, you might consider a much smaller shed of about $3\frac{1}{2}$ feet square with double doors. Although not large enough to step into, the advantage of such a shallow shed is that storage is easy to organize and there are no dark depths for things to get lost in.

A larger shed with plenty of window light (and perhaps an electricity supply) will give you enough room to set up and organize a permanent workbench.

The size of shed you choose may be influenced by where you intend to site it – think carefully about this. Sheds are often put at the far end of a garden where they are out of sight; but it may be more convenient to have a shed much nearer the house, where there is a dry, mud-free path and it is fairly easy and not too expensive to get it fixed up with an electricity supply.

Choose a site which is level and avoid parts of the garden that tend to be wet or boggy. Position the shed out of the main lines of view from the house; if it has to be built in sight, arrange rambling plants such as evergreen clematis or honeysuckle to soften the harsh lines of the design.

If you want to use your shed as a greenhouse, make sure the windows get good sunlight; otherwise put your shed in shade so that the sunnier parts of the garden can be used for flowerbeds. Think about the way the door will open and aim to have the opening away from the prevailing wind.

BUYING A SHED

Before committing yourself to buying a particular shed, have a look at a sample that has been erected (even mail-order firms have showrooms where their sheds are available for inspection). Look for a shed that has all the features you want and then check that the structure is sound while you are examining it, take particular note of the following points:

Roof: There are two types of roofs: apex – with sloping sides on either side of a ridge; and pent – with a slope in only one direction. Pent roofs are used on shallow sheds and on low-priced ones of average size – they look best when a shed is installed with a wall or fence behind; a shed with an apex roof looks good whether freestanding or alongside a wall.

Siding: The wooden siding of the shed walls can be simple overlap, rabbeted or tongue-and-grooved. Overlapping siding is most

economical and used on cheaper sheds; rabbeting gives better waterproofing and, provided good quality wood is used, tongue-and-grooved is more weatherproof still. You may come across *shiplap* siding; this can be rabbeted or tongue-and-grooved – the name describes the shape of the board.

Floor: A boarded floor on framing joists is available as an optional extra with most sheds. These are useful if you are installing the shed on sleeper walls or if you want a floor that is "warm" underfoot. A shed on a concrete slab base can be constructed without a boarded floor.

Timber: Sheds are available in redwood and Western Red Cedar. The first is a softwood, which needs treating with preservative for durability. Some sheds are sold untreated for you to do yourself, but a shed will last longer if it's professionally treated, and it is worth paying the extra for a shed that has been pressure-impregnated with a preservative.

Western Red Cedar is naturally durable. Left untreated, it weathers to an attractive gray; if you prefer the wood to be light brown you will need to revive the surface with an occasional brushed-on cedar treatment.

Doors and windows: Apex roof sheds usually have the door at the center on one end. Pent roof sheds may have the door on an end or on the front. A front-opening door is ideal for a shed to be used only for storage, but if you want a workbench or a shelf for plants, an end door is better as it leaves the long side uninterrupted. Doors are normally single ledged-and-braced, but sometimes part glazed durable doors are offered. The windows are normally along one side.

If you want to use your shed partly as a greenhouse, look for a shed with windows at 45° above a cantilevered shelf to give even light to plants. If you want opening windows for ventilation, look for top-hinged ones that can be left open in the rain.

To check the structure of the shed, shake the walls, slam the door, and jump on the floor – if it bends or feels fragile look for another shed. Check construction as well: are nails straight, holes properly drilled and so on?

It is very important to choose the correct site for your shed, on level ground, and, if you want to make it your office-cum-hideaway, a special place to grab an hour on your own, in a quiet, sheltered position.

USEFUL NAMES AND ADDRESSES

CABINETS

Allmilmo Corporation
P.O. Box 629
Fairfield, NJ 07006

Kemper & Quaker Maid
701 S. N Street
Richmond, IN 47374

Millbrook
Route 20
Nassau, NY 12123

Mutschler
302 S. Madison Street
Nappanee, IN 46550

Poggenpohl USA Corporation
P.O. Box 10 KB2
Teaneck, NJ 07666

Riviera Kitchens
Dept. KBB-7. Suite 200
825 Greenbriar Circle
Chesapeake, VA 23320

H. J. Scheirich Company
P.O. Box 37120
Louisville, KY 40233

SieMatic Corporation
P.O. Box 2536
Santa Barbara, CA 93118

St. Charles Manufacturing Company
1611 E. Main Street
St. Charles, IL 60117

Wood-Mode Cabinetry
Kreamer, PA 17833

CABINET STORAGE ACCESSORIES

Amerock Corporation
4000 Auburn Street
Rockfield, IL 61101

Feeny Manufacturing Company
P.O. Box 1130
616 Mulberry Street
Muncie, IN 47305

Grant Hardware
High Street
West Nyack, NY 10994

Háfele America Company
P.O. Box 1590
High Point, NC 27261

CORIAN

E. I. Dupont & Company
Tatnall Bulding Products Information
   Section
Wilmington, DE 19898

DOORS

Andersen Corporation
P.O. Box 12
Bayport, MN 55003

Customwood
4840 Pan American Freeway N.E.
Albuquerque, NM 87109

Forms & Surfaces, Inc.
P.O. Box 5215
Santa Barbara, CA 93108

Georgia-Pacific Corporation
133 Peachtree Street, N.E.
Atlanta, GA 30303

Louisiana-Pacific
1300 S.W. Fifth Avenue
Portland, OR 92701

Pella Doors
100 Main Street
Pella, IA 50219

FAUCETS

Chicago Faucet Company
2100 S. Nuclear Drive
Des Plaines, IL 60018

Delta Faucet Company
Division of Masco Corporation of Indiana
P.O. Box 40980
55 E. 111th Street
Indianapolis, IN 46280

Elkay Manufacturing Company
2222 Camden Court
Oak Brook, IL 60521

Grohe
Division of Flygt Corporation
1591 Elmhurst Road
Elk Grove Village, IL 60007

Kohler Company
Kohler, WI 53044

KWC Faucets
Western States Manufacturing Corporation
6900 Eighth Street
Buena Park, CA 90620

Moen
Division of Stanadyne
377 Woodland Avenue
Elyria, OH 44035

Price Pfister
13500 Paxton Street
Pacoima, CA 91331

U.S. Tap
P.O. Box 369
Frankfort, IN 46401

FLOORING

Armstrong Company
Liberty and Charlotte Streets
Lancaster, PA 17604

Bruce Hardwood Floors
16803 Dallas Parkway
Dallas, TX 75248

Congoleum Industries, Inc.
195 Belgrove Drive
Kearny, NJ 07032

Connor Forest Industries
P.O. Box 847
Wausau, WI 54401

GAF Corporation
Floor Products Division
1210 Massillon Road
Akron, OH 44305

Kentiles Floors, Inc.
979 Third Avenue
New York, NY 10022

Mannington Mills, Inc.
P.O. Box 30
Salem, NJ 08079
(sheet goods only)

HARDWARE

Artistic Brass
4100 Ardmore Avenue
South Gate, CA 90280

Belwith International, Ltd.
7600 Industry Avenue
P.O. Box 1057
Pico Rivera, CA 90660

Forms & Surfaces
P.O. Box 5215
Santa Barbara, CA 93108

Home Hardware
1900 E. Orangethorpe Avenue
Fullerton, CA 92631

The Ironmonger
446 N. Wells
Chicago, IL 60610

Paul Associates
155 E. 55th Street
New York, NY 10022

Valli & Colombo, Inc.
1540 Highland Avenue
Duarte, CA 91010

LAMINATED PLASTICS

Dura-Beauty
Consoweld Corporation
700 Durabeauty Lane
Wisconsin Rapids, WI 54494

Formica Corporation
120 E. Fourth Street
Cincinnati, OH 45202

Laminart
6430 E. Slauson Avenue
Los Angeles, CA 90040

Nevamar
Division of Exxon Chemical Company
Telegraph Road
Odenton, MD 21113

Wilsonart
600 General Bruce Drive
Temple, TX 76501

LIGHTING

Halo Lighting Division
McGraw-Edison Company
400 Busse Road
Elk Grove Village, IL 60007

Lightolier
346 Claremont Avenue
Jersey City, NJ 07305

Trak Liting, Inc.
14625 E. Clark Avenue
City of Industry, CA 91746

MOLDINGS

Focal Point, Inc.
2005 Marietta Road
Atlanta, GA 30318

Fypon, Inc.
108 Hill Street
Stewartstown, PA 17363

Maple Brothers, Inc.
1295 W. Lambert Road
Brea, CA 92621

Western Wood Products Association
Yeon Building
Portland, OR 97204

SINKS

American Standard, Inc.
P.O. Box 2003
New Brunswick, NJ 08903

Delta Faucet Company
P.O. Box 31
Greensburg, IN 47240

Eljer
Division of Wallace-Murray Corporation
3 Gateway Center
Pittsburgh, PA 15222

Elkay Manufacturing Company
2222 Camden Court
Oak Brook, IL 60521

Franke, Inc.
Kitchen Systems Division
212 Church Road
North Wales, PA 19454

Jensen-Thorsen Corporation
301 Interstate Road
Addison, IL 60101

Kohler Company
Kohler, WI 53044

Moen
Division of Stanadyne
377 Woodland Avenue
Elyria, OH 44035

Villeroy & Boch
P.O. Box 103 DW
Pine Brook, NJ 07058

SKYLIGHTS AND CONSERVATORIES

Four Seasons Solar Products Corporation
425 Smith Street
Farmingdale, NY 11735

Lord & Burnham
P.O. Box 255
Irvington, NY 10533

Ventarama Skylight Corporation
140 Cantiague Rock Road
Hicksville, NY 11801

TILES

American Olean Tile Company
1000 Cannon Avenue
Lansdale, PA 19446

Country Floors, Inc.
300 E. 61st Street
New York, NY 10021

Designers Tile International
6812 S.W. 81st Street
Miami, FL 33143

Elon, Inc.
964 Third Avenue
New York, NY 10022

Emser International
1660 S. State College Boulevard
Anaheim, CA 92806

International Tile
1288 S. La Brea Avenue
Los Angeles, CA 90019

Latco Products
3371 Glendale Boulevard
Los Angeles, CA 90039

Summitville Tiles, Inc.
Summitville, OH 43962

Walker & Zanger, Inc.
179 Summerfield Street
Scarsdale, NY 10583

WALLCOVERINGS AND PAINT

The following companies offer customer
literature.

Ameritone Paint
P.O. Box 190
Long Beach, CA 90801

Laura Ashley
714 Madison Avenue
New York, NY 10021

Charles Barone, Inc.
9505 W. Jefferson Boulevard
Culver City, CA 90230

Clarence House
111 Eighth Avenue, Room 801
New York, NY 10011

Du Pont De Nemours
1007 Market Street
Wilmington, DE 19898

Fashion Wallcoverings
4005 Carnegie Avenue
Cleveland, OH 44103

General Tire & Rubber Company
979 Third Avenue
New York, NY 10022

S. M. Hexter
2800 E. Superior Avenue
Cleveland, OH 44114

F. Schumacher & Company
939 Third Avenue
New York, NY 10022

Sinclair Paints & Wallcoverings
2500 S. Atlantic Boulevard
Los Angeles, CA 90040

Albert Van Luit & Company
4000 Chevy Chase Drive
Los Angeles, CA 90039

WINDOWS

Anderson Corporation
P.O. Box 12
Bayport, MN 55003

Caradco Windows & Doors
Division of Scoville Manufacturing Company
1098 Jackson Street
Dubuque, IA 52001

Lord & Burnham
P.O. Box 225
Irvington, NY 10533

Marvin Windows
Warroad, MN 56763

Pella Windows
100 Main Street
Pella, IA 50219

Southern Cross Lumber & Millwork
143 Brown Road
Hazelwood, MO 63042

INDEX

ACKNOWLEDGMENTS

Addis: 139.

Allmilmo: 7(b) 'Torino', 73 '3D Design', 81 'Roma White Gray', 100/1.

Alno: 79(tr,b).

Amtico: 83 'Bucks Country'.

Banbury Conservatories: 34.

Paul Beattie: 60(t), 61(l), 64(t), 65, 156.

Bosch: 32, 82 'Flair', 85, 88 'Sixty Kitchen Program', 127 'Alpha White', 134 'Alpha Module 80', 174.

Richard Bryant/Arcaid: 103.

Camden Studio: 10.

Camera Press: 5, 6, 14(l,r), 15(t,b), 16(tl,tr,b), 17(t,b), 33, 35(b), 38(b), 48, 71(t), 86, 98(b), 109, 110, 113, 135, 162, 163(t,bl,br), 165, 170(t,b), 171(tl,tr,b), 175, 178/9, 179(t,b).

Condor Public Relations: 57, 94.

Cover Plus Paint: 40.

Crosby: 74 'Chiltern Mist Gray'.

Crown Paint: 4, 11, 12(t,b), 90, 106, 121, 159.

Crystal Tile: 126 'Tigriss', 129(t) 'Bloomsbury', 141 'Ocean'.

Dolphin Showers: 153.

Barbara Douglas: 148.

Dulux Paints: 31, 50, 51, 60(b), 91, 93, 122, 145, 157(t).

Ray Duns: 25(t,b), 61(r), 64(b).

Eurostudio: 62, 63(l), 152, 155(t).

Futon Company: 147(b).

G. Plan Furniture: 19.

John Heseltine: 182.

Tony Hurley: 154.

Junkers: 97.

Dave King: 38(t), 45(b), 49, 114, 116, 132, 157(b).

Ken Kirkwood: 7(t), 37, 56, 68, 92, 98(t), 102, 115(b), 142, 176.

Kirsh Contour: 41.

Steve Lyne: 20(t,b), 42, 43(tl, tr, b).

Maples, Waring & Gillow; 44(tr) 'Valero'.

Alan Marsh: 47.

Marston & Langinger: 35(t) 'Barney', 36 'Mathieson'.

Miele: 78(l,r), 84(t) 'Program 60', 172 'Oyster Program 27'.

Michael Murray: 71(b), 146.

Next Interiors: 52/3, 104, 108, 147(t), 151.

Jan Orchard; 13(t,b), 26, 96, 123, 155(b).

Roger Payling: 124.

Poggenpohl: 79(tl), 84(t), 89.

Rubans Fleuris: 120.

Sandersons & Sons Ltd: 149, 150.

Sharps Individual Bedroom Designs Ltd: 54, 160.

Smallbone Kitchens: 18, 59, 69, 76.

Harry Smith Horticultural Collection: 181, 183.

Spur Shelving: 112.

Jessica Strang: 9(l) Sagna Waddell, 58(r) Sagna Waddell.

Swingform by Behr: 45(t).

Tapestry Color: 105.

Twyfords: 136.

Elizabeth Whiting & Associates: 24, 29, 44(tl), 46, 66/7, 129(b), 138, 143, 158, 164, 166, 167, 168(l), 168/9, 172, 177.

Micheal Warren: 180.